'This book plots, historically, the journey of the birds of passage – the migrants – and their refusal to fly away from a city that pretended they did not exist. A cultural memory transported from villages to new geographies only to be converted into trade-able cultural goods and services.'
– BONGANI NGQULUNGA, AUTHOR OF *THE MAN WHO FOUNDED THE ANC*

'*Maye? Maye!: The history and heritage of the Kwa Mai Mai market* is the piece of gold we have been waiting for. It is a treasure that intrigues one's intellect with its digging into the shafts of the history of gold in South Africa. *Maye! Maye!* is indeed a cry for help for the abandoned Mai Mai Market, a potential left to decay without its fulfilment.'
– HOMBAKAZI MERCY NQANDELA, AUTHOR OF *DON'T UPSET ooMALUME: A GUIDE TO STEPPING UP YOUR XHOSA GAME*

'Here we have a real people's history written by a public intellectual who has dedicated years to recording and researching the story of the residents of Johannesburg's famous Mai Mai market. What those arrivals in that tough city have *really* accomplished is to make something both economically and culturally significant out of practically nothing. Where there were once stables, for decades has thrived a residential production site for the best in African indigenous costumery and medicine available anywhere in South Africa. Sithole has also looked the perfidious mismanagement and discrimination the residents and craft artists of Mai Mai have had to endure. This book is not only of great sociological and cultural import, it is also an exciting, nitty-gritty read. Do yourself and the city a favour and read it.'
– DAVID B. COPLAN, PROFESSOR EMERITUS IN SOCIAL ANTHROPOLOGY, UNIVERSITY OF THE WITWATERSRAND

# Maye! Maye!

# Maye! Maye!

## The history & heritage of the Kwa Mai Mai market

Sipho Sithole

The financial assistance of the Johannesburg Institute for Advanced Study (JIAS) towards this publication is gratefully acknowledged.

First published by Jacana Media (Pty) Ltd in 2023

10 Orange Street
Sunnyside
Auckland Park 2092
South Africa
+2711 628 3200
www.jacana.co.za



ISBN 978-1-4314-3294-3

Cover design by publicide
Editing by Ali Parry and Isabelle Delvare
Proofreading by Isabelle Delvare
Indexing by Ali Parry
Set in Ehrhardt MT Std 11/15pt
Printed and bound by ABC Press, Cape Town
Job no. 004026

For a complete list of Jacana titles, visit www.jacana.co.za

*To the memory of my sister,*
*Nelisiwe, who taught me how to read*

# Contents


Acknowledgements                                              ix

Prologue                                                     xi

1   Maye! Maye!                                               1

2   Wrapped in gold                                          13

3   Condemned                                                37

4   A Bantu affair                                           63

5   Kwa Mai Mai: Not your usual hostel                       87

6   Meet the cultural entrepreneurs                         109

7   Converts and diviners at the crossroads                 151

8   At loggerheads                                          195

9   Betrayed, but not defeated                              221

10  Formalising the informal?                               231

11  Conclusion                                              247

Notes                                                       253

References                                                  257

Index                                                       265

# Acknowledgements

To my wife, Velile, for tolerating me writing into the wee hours of the morning. To Dr Bongani Nqulunga – *nsizwa yakithi, uyiqhawe wena* – thank you for the support and for believing in me. To the Honourable Minister, Nathi Mthethwa, thank you for encouraging me not just to write an article on this topic, but to go full throttle and produce a book, which has since given birth to a documentary and a stage play – I am truly honoured. To Ali Parry and Isabelle Delvare – I still do not know how you are able to spot even the tiniest error; your edits are unparalleled. To the anonymous peer reviewers, thank you for pushing my scholarship to the limit.

Lastly, to the Department of Sports, Arts and Culture and the Johannesburg Institute for Advanced Study – without your financial support the story of Kwa Maye Maye would not have been told.

To the reluctant migrant workers turned economic hustlers in this concrete jungle – keep on keeping on.

Jacana! Let's do this more often.

# Prologue

Kwa Mai Mai is the embodiment of everything Johannesburg is meant to be – the City of Gold, a place where dreams deferred come true. It is a constellation of people's cultures, imbued with beautiful memories of life in villages left behind but cherished by those who refuse to forget, lest they lose themselves in the concrete jungle that knows no mercy.

This book tells the story of how cultural memory, sacredly preserved and transported to new geographies, can be employed both as a cultural weapon to resist subjugation and as an economic weapon to turn those priceless traditions into tradeable commodities. The book explores how the keepers of cultural memory can use it not only to survive but also to invoke the entrepreneurial and creative spirit buried deep within their souls. Moreover, it builds on the assumption that if cultural memory can be stored and retrieved through artefacts, sites, ceremonies, myths and rituals, then Kwa Mai Mai is the place where these elements converge in inspiring displays of craftsmanship, worship and healing.

Yet Kwa Mai Mai has a darker side. It is a place of painful memories and ignored pleas – where its members are in a constant battle to be acknowledged by the city that created it.

This book records my collective observations and interpretations from the ethnographic work that I conducted over a period of four years among Kwa Mai Mai traders and residents – those who reluctantly remained in the City of Gold when they were faced with no alternative, short of admitting defeat and returning to the villages.

Since the middle of the 19th century, that is, for more than 170 years, generations of Africans from far-flung villages in South Africa and southern Africa have flocked to Johannesburg in search of fortune. Not everyone has found the proverbial pot of gold, let alone remnants left behind by those fortunate enough to strike it rich. Many fortune seekers extracted African labour from the villages and employed it to dig out the mineral wealth that lay deep within the earth's belly, never sharing their new-found fortune with those who had brought it to the surface.

My acquaintance with Kwa Mai Mai began with a visit to this hub of Zulu culture where, as a Zulu migrant, I found myself in an ethnographic wonderland where the language spoken by the traders was pure and beautiful. I met several Zulu migrants whose passion for culture and tradition was almost palpable. I formed strong bonds with some of the traders who held dear, and took pride in, the businesses they had inherited from their forebears.

I listened to inspiring stories of how great-grandfathers and grandfathers had arrived in the city in the 1920s and defeated a system that, unchallenged, would have seen them returning to their villages with nothing. I spoke to old women who, with little-girl demeanour, spoke fondly of the fathers who had first come to Kwa Mai Mai in the 1950s to set up the businesses that they now ran. I also spoke to men old enough to be grandfathers, who shared with me how their fathers had taught them the trade from a young age and had moved them to the city so that they could inherit the business. Having become heirs to their family business and custodian of its legacy, they all vowed never to disappoint their departed parents.

Despite the difficult trading environment and the many economic hurdles that suddenly confronted them, they displayed an unwavering determination to carry on the trade in those goods and services that had been inspired by their culture and tradition. I engaged with traders who unflinchingly and unequivocally stated that even if no customers came, they would still wake up every morning and open the doors of their shops, anxious to show their departed parents that the businesses they had left behind were still operating.

Not everyone at Kwa Mai Mai inherited their businesses from their parents or grandparents. Legend has it that one prominent herbalist, who was also the headman of the hostel, had practically given up hope of finding employment in Johannesburg, when he was suddenly confronted by a white man who threatened him with a gun while he was job hunting in the suburb of Kensington. He vowed never to work for a white man after that. Similarly, Mshengu, a panel beater, made a decision to move to Kwa Mai Mai in the 1980s when he realised that he would never work for a white man, if at all possible.

It was touching to see young children of various ages playfully running around the paved corridors of Kwa Mai Mai, oblivious of the historical turn of events that had resulted in their being born in the hostel that had once been a horse stable. They seemed to be unconcerned about the concrete jungle of the inner city just beyond the gate. Playing happily and pushing crates which they imagined to be automobiles, these children helped to lighten the mood of the traders who, as parents, suddenly felt a renewed determination to succeed in their chosen profession to help their children find a better life.

Several of the children born at Kwa Mai Mai attended schools in and around Johannesburg. Some successfully passed their matric but have since retreated back to Kwa Mai Mai, having failed to go on to university or find work. With doors closing behind them, their prospects look bleak. Yet a few young residents still hope that their parents may strike it rich in their businesses and help them to escape their plight.

Over the four years of my ethnographic study, I could not help but notice that some of the residents of Kwa Mai Mai were old enough to be permanently back home in the villages, tending to their homestead, livestock and crops. Someone like uMama uMaNhlangwini Zakwe from eMaChunwini eMsinga could pass for a double pensioner, but she keeps on going, against all odds. Unfortunately, there is no fixed timeframe for coming to Johannesburg in search of opportunity and fortune and then returning home to live in comfort, enjoying the spoils from their time in the city. Sadly, too, many of the Africans who left their villages towards the end of the 19th century, hoping to 'make it' in the city, resisted going home every year for fear of being ridiculed, and eventually ended up staying in the city indefinitely – always waiting for the right time to return but never finding it.

This book reveals how the subversive socio-economic order that epitomised Kwa Mai Mai turns class theory upside down. In an interesting reversal of roles, the Kwa Mai Mai community, who used to be a migrant working class, wrested the power and control over the means of production from the dominant class. Through their heightened cultural consciousness, this marginalised migrant community has reimagined new economic realities and possibilities, forever distancing itself from the painful, repressive past.

This book is dedicated to marginalised communities and those who, despite operating on the fringes of the economy, have sought to create their own fortune and destiny, using their cultural currency and traditions transported as memories or through artefacts from the villages.

This is the story of Kwa Mai Mai – an economic trade zone and home to people who dared to dream.

# One
# Maye! Maye!

When traders at Kwa Mai Mai speak of their grandparents or parents who started their own businesses and later passed them down to the next generation, their eyes glisten and tears trickle down their cheeks. They are reminded of the days when their grandparents or parents plied their trade in a place that was run like a camp – under lock and key. They recall the security and compound police who enforced the law to the letter. Only permitted Africans or so-called 'natives' were allowed in the compound.

In their fight to survive, these migrant workers created 'social spaces of distraction' (Harvey 1989:234) by using culture as a day-to-day focal point and as a raft to keep them buoyant in a city that would have preferred them to remain anonymous. As they became aware of the constant struggle between capital and labour, a cultural community was created, with people forming bonds that transcended their individual differences. By burying their personal and ethnic differences, they forged a solidarity that allowed them to withstand the threat of social exclusion and anonymity in a city that was full of life.

To avoid being mocked as urban outcasts, these migrant workers had to develop a sense of transnationalism or a cosmopolitan disposition, which overrode their cultural origins and propelled them into a socio-economic space to survive urban marginality. These 'transnational villagers' (Levitt 2001) redefined the concept of diaspora or cross-border migration as a form of 'mobile sociology' (Urry 2010) whereby they assumed a diasporic status within migrant communities, with 'cultural, economic, political and social formations in process' (Werbner 2004:896).

Culture and the memory of one's antecedents can only thrive within the context of collective remembering, especially where identity formation is in conflict with that of other social groups. Moreover, collective remembering involves individual minds (Wertsch and Roediger III 2008) – out of a sense of joint marginality and alienation from other dominant groups – sharing a common set of cultural tools to register their presence and 'privilege identity formation' in a space that would otherwise render them invisible.

Using cultural memory and collective remembering to respond to their new and unfamiliar socio-economic and political environments, these migrants have formed their own communities. By maintaining their social independence, and trading in their own cultural goods and services, they have displayed the 'highest level of self-sufficiency relative to its environment' (Parsons 1971:8), as dictated by the prevailing socio-economic and political circumstances.

Those who reluctantly returned to the city came to refer to it as *esilungwini* (the place of the white man). Disassociating themselves from the city was a clear indication that they had no intention of bonding with it and its way of life, which they found foreign. By calling it a place of the white man, migrant workers disengaged from the city, creating psychological and social boundaries in their interpretation of and engagement with it.

To these migrant workers, the city became a necessary destination after a journey, but not a desirable place to settle. McClendon (2002:118) correctly captures this sentiment when he remarks, 'By the late 1930s, the resurgence of urban economies … led increasing numbers of young men seeking new opportunities in urban areas.' McClendon (2002:101) further observes that land dispossession resulted in Africans having fewer cattle than before, which prompted increased migration by young men, who needed to earn cash 'if they were to accumulate cattle for *lobola*'.

However, the city was also known for converting village men of stature into *amabhunguka* (those who abandoned their homesteads, women, children and livestock and opted for city life, never to return home). To most reluctant migrants, however, who refused to be seduced by the wicked ways of metropolitan life, the city became just a place to earn enough money to enable them to pay the colonially imposed government taxes. The city was a place in which to accumulate the financial resources needed to enjoy the ultimate village life, both during and after their time spent in it. These migrant workers refused to abandon their sense of loyalty to their heritage and tradition back home in the villages. Yet they also felt a commitment to making things work in their new place of residence (the metropolis) without selling their soul.

By retaining their old identity, albeit in the new urban setting, they created what Cohen (2006:7) calls a 'syncretic compromise between old and new', that is, a blend of rural and urban, giving rise to a new ethno-urban man. Cognisant of their rural persona and sticking out like a sore thumb in their new urban setting, they refused to fit in. Their heritage and tradition helped them to develop survival strategies and tactics in a city that would gobble up any migrant worker who arrived in Johannesburg culturally and mentally ill-prepared – who displayed even the slightest signs of weakness.

The vantage point from which they viewed and imagined the city presupposed the existence of a multi-layered construction of hierarchical race and class structures, where the relationship between social structure and residence-based differentiation was clearly defined. Therefore, upon arriving in the city, they opted for a simple life, often preserving their meagre savings for a dignified life back home when they reached retirement – if they were lucky enough to keep their jobs until then.

These 'birds of passage', as Wacquant (2008:163) calls them, defied the temptation to settle in the city. They clearly showed no affinity with, or intention of settling permanently in, their host town, and would go home whenever an opportunity presented itself so that they could be reunited with their families, even if only for a short while. This is best captured by Callinicos (1994:95), who says, 'Each time they went back to work, they would hope it was for the last time. They hoped that this time they would save enough money to support the family so that they could stay home and go back to farming. But most men remained migrants until they were too old to work for themselves again.'

A visiting journalist would come to testify that Johannesburg grew from being 'a City of unbridled squander and unfathomable squalor' (Britannica 1999) to a place where migrant workers found themselves at the bottom of the ladder, seriously affected by residential differentiation. Forced to live in squalid conditions, confined to the compounds which were 'bounded and segregated spaces' (Wacquant 2008:169) and made to feel redundant over weekends or on their off days, they grouped themselves into formidable social structures, joined at the hip through their heritage, tradition and collective suffering. As Harvey (1989) argues, the relationship between their shared values, consciousness and collective life experiences is what bound this community together as a distinct social class with their own aspirations and expectations.

Refusing to allow these compounds to become labour camps where they would merely sleep, wake up and go to work, the migrants converted them into shrines to culture and entertainment, especially over weekends when they took time off from their hard labour. Typically, each ethnic group brought with them their traditions, customs and beliefs, carefully preserved in their memories, from their remote villages across the hinterland of South Africa. Some also brought various traditional objects and artefacts, used or worn, to showcase their colourful village life, much to the envy of others.

As migrant workers flocked to the city in large numbers, the environment was abuzz with different ethnic groups, including the Zulu, Xhosa, Sotho, Ndebele, Shangaan and Venda, to name a few. While migrants wore traditional garb, each reflecting their own unique and interesting way of life, the compounds also became a magnet for other city dwellers who were keen to learn about the ways of the village.

These marginalised communities presented to the open market what made them distinctive, and they began to trade amongst themselves. In the process they mastered the social economics of poverty, its alleviation and ultimate conquest. An important dimension of their common identity was their culture and related artefacts, which could be monetised. It is this socio–cultural fabric that gives rise to what

Barrett (2005a:2) calls the emerging 'social economics paradigm', where groups bound by a common heritage and strong identity choose to fight poverty and unemployment by creating an economy out of their social life. Barrett (2005b:217) argues that 'collective, shared identities create groups and communities' from which a pool of creative and shared resources, ideas and knowledge are mobilised to produce goods and services for the sustenance of these groups or communities.

It was inevitable that the compounds would become cultural melting pots where the Sotho (with their brightly coloured blankets) and the Ndebele (with their neck rings, beadwork and striking traditional blankets) mixed with the Venda, the Tsonga, the Zulu and the Xhosa. What had originally been basic items of clothing and accessories that these migrants had brought to the city soon became the envy of other ethnic groups and races. Mining company and other industry bosses, together with their wives and children as well as tourists, began spending their leisure time visiting the open cultural spaces at these compounds.

From the fascinating mix of cultures sprang magnificent displays of dancing evoking ancient times, hair-raising warrior songs about migration and riveting visual showcases of the country's diverse ethnic traditions. The Zulu wielded their shields and spears in rhythmic dance moves to the roar of drums, while singing war songs (*amahubo*). Meanwhile the Xhosa, in their elaborate outfits, kept audiences spellbound with their captivating melodies and ethnocentric mannerisms. Momentarily, the migrant workers' pain – a testimony of years of hard labour and indignity suffered at the hands of colonial masters – would be suspended as they danced themselves into a trance-like state, consumed by the omnipresence of their ancestors.

Not surprisingly, a market culture also began to emerge in these compounds, where the different ethnic and cultural groups started exchanging some of their attire and accessories. Craft markets sprang up, where folk art (such as beadwork and pottery) and functional items (such as sleeping mats, baskets, spears, shields, sticks, animal-hide clothing and traditional footwear) were sold to tourists.

Some migrant compounds became deserted as more formal, structured settlements were built in the city. The establishment of townships away from the economic hubs eventually saw those who had been living in compounds eventually move to the townships. Similarly, as new modes of transport were introduced in the city, horses and horse-drawn carriages faded over time. Horse stables were eventually converted into different types of dwelling. For example, a horse stable built at the turn of the 20th century eventually became a place of residence for the 'birds of passage' or urban outcasts.

Set against the above backdrop is the story of Kwa Mai Mai, an economic trade zone that captured the imagination of people who dared to dream.

Velicu (2011:1) argues that 'the manner in which a community relates to the past involves notions and actions such as connectivity, storage, retrieval, transmission and interpretation'. This is further confirmed by Verovšek (2016:529) who remarks that 'politicians frequently make use of mythologized understandings of the past to mobilize memory as an instrument of politics in the present'. This book sets out to discover how a community of migrant workers, when faced with their harsh, urban reality, used their collective memory and connective marginality to retrieve past memories and attain a heightened cultural consciousness that allowed them to redefine how they would survive in a city where they were not welcome.

The exclamation 'Maye Maye', colloquially referred to in this book as 'Mai Mai', denotes shock, disbelief or exasperation and stirs instant awkwardness and discomfort among those who choose to walk through the gate. However, behind the gate is a place that defiantly contradicts the emotions that the term evokes: a thriving economy built from the ground up by marginalised members of society who have been rejected by the formal employment system.

Kwa Mai Mai is a trade zone-cum-hostel that has managed over the years to create its own informal economy where culture, heritage and tradition converge and find expression in the creative work of defiant and non-conformist migrant workers. This is a place that has become a refuge for those who left their villages to look for formal employment but soon abandoned the search when it became clear that such opportunities were beyond their reach. This anthropological phenomenon of a people dedicated to producing material goods and services, using their connective marginality to create a culture-based economy, is what has made Kwa Mai Mai such an interesting site of study for those interested in the creative zeal of people from the margins of society.

Kwa Mai Mai has turned the class theory upside down in the sense that control over the means of production has been prised away from the dominant class by the rural migrant working class. Whereas the entire class structure of marginalised urban workers has been reconfigured within the labour relations system, its social structure has not been changed. Instead, it is through an awareness of their marginal status in a city that sought to reject them that they have managed to retain their strong cultural identity and tradition, and to use these to imagine a new economic reality.

This is a story of how cultural memory, sacredly preserved and transported to new geographies, can serve as a cultural weapon to resist subjugation and as an economic weapon by turning priceless traditions into tradeable commodities. It is a story of how those who are the keepers of cultural memories and tradition can use them not only as tools of survival but also as levers to unlock the creative and entrepreneurial talents that are buried deep within their souls.

This book argues that if cultural memories can be stored and retrieved through artefacts, sites, ceremonies, myths, rituals and texts, then Kwa Mai Mai is a place in which they all converge in the spirit of worship and celebration. The book further posits that the holders of these village memories are also astute practitioners who have turned priceless traditions into tradeable commodities as a means of survival.

In a fetishised fashion, many idolise Kwa Mai Mai as a site of cultural validation, a place that brings them closer to a culture that defines their identity, which is so different from that of the urbanites. It is also a place of cultural worship for those whose hypervisibility has been eclipsed by those who would rather denounce them as urban outcasts confined to hostels as migrants. Against all odds, this is a place of connective marginality where cultural memories, having been transported from the villages, are retrieved, repackaged and systematically revealed, for the purpose of idolisation or commercial consumption.

When consistent attention is given to texts, images and rituals, they lead to the establishment of a canon which helps to define the identity of the community (Velicu 2011). As a site of memories, Kwa Mai Mai has become the glue and placeholder for the collective rural experiences of migrant workers who came to Johannesburg armed with a pick and a shovel, only to discard these for the culture and tradition that were stored in their collective memories.

This book examines how traders and hostel dwellers in Kwa Mai Mai have constructed an economic community by appropriating their own culture and turning the place into a production site for goods and services. The book sets out to unravel how a migrant community's unintended, subversive vision to assume control over a space from which they were socially excluded has given rise to a site of vibrant economic activity. Building on Lefebvre's (1974) argument that control over the creation of space also confers a certain power over the processes of social reproduction, Harvey (1985) asserts that the ultimate command and control over the use of the space become crucial for the reproduction of social power relations.

The story of Kwa Mai Mai highlights how village migrant workers, comprising both men and women, have defied a system that was designed to break their dignity. Instead, they have turned the site into a socio–economic engine, which they own and control. In their determination to retain their cultural memories and identity, and by setting their own economic agenda, these reluctant migrant workers have waged a cultural war to fend off a system that sought to denigrate them, a system designed to disengage them from their social network back in the villages and turn them into perpetual urban workers.

Determined to reimagine new possibilities and craft a new social agenda and creative economy in the post-colonial era, they are a people who have skilfully used their connective marginality, supported by their heritage and tradition. By creating a culture-based economy, they have declared war on poverty, unemployment and inequality. Kwa Mai Mai has become a place where the money economy dominates and the exchange of goods and services defines social relations in a manner not seen in rural life.

To understand how the Kwa Mai Mai community have fought for their survival over the decades, it is important to explore how the 'metropolitan man' or urbanite intentionally or unintentionally alienates migrants in the city. The unwavering bond that unites the members of the Kwa Mai Mai community is the latter's response to the cold reception they received from the city. The metropolitan man displays a certain degree of apathy and indifference towards migrants in the city. As Casserley (1955:338) testifies, the metropolitan man 'evokes no recognition of personality and individuality in the other man', in that 'the depersonalizing of the personal is the essence of apathy' in the metropolitan man. The village migrant, in turn, disengages from the metropolitan social character by paying scant attention to the impersonality of the city.

Out of resentment for their alienation, their 'mode of life and state of mind' (Wirth 1964:225) reject neoliberal urbanism. As urban social life, according to Wirth (1964), bears some resemblance to an earlier folk society, the majority of those who migrate to the city are unlikely to abruptly drop their rural personality. However, by rejecting urbanism, village migrant workers assume total control over their existence in the city, with Kwa Mai Mai acting as the site of urban resistance and cultural resilience.

According to Casserley (1955:336), 'urbanism not only comprehends rural life [in relation] to its categories, it also seeks to subject it to its power'. When read carefully, this suggests that migrant workers can easily succumb to urban loneliness if they adopt the characteristics of apathy, as displayed by the metropolitan man.

In response to this alienation and rejection by the metropolitan man, the traders and residents of Kwa Mai Mai have taken their socio-economic struggles right onto the doorsteps of the city. Simmel (1964:36) argues that once in the city a man assumes a different and more discriminatory character than if he were in a rural setting. Against all the contending forces of life in the city, the need to 'preserve the autonomy and individuality of his existence in the face of overwhelming social forces, of historical heritage, of external culture, and the technique of life' (Simmel, 1964:35) characterises Kwa Mai Mai traders' determination to survive life in the metropolis. It is through their consciousness of the need to survive life in the city and the struggle between capital and labour exploitation that they have morphed into 'ethnic entrepreneurs' (Keith 2005), by using their ethnic narrative to reimagine themselves in a multicultural community and multiracial environment. These ethnic entrepreneurs have converted their cultural and living spaces into sites of consumption and have assumed control over the means of production.

How they have converted their culture into a viable economy, in an urban setting that rejects them, speaks to Watson (2009) and her views on the importance of social associations in keeping even the most neglected public places as vibrant trading places. 'As culture is not unitary, artefactual or auxiliary,' Walton (1984:88) argues, 'it follows that there are cultures associated with the major contending social groups whose collective action shapes the urban environment.' This is what one could call cultural adaptation and survival tactics in the city.

As Harvey (1985) states, converting and appropriating living spaces into sites of consumption has a liberating effect in the sense that the least privileged in the social order reconstitute the space in new ways, ring-fencing it and protecting it from external influences. To the extent that these spaces are appropriated, Harvey (1985) further argues, such fragmentation, which accompanies its homogenisation, allows the formation of protected islands that escape direct social control.

This book aims to explore and understand the cultural milieu of rural migrants in the city and the economic structures and social bonds that they have forged to guard against being sucked too deeply into urban life, where they will simply end up becoming perpetual workers at the mercy of the 'lowest available bidder'. By investigating the historical context of rural–urban migration, the book also seeks to understand rural migrants' day-to-day struggle for 'urban citizenship' (Schilliger 2019:35) in their fight for economic and social inclusion.

This book also seeks to determine whether the rights and access to the city are, either by default or by design, exclusionary and alienating to rural migrants. It further interrogates whether, in an urban capitalist society, the social system of rural migrants and their struggle for survival inevitably creates a new form of resistance and cultural resilience. Finally, it offers insights on whether, by 'formalising the informal', the rural migrant is redefining the city's material structures by creating cultural economic corridors.

Intangible cultural heritage has resisted and survived trans-Atlantic slavery, wars, religious conflicts and human migration. However, it remains fragile and susceptible to neglect, deliberate destruction, looting and illegal trafficking. Its ongoing survival is in the hands of those who appreciate it and are willing to preserve it for future generations – albeit in new and reimagined forms.

Ultimately, this book hopes to present new scholarship on post-coloniality, decoloniality and the re-imagining of cultural treasures to ensure that such treasures and the unique identities that have given them their special shape and form do not disappear into the mists of time.

# Two
# Wrapped in gold

'We must have labour. The mining industry without labour ... it would be to imagine that you could get milk without cows.' *(President of the Chamber of Mines, March 1912)*

## The gold rush and the making of the city

No amount of anthropological objectivity can adequately explain the dehumanising effect, humiliation and indignation suffered by a people who once strolled through their villages triumphantly but suddenly had to succumb to forced economic migration as a way to survive. The arrival of migrants in Johannesburg cannot be understood without first reflecting on the propitious discovery of gold on the Witwatersrand in 1886. The systematic extraction of African men from villages to supplement the much-needed cheap labour in the urban areas was a carefully constructed plan by Europeans who had descended on these shores to seek their fortune.

It all began in the Transvaal, a struggling territory under the control of the Afrikaners before 1886 when gold was discovered, but which suddenly became an economic stronghold with the world's richest gold reserves. A small emerging town, soon to be called Johannesburg, became the site of weekly pilgrimages for throngs of people descending on the 'Rand' as prospectors, labourers or traders. Suddenly, everyone had a mission, which was to make money from those who made money from mining that elusive gold, buried deep in the belly of the earth.

There were plenty of get-rich-quick schemes, including landowners selling their land to prospectors. Even those who owned means of transport, such as horse-drawn carriages or ox wagons, made money by transporting those who were looking for ways to make money. For essential goods and services, store owners, barbers and hawkers were on hand to keep everyone satisfied. Meanwhile, solicitors made money from all the commercial transactions that were necessary to kickstart an industry on a previously unheard-of scale. A city built from hustling was in the making.

Potenza (2016) observed in *All That Glitters*:

One summer's day in 1886, two prospectors discovered gold on a Transvaal farm called Langlaagte. Gold was not new to the Transvaal, Africans had mined gold hundreds of years earlier. More recently, gold had been found in the Eastern Transvaal. In most cases this gold ran out, forcing small mining towns to close down. The gold found at Langlaagte was different. The gold discovered there ran for miles and miles underground, 'an endless treasure of gold'.

De Kiewiet (1941) concurs that the discovery of gold in 1886 had an impact on the Witwatersrand that far exceeded expectations. According to him, it was the greatest gold discovery in history, both ancient and modern. Consequently, the story of South Africa was, for a considerable period of time, wrapped up in gold, and she glittered (De Kiewiet 1941).

It is no coincidence that the Kwa Mai Mai compound today is right on the banks of the *spruit* (small river) where gold explorers from Natal established their base. What makes this site fascinating is that, at a time when horses were the only mode of transport for people and goods, a horse stable had to be built to keep the hundreds of horses that were needed in this up-and-coming town. The area was soon abuzz with horse-drawn carriages and ox wagons, transporting either goods or people going about their business and negotiating deals in a city that was clearly not for the faint-hearted. The deafening and inescapable sounds of hammering and drilling had descended on the place, with many racing against time to strike it rich before the proverbial sun set. Interestingly, the then present-day Kwa Mai Mai compound was once a horse stable.

*Early hustlers in Market Square circa 1892 (Source: Davies Brothers)*

As the search for gold deposits continued, with the work so strenuous and tiring that it required almost herculean strength, a town was being built, brick by brick. Originally considered to be a wasteland, the area where Johannesburg is situated today developed by accident but forever changed the socio-economic and political landscape of South Africa. Sandwiched between Braamfontein, Doornfontein and Turffontein, the area was initially called Randjeslaagte – a mining village originally owned by the state and comprising 600 farm stands. On 8 September 1886, farm owners were coerced into entering into prospecting agreements with gold scavengers. Nine farms, from Driefontein in the east to Roodepoort in the west, were declared sites for public diggings, under the supervision of a committee formed on 8 November 1886 to assist the mining commissioner in playing an oversight role (Shorten 1970).

As part of the scramble for Africa, and in no time at all, the European settlers had carved out beautiful pieces of land, allocating 3 100 acres (1 500 morgen) amongst themselves as farms, including Langlaagte, Turffontein, Doornfontein and Braamfontein – the area that was to become Johannesburg, the City of Gold.

Those prospectors who originally thought that this would be a quick smash-and-grab exercise, and that they would soon be on their way out of the city with bags of gold loaded onto their horse-drawn carriages, soon realised that a collective approach was required. They therefore dispensed with the notion of possessive individualism and exclusivity, a theory advanced by Macpherson (1961). It was clear that individuals who saw themselves as the proprietor of their own person and as owing nothing to society were not going to emerge as winners in this gold rush. While they first thought they could undertake this gold-digging mission on their own, it suddenly dawned on them that, without sophisticated, industrial tools, this would not be possible. The gold prospectors and diggers owed this precious metal to society, and the world waited with bated breath for its timeous extraction. Not only did they need the right machinery to drill down into the barren earth, they also needed skilled and unskilled labour for the task at hand.

This type of endeavour was obviously not for small-time miners or diggers. It was a capital- and labour-intensive project. Therefore, striking it rich and creating wealth could only be achieved by employing more sophisticated and capital-intensive mining instruments and going deeper underground (Cameron 1986). In the face of this unpalatable truth, individual mining efforts were soon abandoned in favour of collective ones. Consortia were formed, which led to some consolidation of mining activities.

The amalgamation of smaller mining groups became increasingly common, and by 1895 a limited number of large, monopolistic companies dominated the scene. Consolidated companies were established, such as the Wernher–Beit–Eckstein group, Consolidated Goldfields, the JB Robinson group, the S Neumann group, the Albu group, the A Goerz group, the Anglo–French group and the Lewis–Marks group. Of these, Cecil John Rhodes' Consolidated Goldfields was the most important (Cameron 1986). Not all of these companies would survive, but a few stood the test of time and lived on to shape the social fabric and race relations of this country.

Eventually the Afrikaners, who had been holding onto this part of the country and had created their own Zuid-Afrikaansche Republiek

(ZAR), also known as the Transvaal Republic, could no longer fortify what later became the single biggest gold-producing region in the world, contributing 27.5 per cent of GDP by 1898 (Cameron 1986). Johannesburg was no longer an *uitlander* (foreigner) enclave (people were mostly from elsewhere, but were numerous) with a few gold diggers using primitive tools to remove the gold deposits from the rocks. Even Africans, who had been extracted from the villages to work as labourers, were part of the city that was not theirs. By 1892, the city was connected by rail to destinations as far afield as the Cape, Durban and Lourenço Marques (present-day Maputo). Stowaways, ex-convicts, runaways, sex workers and job seekers soon started to converge on the city – the ultimate encounter – in search of fortune.

## The shaping of the city

What had started out as a small, crudely built collection of dwellings was becoming an industrial zone. How this area, which would eventually become Africa's economic hub, came to be known as Johannesburg actually remains a mystery. A legend gathered around the name 'Johannesburg' and the person of Paul Johannes Kruger, who was president of the ZAR between 1883 and 1900. In 1892, he was awarded the Order of the Immaculate Conception of Vila Viçosa by Carlos I, King of Portugal. The renaming of Randjeslaagte as Johannesburg was then interpreted by some as associated with the honour conferred on Paul Kruger by Portugal. Boosting the idea of a link was the fact that coins minted since the reign of João V in Portugal (especially a famous, valuable gold coin) carried the name 'Joannes' and sometimes even 'Johannes' alongside the relevant king's profile at the time. (When relations between the Boer Republic and the Portuguese broke down in 1899, Paul Kruger returned the Order and was struck off the roll.)

Other commentators attributed the name of the city to three officials: Christiaan Johannes Joubert, who was the acting surveyor general and vice president of the Republic in 1896; Johann Rissik, who had stood in for the surveyor general; and Johannes Meyer, the once acting mining commissioner who oversaw law and order in the new goldfields.

By now, the fledgling town had been named Johannesburg. And by adding 'burg' to 'Johannes', the officials of the Transvaal Republic were satisfied that they had fortified the city, as the word symbolised their language, Afrikaans. Afrikaans was spoken by the Dutch settlers who had come from Holland, but it soon acquired its own distinguishing characteristics in the South African context. Where the name Johannesburg came from or to whom it must be attributed are still the subject of speculation. However, mention of the city being named Johannesburg can be traced to Reference No. R4996 of 1886, in City Council minutes. Yet the actual record of R4996/86, containing the details of the naming of the city, has not been found.

Nevertheless, with or without a name, the discovery of gold in 1886 was not going to deter explorers from flocking to this piece of land which would in time forever change human relations and, indeed, the world. This discovery separated the greedy from the generous, the schemers from the upright, the haves from the have-nots, and – more importantly – the Africans from the Europeans, who became the proletariat and the bourgeoisie respectively. The discovery of gold would later give birth to a classist society, racial segmentation and, eventually, racial segregation. The power relations between wage earners and payers of wages eventually defined the race relations in the City of Gold.

This multifaceted story finds its expression in the myriad and varied experiences of those who came from across the world, from colonies and disparate communities, who witnessed the scramble for this precious metal, either as willing or less willing participants in what was to become one of the world's greatest discoveries. In this story is a multiplicity of players, including those who travelled on horseback or in an ox wagon, and those who made their way through the treacherous forest to reach the Transvaal. Some living in the Kwa Mai Mai community today are the descendants of the first Africans who came to the city at the end of the 19th century.


## By hook or by crook – the hunt for labour

The dramatic economic story that unfolded in the Transvaal goldfields had a huge impact on social and human relations and would forever change the socio-political face of South Africa and the socio-economic structure and status of Africans.

*The two documents, respectively dated July and September 1896, leave no doubt that Johannesburg was named after Vice-President Christiaan Johannes Joubert and Johann B F Rissik of the Surveyor-General's Office. The letter on the left was written in German by one Erhardt Johannes from Prairie City, Missouri, on 18 July 1896, to enquire about reports he had read that the property of the founder of Johannesburg had been confiscated. Government officials in Pretoria misunderstood his letter and the response, dated 11 September 1896, quotes a note (right) by Surveyor-General Johann Rissik saying that Johannesburg was founded by the Transvaal Government and named after himself and Christiaan Johannes Joubert. This is the only extant official statement on the origin of the name. (Source:* Johannesburg One Hundred Years*)*

What caused the migration from the rural areas to the cities has been the subject of much debate. There are two schools of thought in this regard. Some people contend that the exodus to the cities was voluntary because of 'backward local economies in tribal areas' while others argue that it was 'conquest, dispossession of land, increasing taxes aided by draconian pass laws, and centralised recruiting' that drove Africans into the cities and ultimately into the compounds (Delius 2017:11). Therefore, the changing socio-economic and political landscape of the rural communities played into the demand for labour in mining operations and other labour-intensive sectors.

South Africa's migrant labour system redefined the urban experiences of those forcefully extracted from the villages to work in the mines and become perpetual urban workers. Retrieving the precious metal from deep within the belly of the earth required a substantial labour force, which at the time was not available within the vicinity of the gold mines. Sourcing labour from African communities in far-flung areas and the hinterland was not only the last resort but also the only option.

A shortage of labour, particularly cheap labour, was a nightmare for mine bosses and had to be resolved with the collaboration of the Afrikaner government in the Transvaal and the British colonial regimes in the Cape Colony and Natal. Acquiring skilled workers to get the mines going was not a problem, as they had already arrived in droves from Australia, North America, Europe and Great Britain. However, there was a dearth of unskilled labour, who were required in numbers that exceeded those of skilled labour. Luring Africans to work in the mines could not have occurred without some treacherous scheme, as few Africans were willing to abandon their way of life in the villages and the things they held dear, such as their livestock, and planting and harvesting.

Pulling Africans out of the villages did not happen in isolation; nor was it driven by the mines only. There was clearly a well-conceived plot to leave Africans with no alternative but to abandon village life or face retribution from the colonial officials. The imposition of all sorts of taxes on adult men, such as a poll tax, a hut tax and a dog tax (Guy 2006), was clear evidence of colonial officials' desperate attempts to drive Africans from their villages to become a source of much-needed labour. The requirement that such taxes be paid in monetary terms and not in the currency that the African had in abundance (livestock) meant that adult men had to leave behind their village way of life to seek employment elsewhere.

As would become increasingly evident, an uninterrupted supply of cheap labour came at enormous cost to Africans. This needs to be understood within a socio-political and historical context. The concerted efforts of the colonial agents and the mining industry to attract Africans to the mines were evident in the spike in the number of arrivals from 1890 to 1899 in the Transvaal. Through their recruitment agents, the mines were receiving Africans at a fast pace, as the latter joined the labour force in droves. It is also important to contextualise the arrival of Africans in the city, as they came from villages and native reserves that were the product of land dispossession by Europeans, particularly in Zululand. Africans did not come to the city of their own accord; they appeared to have no other option but to leave their villages.

The partitioning of Zululand in 1883 into 13 districts, the ultimate annexation of Zululand into Natal in 1887 and the Natives Land Act (No. 27 of 1913), which saw the allocation of only about 13 per cent of arable land to Africans, leaving more fertile land for whites, made the villages and reserves less and less attractive to Africans. As much as 80 per cent of the arable land was allocated to white people (western Zululand for the Afrikaners and eastern Zululand for the British), who made up less than 20 per cent of the population. The Zulus, who had enjoyed and observed traditional customs and were governed by kinship relationships and respect for traditional authority, were turned into farm tenants and, subsequently, farm labourers. Africans soon found themselves squatters on the land of their forefathers, which was now under the control of white settlers.

Migration to the city must therefore be seen and understood within the context of years of fighting exhausting anti-colonial wars, which could not be won. The ongoing tribal wars and rivalries between the chiefs and the falling African kingdoms, which stemmed from the colonial wars, came in handy for both the Afrikaners and the British, who used the opportunity to dislodge Africans from the village social system and create a captive labour reserve. In Zululand, defeating and dismantling the Zulu Kingdom contributed greatly to the development of the migrant labour system and the supply of cheap labour to the mines and surrounding cities.

According to Laband (1995:376), 'The Zulu lost nearly all the highland grazing and valuable mixed veld in the upper reaches of the great rivers.' By 1887, the British colony of Zululand had been established, which totally transformed the social make-up and power relations in what remained of the kingdom. This was the ultimate assault on the social system of the Zulu, while their economy and sense of cohesion were shaken to the core. This would have had a massive, devastating impact on the life and livelihoods of the Zulu people, while dealing a deadly blow to the social system of Africans in general.

The explorers, soon to become mine owners and bosses, conspired with the government to extract African labour from the villages by introducing all sorts of schemes that would make Africans vulnerable to capitalist ploys. As mentioned earlier, one of the tactics devised by the government to promote the interests of the mining industry was the imposition of taxes on adult men living in villages to force them to seek work in the cities. As taxes had to be paid in cash, the only way for Africans to avoid imprisonment was to join the expanding labour force which was needed in the mines. The imposition of taxes also helped to finance the struggling colonial government administration in Natal.

The colonisation of Natal and the supply of much-needed labour to emerging industrial sectors also produced a labour supply for the territories in which the Natal colonialists had commercial interests. The number of African workers who flocked to Johannesburg from Natal suggests that the region had become a labour reserve and a conduit for the supply of labour to serve the interests of mining magnates who had acquired claims on the farms that previously constituted land belonging to Africans.

Given the large and growing need for cheap labour, Africans were soon regarded as better suited for pick-and-shovel work, particularly in the early period of open-cast mining. With dwindling options open to them in the villages, many of the young, able-bodied African men saw this as a more attractive alternative to becoming permanent labourers on white-owned farms. Not only did the responsibility for paying taxes, often on behalf of their aging fathers as well, fall squarely on their shoulders, but many needed to earn money to pay the traditional bride price.

For many years, most labourers did not come to the mines with a view to staying permanently; they intended to return home as soon as they had earned enough money – a tradition that is still upheld today. Others hoped to find jobs so that they could acquire the new, material items that Westerners had introduced to African communities, including various types of clothing, which were still foreign to them. Still others wanted to access tools such as hoes and ploughs to use on their rural lands. Those who were not fortunate enough to make it in the city either got lost in the concrete jungle or figured out other ways to make a living, either legally or illegally.

The forced labour migration system had been so carefully crafted – by stripping Africans of their means of survival in the villages – that migrating to the city seemed to be the only viable option for them. Over time, the systematic extraction of Africans from villages, which was designed to turn young and proud men into a conformist working class and an ongoing source of cheap labour, became the backbone of a capitalist-driven urban economy.

Africans seeking employment in the city also served the interests of the Natal colonial government which was facing serious financial difficulties, with a budget deficit standing at 17 per cent. Natal was struggling to secure a loan of at least £1 million to meet the colony's capital expenditure requirements.[1] In fact, the fiscal situation in the colony was so dire that the collapse of its administration seemed imminent. The colonial government was not collecting enough revenue from customs, the post office and telegraphs or the railways.[2] The only solution that the government seemed prepared to implement was to increase taxes for the black population, who had played no part in creating the deficit. The existence of a well-established tribal system in Zululand and Natal was fortuitous, and the colonial government did not have to look any further for a financial solution.

# A captive native community and the reluctant migrant worker

The process of pulling African labour out of the villages was facilitated by taking advantage of the hierarchical social structure of the village, particularly in Zululand (which was subject to traditional rule) and parts of Natal. The conversion, through conquest and compliance, of the tribal chiefs into administrators and enforcers of Natal's colonial policies on natives in native reserves and farms, under the so-called supreme chief, proved to be an effective way of bolstering the depleted coffers of the colony. In this regard, the tribal system and the role of chiefs and headmen helped to ensure the implementation and administration of colonial policies. King Shaka's building of a powerful and organised tribal system, which made it easy to communicate and send messages as and when needed, became the Achilles heel of the Zulus.

The imposition of taxes on adult men and the collection thereof through traditional chiefs, who had been forced to become administrative agents for the colonial government, made tax collection simpler than it might otherwise have been. Over 227 Natal chiefs were under the control of the colonial government, together earning a total of £2 618 in a year as compensation for administering and collecting taxes. With such a system in place, adult men were not going to escape paying taxes. What better way to impose and collect taxes than through the conforming chiefs, who had simply become administrators of colonial laws and policies that had been shoved down the throats of the 'natives'. In 1879, the Zulu Kingdom was broken up into 13 sections and in 1887, Zululand was annexed into Natal, with all chiefs now falling under the governor of the colony, who had become the supreme chief.

As the 'new king' of the colony, the governor needed only a well-organised tribal system to ensure that messages trickled down to the last person in the tribe. With the assistance of the magistrates (the new white chiefs), such messages could easily be passed on through the hereditary or appointed chiefs, who in turn would send the messages further down the line. Depending on the size of each tribe or clan, the chief would pass on such information to the headmen (*iziNduna*), the overseers of the chief's territory, who played a supervisory role in the tribe and deployed the information according to the number of wards or *izigodi* under the chieftaincy. The tribal headmen would then pass the relevant message to each individual homestead (*kraal*) or via the *oBhekeni* (those who oversaw young adult men), for the attention of, and action by, the head of the homestead.

The above was best described by Stuart (1913:29), who had become Under-Secretary of Native Affairs in the colony:

> After Zululand was annexed to Natal (December, 1887), the office of the Resident Commissioner and Chief Magistrate of that territory was converted into Commissioner for Native Affairs. Under the Under-Secretary and Commissioner came the Magistrate, the thirty of Natal proper, as ex-officio Administrators of Native law, coming under the former, and the eleven of Zululand under the latter, officer. After the Magistrate came the Chiefs of tribes, 238 in Natal proper, and 83 in Zululand. Salaries and allowances were paid to 227 of the Natal Chiefs, and stipends to seven of those in Zululand. All Chiefs were required to control their tribes in accordance with the tribal system and keep in close touch with the Magistrate of their respective wards.

The colonial government's understanding of the social and political structure or of the organisation of the tribal system extended no further than an organogram depicting a hierarchical structure. The locations and reserves became mere statistics that could be presented as simple numbers: the number of chiefs in the colony, the number of *iziNduna* (headmen), the number of men and their wives and children, the number of huts belonging to each homestead, and the corresponding taxes that stood to be collected.

Given the colonial understanding of the Zulu social system and the organisation of a homestead, it was easy to deduce how much tax could be collected from the natives in Zululand and Natal. Assuming the existence of polygamy, which was prevalent in those days, each wife in a polygamous marriage would have had her own hut. Assuming, too, that a man had about four wives, there would have been five to six huts, if not more. This is the captive Zulu social system that the colonial system used to its advantage. Coercing adult men to pay tax and using the command structure underpinning the social and military organisation of the Zulu, while working through headmen and chiefs to collect and administer taxes, was an easy route for the colonial government to follow.

The desperation of the colonial government to collect a poll tax to provide much-needed financial relief was evident in the speed with which the government conducted meetings throughout the colony. By October, two months after the passing of the Poll Tax Act, the magistrates had conducted meetings within their jurisdictions, much to the displeasure of the Africans on whom the tax had been foisted. Africans were informed by the magistrates that the collection of the poll tax would take place on 20 January 1906, or as soon as possible thereafter.

Needless to say, while this book does not deal in detail with the administration and execution of the Act, it is important to point out that without the assistance of the colonial magistrates and the chiefs, these tax-collection efforts would have been stillborn. As such, it would probably not have been possible to recruit native labour or set in motion such a large exodus of Africans from the villages to the cities. Yet, as soon as the Act was passed, the Minister of Native Affairs issued very clear directives to the magistrates to ensure that chiefs in the colony were apprised of the Act and that they understood its provisions.

As if the poll tax was not enough for the Africans, whose lives and livelihoods had been disrupted by the contraction of their land, the proposal – by Theophilus Shepstone in 1849 – to levy an additional 7 shillings on every native hut was a financial blow to village men (McClendon 2010). Taking into account the polygamous nature of Africans at the time and the size of a typical homestead, which averaged three wives or upwards and their children, this was a tall order. The imposition of such taxes meant that Africans could no longer remain in the villages. As McClendon (2010:13) argues, 'The crucial change introduced as the colonial state began to tap the productive capacity of this social system was the requirement the tax be in cash, thus steering Africans toward wage labor, production for the market, and the commercialization of social relations.'

As was evident from this Shepstonian revenue-generation scheme, whether they resided on the reserves or farms or in locations, the natives were not about to escape the strategy that sought to turn them into perpetual labourers. Those who remained on the white farms were also forced to pay rent and hut tax, thus forcing them to sell their labour to serve the agricultural interests of white farmers, on land that had been expropriated for commercial purposes. Much as the natives argued that the imposition of all sorts of taxes was merely a ploy to satisfy the labour demands of white farmers, in that blacks were forced to work as farm labourers, this Shepstonian policy had reached a point of no return.

To extract rent from natives residing on white farms – who by virtue of land dispossession had become tenants on the land of their forefathers – the farmers employed all sorts of tactics. Rent, which had become a burden for the farm tenants, had to be paid one way or another. Some farm landlords demanded service in lieu of rent, in the form of labour; others paid wages to the tenants for working for half the year and then freed them of the need to work for the other six months, but still charged them rent. Some farmers saw rent as a useful source of revenue for their farms and demanded nothing but rent from their tenants.

By 1906, the annual rent per hut could be as low as £1 and as high as £12, but it averaged between £2 and £3 per hut. Those who failed to pay rent were evicted and forced to find a place on a nearby farm where they would become tenants of the new European landowners and landlords. This had been the land of the Zulu under the respective reigns of Shaka, Dingane, Mpande and Cetshwayo and the last warrior, King Dinuzulu. As tenants of white landlords, they would be forced to act as labourers in return for receiving lodging on their ancestral land. Heavy fines were imposed on those who failed to pay their taxes, regardless of their economic circumstances. Many villagers slid deep into debt or were subjected to flogging or jail terms.

As if the imposition of taxes was not difficult enough, a series of natural disasters altered the social and economic life of the Zulu. These disasters not only negatively impacted the production of crops, but they also decimated cattle herds. Between 1895 and 1907, ploughed fields were attacked by a swarm of red locusts, while serious drought swept through the remaining viable land, obliterating any hope of harvesting. Cattle diseases such as rinderpest swept through Zulu cattle herds in 1897, followed by a tick-borne disease. These struck a deadly blow to the heart of Zulu pride – their cattle. As Laband (1995:437) observes, 'The sudden nigh obliteration of their cattle shook the Zulu to their roots.'

The British colonialists devised a similar labour taxation scheme in the Cape Colony. In 1894, a law was passed in the Cape by the then prime minister, Cecil John Rhodes, called the Glen Grey Act. It, too, forced Africans into the migrant labour system by imposing a tax on them, with the option of working for three months a year in exchange for wages. This was a Catch-22 situation, because to pay tax every year Africans had to earn wages one way or another.

The inevitable had now become a reality: stay in the village, fail to pay your taxes and face imprisonment; or move to the city and sell your cheap labour to cover your tax payments.

## A social fabric destroyed

The ultimate winners were the industrialists, the government and everyone who, in pursuing their commercial or personal interests, needed cheap African labour. As Africans flocked to the cities from the rural areas, the social fabric of a community – whose life revolved around subsistence farming and who grew just enough food to feed their families, complemented by the regular hunting of wild deer, rabbits and birds, and the gathering of wild fruit – was severely disrupted. The social and economic organisation of the village meant the world to its residents. Their world was the village, the surrounding grazing lands for their livestock, the fields for crop production and the forest, which was both a hunting ground (for antelopes and other animals) and a source of energy (firewood).

Krige (1950:35) regards a vibrant village economy, which is held together by a strong social fabric, as 'a self-contained economic unit in which a complete life can be led. Each village has its own cattle that supply the milk, and its own fields, in which sufficient corn and vegetables are to supply the needs of the inhabitants'. There is no excess labour to expatriate to the cities, for example, because everyone has a distinct role to play in the village. Yet labour *was* expatriated to support the growth of mining and other industrial activities in the urban areas, upsetting the natural socio-economic order in the villages and causing irreparable harm.

The division of labour in the villages ensured that men and women of varying ages executed their specific duties and chores, which kept the community alive and thriving. While women tended to the fields, fetched water and firewood, and prepared meals, men went on hunting expeditions in what was known as *ukuphuma inqina*, hunting rabbits, antelope and buck. Similarly, young boys tended to the cattle and goats and performed other chores. Outside of this world, nothing mattered. It was this village system and way of life that the migrant labour system sought to disrupt.

Without the use of force and other threats, the extraction of labour from the villages would have proven to be a mammoth task. Although Africans were deeply entrenched in their simple life in the villages, any attempts to resist the imposition of taxes proved to be futile, with sometimes dire consequences. Even when defiant chiefs, such as Bhambatha ka Mancinza of the Zondi clan, fought fearlessly against the poll tax and refused to force adult men under his chieftaincy to pay tax, their rebellion was eventually extinguished.

The crushing of traditional rule left villages in disarray as the chiefs who had been associated with the rebellion were tried in court, imprisoned or deposed and replaced with government-appointed chiefs whose job was to advance the interests of the colonialists. Those who succumbed to colonial control were given the responsibility of ensuring compliance with the tax-collection system, which was meant to swell the rapidly diminishing coffers of the colonial government.

Where else would young men, some younger than 18 years of age, go except to the mushrooming goldfields that offered a more attractive value proposition than working for meagre wages as farm labourers? And so, they left in droves for the city. Ultimately, the unrelenting colonial wars against innocent Africans prevailed.

## The village exodus and the rise of the migrants

The new tax burden meant that natives were caught between the proverbial rock and a hard place: they had to choose between toiling and possibly dying on white farms or escaping to the city (Johannesburg) and seeking employment in what was fast becoming the economic heartland of Africa.

The sudden discovery of mineral resources resulted in villagers being forced to sell their labour in exchange for wages, which turned the social system of the African upside down. Whether they stayed behind in the rural areas and worked as farm labourers or converged on the cities, Africans became trusted sources of labour for those who had come to seek their fortune in the scramble for Africa. Africans eventually filled the cities to the brim and their labour was up grabs in the mining and industrial communities.

Callinicos (1994:96) observes, 'At first, only the young, unmarried men left. They were sent by their chief who needed their wages to pay taxes. These taxes had been imposed on the people by the government. A few young men left on their own accord.' Therefore, the fact that many young men entered the Witwatersrand labour market was no coincidence; in fact, it can only be described as forced migration, with these men being reluctant or circumstantial migrant workers. Even those who decided to return home, because they struggled to adjust to life outside the villages, found themselves being lured back to the cities, unable to escape the almost magnetic control they had over them as providers of always-in-demand labour. A permanent labouring class was beginning to form, but one that was also seasonal in some respects as it still had to contend with and maintain a 'traditional economy based on homestead production and cattle-keeping'.[3]

As was to be expected, compelling natives to pay various taxes, including rent for their tenancy on farms, eventually forced young men to leave their homesteads and find work elsewhere so that they could meet the financial obligations of their fathers. Large numbers of young men left Natal and Zululand to seek employment in the mines in Johannesburg, while their fathers eagerly waited for their sons' hard-earned wages to be sent back home to cover rent and taxes. This also redefined the relationship between a new migrant working class in the city and those remaining behind in the villages – a subject that is explored later in this book.

As the migrant labour system gained traction, the numbers of

Africans arriving on the Witwatersrand began to grow. The recruitment efforts of the Witwatersrand Native Labour Association (WNLA) played an important part in this regard. From the initial cohort of 14 000 Africans who had come to work in the mines, the number had risen to 88 000 by 1890. By 1899, there were 100 000 African mineworkers.

By 1898, a year after Zululand was annexed into Natal, large numbers of young men had already left Zululand in search of employment opportunities in the city. By 1904, just over 17 000 Zulu men had left Zululand and become migrant workers in faraway towns and cities, including working as miners in Johannesburg. This active recruitment of African mineworkers by the WNLA, which by then enjoyed exclusivity, was designed to eliminate competition and keep wages as low as possible. By 1910, the WNLA was delivering 200 000 unskilled Africans to the Witwatersrand each year.

Not surprisingly, the large influx of migrant workers in the city created tensions and eventually manifested in a war of the classes – a war between the underclass and the upper class. This would ultimately dictate who stayed in the city and who had to go.


## A human settlement nightmare

The need for cheap African labour and all its ramifications had not been given proper consideration. With more and more African migrant workers flocking to Johannesburg, the city was battling to accommodate them all. The rate of urbanisation and the need for housing settlements for emerging urbanites, particularly blacks, was becoming a growing concern of those engulfed in the politics of fear. The increasing numbers of Africans migrating from rural areas and the need to provide housing for them became a political and ideological conundrum in that the city was damned if it did and doomed if it did not. The city nevertheless escaped doom – if not damnation.

Housing was needed in the areas where blacks worked. While certain types of work, such as domestic work, necessitated black labourers being in the city for as long as they worked there, it also became apparent that they could not be accepted as residents of the city. Grant and Flinn (1992:139) argue that 'the cause of Black housing problems was, in fact, largely due to the political and ideological framework which determined all major housing policies relating to housing, and which was contradictory to the natural process of urbanisation'. The same cheap labour that whites and big businesses needed was not welcome to reside in the vicinity of their employers.

Yet, as early as 1896, a census conducted by the city showed that Johannesburg already had 102 078 inhabitants, of whom approximately 61 292 were residing within a three-mile radius of Market Square. The area around Market Square was home to 50 907 Europeans, made up of 24 489 whites born in Europe, of whom 12 389 were from England and Wales, 997 were from Ireland and 2 879 were from Scotland. There were also 24 500 Europeans born in Africa, of whom 6 205 were born in the Transvaal and 15 162 were born in the Cape Colony. Of course, the city extended beyond the city centre, also encompassing the new suburbs of Klipfontein, Forest Town, Hillbrow, Berea, Yeoville, Bellevue, Houghton, Vrededorp, Paarl's Hoop, Robinson, Ophirton, La Rochelle, Rosettenville, Klipriviersberg, City and Suburban, Doornfontein, Bertrams, Lorentzville and Troyeville.

The next group of people living within the three-mile radius of Market Square were 14 195 natives (out of a total of 42 533 in the city), followed by 4 807 people of Asian descent, 952 Malays and 2 879 from other race groups. These various groups of people were accommodated in segregated communities or settlements, termed 'native locations', which had been deliberately established in Johannesburg and classified into three racial groups: the 'Malay Location' (in Pageview, next to Vrededorp), the 'Coolie Location' (near the Braamfontein railway station, an area that was to later become Burghersdorp) and the 'Kaffir Location' (which was close to the railway line, on the south side, not far from the present-day Vrededorp subway) (Grant and Flinn 1992:135). The only other, and the oldest, black residential district in Johannesburg, where the rest of the blacks resided, was Kliptown, which had been established in 1891 (Cripps 2012). Both the 'Coolie Location' and the 'Kaffir Location' were demolished after the bubonic plague in 1904 and their residents relocated to present-day Pimville.

Exacerbating the housing problem was that families of migrant workers were now joining them in areas where there was no, or very little, extra accommodation. In an attempt to limit the influx of Africans into the city, the Secretary of Native Affairs sent a circular to all officers of the Department of Native Affairs, magistrates and full-time special justices of the peace throughout the Union of South Africa, warning the natives against this influx.[4]

Clearly, regardless of the measures adopted to try to limit the numbers of Africans flocking to the city, except for those formally recruited for their labour, blacks were now determined to escape to the sprawling urban spaces. The situation had become a nightmare for the government. Parliament passed the Natives (Urban Areas) Act No. 21 of 1923 to allay the fears of Europeans by ensuring that blacks did not encroach on what whites considered to be their sacred living spaces. The Act also made provision for measures to be put in place to clearly separate habitat spaces and to bar Africans from having any right of access into white urban areas. This included barring them from owning businesses and residing in designated white areas. Putting all this into practice, however, posed a real challenge and it remained to be seen how effectively it could be implemented. However, the government was determined to see the process through to allay the fears of white Europeans.

Furthermore, the Act placed a corresponding responsibility on the local authorities to provide accommodation for those Africans who were lawfully employed and residing in the areas in which they worked. Faced with the unenviable task of finding accommodation for the multitudes of Africans arriving in the city and having to comply with the various provisions of the Act, the Johannesburg City Council established the municipal Department of Native Affairs in 1927. Together with the Council's Committee on Native Affairs, the Department of Native Affairs moved swiftly to settle blacks in designated areas.

The Natives (Urban Areas) Act started to deliver results when the process of resettling blacks outside the city began to take shape, particularly with the establishment of Western Native Townships, later to be known as Soweto. By 1927, the process of moving Africans to residential areas far from the city was gaining momentum, evidenced in large-scale construction and resettlement of blacks in designated African townships.

The establishment of settlements and the provision of housing for the large numbers of people arriving from other parts of the country continued to strain the resources of the city. There were some black settlements in other parts of Johannesburg, such as Alexandra township, Sophiatown and others, yet illegal settlements were still popping up in the city. The municipal Department of Native Affairs and the Council's Committee on Native Affairs, established in 1927 and 1928 respectively, had the task of dealing with the unfolding crisis of spiralling informal settlements and relentless demand for decent accommodation among Johannesburg's arriving migrants.

The establishment of what would later become Soweto started with the purchase of 1 300 morgen of land on which the first township, Orlando, was built to accommodate 80 000 people (Grant and Flinn 1992). By 1930, a total of 2 625 houses had been built in Western and Eastern Native Townships. To enforce racial distance, the whole of Johannesburg was declared a whites-only area in 1933. The immediate implication of this was that blacks (not just Africans but also Indians and coloureds) residing in Sophiatown, Martindale and Newclare found themselves on the wrong side of the recently enacted law. A total of 43 000 people would need to be resettled in areas earmarked for black habitation, which were sufficiently far away to allay white fears.

The 1943 raids by the police in whites-only areas drove home the fact that blacks had suddenly become unwanted in European areas, unless they were coming to work but not to stay. The establishment of townships and other residential areas was becoming more and more of a priority as arrivals of African migrants in Johannesburg continued unabated. However, Africans were frustrated by the restrictions preventing them from buying or leasing property in urban areas or building their own homes. They felt that the Council should not be absolved of the responsibility of providing housing for Africans.

What complicated matters and was a growing dilemma for the city was that European ratepayers had pressured the Council in 1944 to demarcate the areas of Sophiatown, Martindale and Newclare as white residential and industrial areas. As a result, blacks had to be moved to alternative land, which came to be known as Meadowlands, which had been purchased for their resettlement. More than 100 families were initially moved to Meadowlands. By 1968, a total of 22 516 families and 6 469 single people had been relocated. In a triumphant gesture on the part of the city authorities, Sophiatown was renamed 'Triomf' and declared a whites-only area.

Additional land was acquired to the west of Johannesburg to accommodate the ever-increasing numbers of Africans. Between 1948 and 1960, a total of 40 682 houses were built, including schools, administration blocks, clinics and beer halls. The plan was to keep Africans away from European-designated areas – whatever the cost and potential difficulty of raising the necessary finance to execute the plan. In the early 1960s, the group of townships in the south-west of Johannesburg was named Soweto, which stood for South-Western Townships. There was widespread resettlement of blacks to the outskirts of Johannesburg, including to areas as far removed as Katlehong, Daveyton, Tsakane and KwaThema on the East Rand, and Kagiso, Dobsonville, Mohlakeng and Bekkersdal on the West Rand. The township of Tembisa was to serve Kempton Park (Grant and Flynn 1992). Clearly, the City Council was rigorously following and implementing government policy. To the Council, this was a necessary evil that could not be avoided and a natural consequence of urban migration.

However, the Act did not satisfactorily address the issue of labour (whether mineworkers or domestic servants) being needed for work in certain areas but being allowed to reside only in other areas. Blacks living in flats and the servants' quarters of their white employers also needed alternative accommodation. In addition, non-permanent residents (largely African men) – the so-called migrant workers – needed a different housing solution to that designed for urbanites who had made Johannesburg their permanent home but could not be accommodated in the townships.

The compounds, particularly the mining compounds, which were established in the late 19th and early 20th centuries, remained the settlement areas for African labourers. These compounds were scattered across the Witwatersrand in the vicinity of the mines. The Salisbury and Jubilee mining compound, on the corner of Wemmer Jubilee Road, was one of many such compounds. This is where the story of Kwa Mai Mai began, before the compound was relocated to its current site.

# Three
# Condemned

Apart from the townships on the outskirts of the city, to which Africans had been forcibly moved, another housing solution emerged – single men's hostels or compounds. Having natives residing in the city where they were most needed had become a necessary evil, as far as the authorities were concerned, and this in turn called for a different type of habitat.

Not all Africans arriving in the city were required to live in the townships because, for some, their employment was of a temporary or seasonal nature. Those who could not be settled in the townships either had to be accommodated in domestic compounds on their employers' premises or at the so-called single men's hostels or compounds. These hostels were developed to accommodate 'boys' – a disparaging term used to describe natives working as domestic workers such as gardeners who had initially been accommodated on their employers' premises in what was commonly known as servants' quarters.

With mining operations scattered across the Witwatersrand and no place to accommodate the ongoing waves of migrants, particularly Africans arriving from the villages, mining companies had to build compounds in the vicinity of their operations to house the mineworkers. Some of the single men's hostels were situated right in the middle of the city, although the inhabitants of these hostels were locked away from everything that the city had to offer. Their life started and ended inside the compounds, unless they were deep down in the belly of the earth or returning home for a short stay.

The mining bosses even established designated mining stores where the mineworkers could purchase their basic necessities. Confined to the mining compounds, African mineworkers had their lives programmed, from the time they were taken underground in cages to dig for the precious, elusive metal to the time they were brought up again after a hard day's slog. This was to ensure that no unwelcome natives would be found roaming around the exclusive white areas in the city. Confining them to the mineworkers' compounds would allay the fears of whites who perceived Africans as vagrants in the city. After their day's toil, they were barred from exploring the night life and enjoying its pleasures, as they would be arrested for vagrancy if found roaming through the city's new streets after the curfew.

The idea of subjecting humans to living quarters with a panopticon design, a jail-like habitat with a social control mechanism that symbolised authority and discipline, was not new to South Africa. As early as 1785, Jeremy Bentham, an English social theorist and philosopher, proposed this prison-like dwelling which enabled total oversight and control over its inhabitants. With its ring-shaped compound and a viewing tower, the guards had line of sight of the entire establishment (Butchart 1996). Michel Foucault (1977:78), the French philosopher, described these dwellings as symbols of 'power and visibility' whose prison-like observation points were an integral part of the space and design of the buildings. Designed for maximum observation, the buildings were configured in such a way that the inhabitants could be watched from a strategic lookout point, which was key to monitoring and controlling their movements, including their entering and exiting the compound.

According to Crush (1994:309), a good example of how these compounds were arranged and managed is found in the description provided by the Deputy Commissioner of the Johannesburg Police when referring to the City Deep mining compound in 1914:

It is surrounded first of all by a galvanised iron fence. It has barbed wire at the top which prevents anybody from getting in or out...

> The gates are so constructed that they have turnstiles by which each native can file in singly. The buildings are so constructed that from the gold compound manager's office he can see down any direction along the line of huts. The buildings are arranged like the spokes of a wheel with the office as a hub [and] by that means they are able to see exactly what goes on in the compound and practically almost in the rooms.

There were common characteristics in the construction and layout of the compounds, as pointed out by Cooke (cited in Vosloo 2020):

- the Kimberley archetype, where workers were placed in isolation within the mine property;
- the layout of the compound, determined by the efficient operation of the mine and ethnic separation;
- a single entrance controlled by mine police;
- large, visible courtyards as circulatory and recreational spaces which allowed inhabitants to be observed most of the time;
- communal sleeping halls for 16 or more workers, with meagre furnishings, showing a disregard for workers' individuality and freedom of choice, personal space and privacy; and
- communal ablutions and toilets.

With the establishment of labour compounds with the above-mentioned features, the natives' movements could be monitored and controlled without too much effort. Also, the appointment of guards from the same racial group created an automatic psychological hierarchy, where those in control used their superiority to subjugate others in the same group. According to Foucault (1977:201), the effects of the panopticon were 'to induce [in] the inmate a state of conscious and permanent visibility that assures the automatic functioning of power'; and to 'frame the everyday lives of individuals' (1977:77) through the introduction of strict daily routines coupled with discipline meted out to those who failed to conform. Placing these migrants under surveillance also meant that their general behaviour and even their simplest actions and personal gestures could be observed and regulated. Their day-to-day existence was therefore underpinned by a disciplinary regime and a strict programme dictating how and when things had to be done.

It was therefore 'natural' that every mining company in South Africa had a mineworkers compound where new labour recruits, upon their arrival from the villages, would be housed, albeit in squalid conditions. With the discovery of diamonds and later gold in South Africa, the closed compound system was a better way of controlling the movements of newly arrived African migrants. The idea of constructing compounds came from Francis Thompson, a confidant of Cecil John Rhodes. Compounds were intended to ensure the complete isolation of mineworkers (Harris 1954) and to prevent the theft of precious materials.

Turrell (1987) observes that by keeping mineworkers in a controlled human settlement system, mine owners could ensure the productivity and effectiveness of the labour supply. 'It meant the closed compound system was the effective form in which the diamond mine owners came to terms with migrant labour' (Turrell 1987:7). The controlled compound system also gave mine owners the power and discretion to coerce labourers into re-employment arrangements, thereby establishing a steady pool of proficient labourers. Moreover, Vosloo (2020) observes that these mining compounds, because they accommodated black labour only, limited interracial violence and made it easy to practise wage control.

Demissie (1998:445) views the introduction of labour compounds as 'an architectural discourse, a strategy of organising space and an institutional design which has emerged in various forms since the nineteenth century to discipline and regulate industrial labour'. This resonates with Foucault's observation that the buildings in a compound make it easier to exert power and control. Nothing that happened in the compounds escaped the attention of those posted to observe the movements and behaviours of those living inside. Like some other scholars, Demissie (1998) argues that the compounds were used to 'protect' the white communities against the perceived threat of thousands of black male mineworkers living in close proximity to them.

The mining compounds on the Witwatersrand ensured that labour was forever present and, through strict discipline and absolute conformity, became the reservoir for controlled cheap labour. One of these compounds was the Wemmer and Jubilee mining compound, owned jointly by the Salisbury and Jubilee mining companies. It was situated on the corner of Wemmer Jubilee Road and Von Wielligh Street on the east side of town, which extended to Kruis Street Extension in the west. This was the part of downtown Johannesburg that had been proclaimed a suburb by 1921, called Salisbury Claims. The same suburb today reflects a mixture of commercial activities and light industry.[5] The mining compound was therefore not too far from the main reef and the farms where gold deposits were initially found. It was also where the Salisbury Gold Mining Company had laid its claim.

It is worth noting that both the Jubilee and the Salisbury mining companies were registered in 1886 in Natal (a British colony after 1843) before acquiring gold claims on the main reef, in Turffontein and on the Witwatersrand (Skinner 1902). Interestingly, both companies also shared the same addresseses in Pietermaritzburg (11 Timber Street) and in London (96 Gresham House, C.E.), with John Shaw Sheldrick as secretary in both offices (Skinner 1902). This is indicative of a mining syndicate involved in the exploration, acquisition and extraction of mineral resources in Africa, with its exploitative tentacles extending to everything that was sacred on the continent.

However, the mines of Jubilee Gold Mining Company and Salisbury Gold Mining Company had ceased to operate before the First World War. Jubilee's mining operation closed down in August 1911, while Salisbury's closed down in February 1912. As previously discussed, for those Africans who were coming to the city to seek employment and were not regarded as permanent residents, a different sort of housing solution had to be provided by the Johannesburg City Council. Because the Council yet had to make provision for single men working in the city and the surrounding areas, it acquired the old mine compounds at Wemmer and Jubilee, which had originally been rented by single men working in the city. Coincidentally, this was the site of the original Kwa Mai Mai hostel before it was relocated to its current location in Albert Street in the City and Suburban part of Johannesburg. The City Council took over the compound to provide much-needed accommodation for natives who were coming in droves to the city in search of work.

## Leasing the compound

In 1912, the municipality initially proposed buying the Salisbury and Jubilee compound for £25 000 to provide housing for the natives, but subsequently decided to lease it. On 6 September 1913, the business manager at Central Rand Freehold Proprietary Limited, Mr LG Heard, wrote to the Town Clerk agreeing to the leasing of the Salisbury and Jubilee compound for £25 per month for an initial period of 12 months, whereafter the termination of the lease would be subject to three months' notice on either side.[6]

On 25 September 1913, the Mining Commissioner, Mr JL van der Merwe, wrote to the Town Clerk informing him that he had no objection to the proposed takeover of the Salisbury and Jubilee compound. The Mining Commissioner explicitly stated that his support was based on the distinct understanding that the occupation of the compound would be entirely at the Council's risk.[7] The compound was to accommodate job seekers who had a special permit allowing them to look for casual work on a daily basis. These daily labourers, as they were called by the authorities, had no fixed employment. Every time they left the compound, they had to carry a special pass or permit, which had to be signed by the City Council official who oversaw the compound. The permit allowed the daily labourers to be out of the compound to seek employment, but if found without a permit they would be arrested for vagrancy.

On 26 September 1913, the Town Clerk wrote to the Provincial Secretary in Pretoria, informing him that the Johannesburg City Council was proposing entering into a lease agreement with Central Rand Freehold Proprietary Limited to (i) implement the lease and apply surface rights, (ii) house the municipal natives in the compound, and (iii) proclaim the area as a location for the housing of natives other than municipal employees in the compound.[8] It is interesting to note the distinction made between 'natives' and 'municipal employees', as they all in fact worked for the municipality. It appears, then, that natives may not have qualified for classification as 'employees'. The Town Clerk then proposed that the compound should house about 700 natives working at the municipal light and power facility. The same compound would also house those natives who could not be accommodated on the premises of their employers.

By November 1913, the Secretary of Native Affairs had written to the Director of Native Labour in Johannesburg, confirming his support for the lease of the Salisbury and Jubilee compound by the municipality as well as its proclamation as a location to house natives.[9] Similarly, the Provincial Secretary sent a letter on 8 December 1913 approving the Johannesburg City Council's request to lease the compound from Central Rand Freehold Proprietary Limited under the provisions of Section 64 of the Local Government Ordinance of 1912.[10]

On 4 December 1913, the Executive Committee of the Johannesburg City Council passed the following resolution:

> Under the provisions of Section 64 of the Local Government Ordinance 1912 to approve a proposed lease, the details of which are set forth in the Administrator's File No. 2/7596, between the Town Council of Johannesburg and the Central Rand Freehold Proprietary Limited in respect of a piece of mining ground with building thereon known as the Salisbury and Jubilee Compound, required by the Council for the purposes of a combined compound and Native location.[11]

Even though there was considerable opposition from various stakeholders, including churches and ratepayers associations, to the establishment of a native location through the acquisition of a compound in the city, nothing was going to stop the Council from going ahead with its scheme. In response to such opposition, the Council steadfastly pointed out that it was competent, under Section 38(a) of the Johannesburg Municipal Ordinance of 1906, to establish locations wherever it saw fit. The Council also pointed out that the only matter requiring the authority of the Executive Committee was the proposed leasing of the ground required by the Council to give effect to its scheme.

On 20 November 1913, Mr JH Dobson, the general manager of the Johannesburg City Council, wrote to the Director of Native Affairs in Johannesburg: 'Dear Sir, I beg to inform you that the Natives previously housed at the Works (referring to Gas, Electrical Supply, and Tramways Department), have now been transferred to Salisbury and Jubilee Compound.'[12]

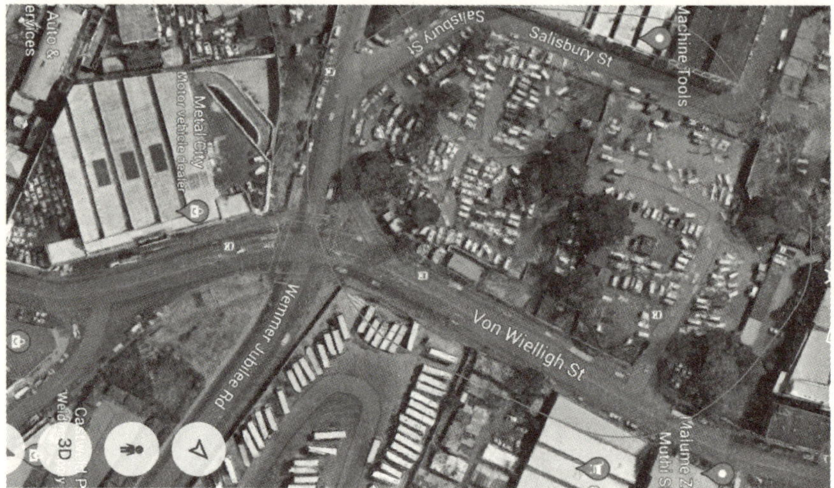

*The original Mai Mai bazaar was on the grounds of the old Salisbury and Jubilee compound, corner of Wemmer Jubilee Road and Von Wiellich Street on the east and Kruis Street Extension on the west.*

## Purchasing the compound

The Salisbury and Jubilee compound was leased by the Johannesburg City Council with effect from 1913. By 1927, the ownership of the compound had changed hands. It no longer belonged to Central Rand Freehold Proprietary Limited; the new owner was Centre Syndicate. The Director of Native Affairs in Johannesburg, Mr HS Cooke, was already seeking permission on behalf of the City Council to purchase the compound outright from the new owner for an amount of £5 500. Mr Cooke argued that the acquisition of this property was a sound business proposition and that the municipality should therefore be afforded the opportunity to make the purchase.

On 24 December 1927, the Secretary for Native Affairs wrote back to the Director of Native Affairs in Johannesburg, confirming his receipt of the request from the Town Clerk for the purchase of four acres in the Salisbury and Jubilee compound for £5 500 plus transfer fees.[13] On 4 January 1928, the Director of Native Labour in Johannesburg wrote to the Secretary for Native Affairs and indicated that the intention of the City Council was to continue using the compound as accommodation for 700 to 800 municipal workers and other natives who could not be accommodated elsewhere.

UNION OF SOUTH AFRICA.

DEPARTMENT OF NATIVE AFFAIRS.

NO: 3814/13/T. 724.　　　　PRETORIA, November 6, 1913. 191

7 NOV 1913

Lease of Salisbury and Jubilee Compound.

The DIRECTOR OF NATIVE LANDS, Johannesburg.

With reference to ... Minute No.2322/13/9782 of the ... Provincial Secretary ... there is no objection ... as this Department ... the Salisbury and Jubilee Compound ... icipality and to the proclamation ... the Johannesburg ... area required for that purpose.

SECRETARY FOR NATIVE AFFAIRS.

*'No objection' letter from the Secretary for Native Affairs, 1913 (Source: National Archives of South Africa)*

Rs/R. 4.12.

THE TOWN CLERK,

JOHANNESBURG.

Sir,

Salisbury and Jubilee Compound.

With reference to your letter No. 12/47 of the 27th. ultimo and previous correspondence, I have the honour to inform you that the Administrator in Executive Committee is pleased under the provisions of Section 64 of the Local Government Ordinance 1912 to approve the proposed lease between your Council and the Central Rand Freehold Proprietary Limited in respect of the Salisbury and Jubilee Compound required by the Council for the purpose of a combined Compound and Native Location.

I have the honour to be,

Sir,

Your obedient Servant,

PROVINCIAL SECRETARY.

*Letter from the Provincial Secretary approving the lease, 1913 (Source: National Archives of South Africa)*

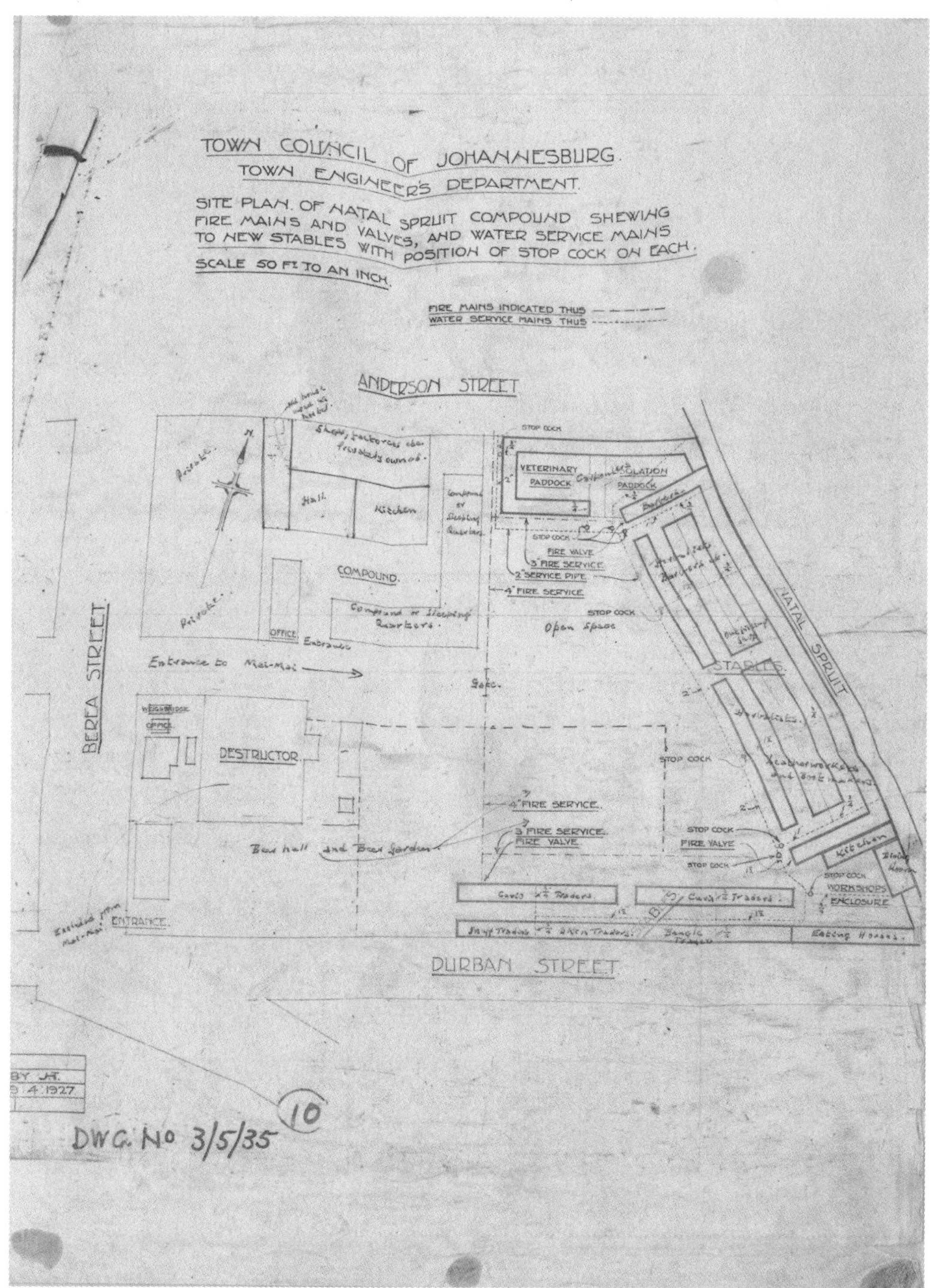



*Town Engineer's drawing of the new Kwa Mai Mai compound, 1927 (Source: National Archives of South Africa)*

It was the Council's intention to eventually dispose of the compound to build an industrial site. This was the first indication that the Council was considering another site in the city to which the natives would be permanently relocated. Mr Cooke wrote: 'It is not the intention of the Johannesburg Municipality to erect substantial building on this property which is considerably undermined, but to utilize it for present purposes as a hostel and, subsequently dispose of it as a[n] industrial site.'

An indication that the original compound would eventually move to the new site was contained in the first town engineer's drawing, dated 19 April 1927 (DWG No. 3/5/35), which was kept in the Office of the Translator in the Department of Interior. This drawing was submitted to the Johannesburg City Council, suggesting the conversion of a section of the Natalspruit compound, which was a stable for horses, into a compound for natives.

## *From a horse stable to a men's compound*

For a long time, the site at Wemmer and Jubilee was the City of Johannesburg's compound for daily labourers. But years of neglect had taken their toll on the Salisbury and Jubilee compound, which now needed serious refurbishment and a general facelift. On top of that, the compound caught fire in the 1940s. The Johannesburg Executive Council took a decision to relocate the whole compound to a new location in City and Suburban, on the corner of Anderson and Berea streets, while keeping its original name of Mai Mai hostel and bazaar.

Even in its new location, Kwa Mai Mai retained its previous formula and served as both a trade zone and a dwelling place for traders who lived and worked in the compound – similar to how the market functioned when it was in its original location. The same rules that applied to the Wemmer and Jubilee compound also applied to the new site, which was sometimes called 'the new Mai Mai'. Again, no native was allowed to leave the compound without a permit proving that they were in the city legally; nor were they allowed to enter the compound without the permit, which confirmed their legal and resident status there.

The task of finding and purchasing a new site to relocate the natives from the old Kwa Mai Mai proved not to be very difficult for the Johannesburg City Council. In Albert Street there was an establishment that used to be a horse stable, situated right on the banks of the Natalspruit, a small river that was subsequently canalised. It was here, just down the road from the old compound, that the City Council identified stands for expropriation, that is, stands 768-9-70 along Berea and Anderson streets in City and Suburban. The acquisition of stands for the purpose of accommodating natives required the approval of the Minister of Native Affairs, as stated in Section 16 of the Natives (Urban Areas) Consolidation Act No. 25 of 1945.[14] In addition, the power vested in the Johannesburg City Council to expropriate the identified stands was provided for in the Municipalities Powers of Expropriation Ordinance of 1903.

As explained, the new compound had previously been a horse stable. Just like humans, who needed compounds for those on the margins of society or castles and mansions for those at the top of the socio-economic ladder, horses needed to be kept somewhere in the city. Horse stables in the middle of the city pointed to an early transport system that had served fortune seekers, explorers, mine bosses and adventurers who used horse-drawn carts, carriages and wagons to get around the city. Horses needed to be cared for. Native labour was therefore required from dusk to dawn, with duties that included washing the horses, walking them for exercise, feeding them and keeping their stables spick and span. Horse minders also needed a place to stay, not far from their horses. Therefore, the compounds – an undeniably condescending term – shortened the distance that mine workers had to travel to and from work, while also protecting them from the bad influences of urban life – at least according to Pirie (1988). Moreover, the horses needed to be kept close to where they were needed.

Interestingly, the new site for the compound used to be the Natal Camp or Meyer's Camp (as it was first called), where gold diggers from Natal first pitched their tents. The Natal Camp was one of three mining camps that were initially set up before the first stands at Randjeslaagte were auctioned off for mining purposes and a permanent town started to take shape. The other two camps were Ferreira's Camp and Paarl Camp. From July 1886 onwards, fortune seekers from all walks of life and from around the world descended on Randjeslaagte and proceeded to establish camps.

*Early mining labourers (Source: AECI Limited Africana Museum)*

*Natal Camp, circa 1887 (Source: Pictorial History of Johannesburg)*

It is interesting that the Natalspruit, on whose banks the new compound was built, acquired its name from the fact that the diggers who set up their bases there, in Meyer's Camp, were all from Natal. By September 1886, there were roughly 500 people living in the camp. The Natal diggers had set up camp near the south-eastern part of Randjeslaagte, in the southern part of Doornfontein, which today is called City and Suburban. Ironically, Kwa Mai Mai today caters mainly for traders who have their roots in KwaZulu-Natal.

On 13 December 1940, with the approval of the Minister of Native Affairs in terms of the Natives (Urban Areas) Act No. 21 of 1923, Treasury Circular No. 1971 was issued, formally establishing the

Natalspruit compound. The approval defined the areas laid out by the City of Johannesburg for the establishment of 'locations for the occupation, residence and other reasonable requirements of natives'.[15] The Natalspruit compound comprised 36 stands in total (Nos. 762, 763, 764, 767, 912, 913, 914, 915, 916, 917, 924, 925, 926, 927, 928, 1068, 1069, 879, 884, 885, 996, 888, 889, 890, 891, 892, 893, 899, 900, 901, 902, 903, 904, 905, 906 and one other), situated in the City and Suburban suburb of Johannesburg.

At the 697th meeting of the Johannesburg Executive Council, held on 25 April 1944, the Council finally considered and approved the submission to convert what used to be an old horse stable into the Natalspruit compound. The conversion involved erecting a small hostel for the 'native' men. Shops would also be built in the compound. This decision by the Council meant that the portions of Salisbury and Jubilee compound that had consisted of a hostel, a bazaar and one part of a brewery and beer hall were to be transferred to the converted compound following proclamation in Government Notice No. 1971 of 13 December 1940. The notice further claimed that the rights of the persons transferred from the Salisbury and Jubilee compound were not only protected but were also extended; and that such people would be accommodated in 'hygienic and attractive buildings'[16] that were to become the Mai Mai hostel and bazaar.

To convert the horse stable into a single men's compound, the Council approved expenditure amounting to £14 221 14s. 8d. A further estimated amount of £316 100 in capital expenditure was approved – which the Council, given its borrowing powers, would raise. At a meeting on 24 July 1945, the Council further resolved, subject to the approval of the Minister of Native Affairs, to expropriate the identified stands at a value of £10 000. This was considered to be a reasonable and appropriate amount to compensate the owners of the stands.

The stands were eventually expropriated and acquired from the Transvaal Graphite Company for the total sum of £10 500, on condition that the Council pay the costs of transfer and that the sellers be permitted to continue to occupy the stands for a period not exceeding two years. This was to give the sellers enough time to identify and acquire another suitable property in the City and Suburban or Jeppe Industrial areas, for the purposes of erecting a new factory for their business.[17] The initial offers for the said stands, before the Council moved for the compulsory purchase, stood at between £12 000 and £15 000, while the market value was between £6 000 and £8 000. The Council decided to invoke Section 6(1) of the Municipalities Powers of Expropriation Ordinance of 1903 and offered £10 500, which it deemed to be reasonable. The mayor was then authorised to process the necessary documents in connection with this matter.

On 5 July 1946, CA Heald, Secretary for Native Affairs, issued a notice to the Director of Native Labour in Johannesburg, informing him of the approval obtained from the Minister of Native Affairs for the purchase by the Johannesburg City Council from the Transvaal Graphite Company of stands 768, 769 and 770 for the sum of £10 500. This kickstarted the establishment of a native hostel at the Natalspruit compound.

The expropriation of additional stands, as discussed below, proved that there was not enough accommodation to house the steady stream of Africans flocking to Johannesburg from the villages. Again, this was clear from correspondence from the Native Commissioner, dated 22 May 1946, to the Director of Native Labour, in which the Commissioner sought approval from the Minister of Native Affairs for the acquisition of further stands – Nos. 759, 761, 765 and 766.

The above request was granted by the Minister of Native Affairs on 12 July 1946, under the provisions of Paragraph (a) of Subsection (1) of Section (16) of the Natives (Urban Areas) Consolidation Act No. 25 of 1945. Again, this was in connection with the establishment of the so-called native hostel.

The Kwa Mai Mai hostel and bazaar was then established as a trade zone and marketplace, but it had limited hostel accommodation. Originally 300 beds were reserved for stall owners and their employees. The so-called Nguni (consisting of Zulu, Swati, Xhosa and Ndebele people) constituted 85 per cent of the residents, while the Sotho constituted only 5 per cent and other ethnic groups accounted for the remaining 12 per cent. However, Zulu traders always had the biggest slice of the pie in terms of the number of hostel places.

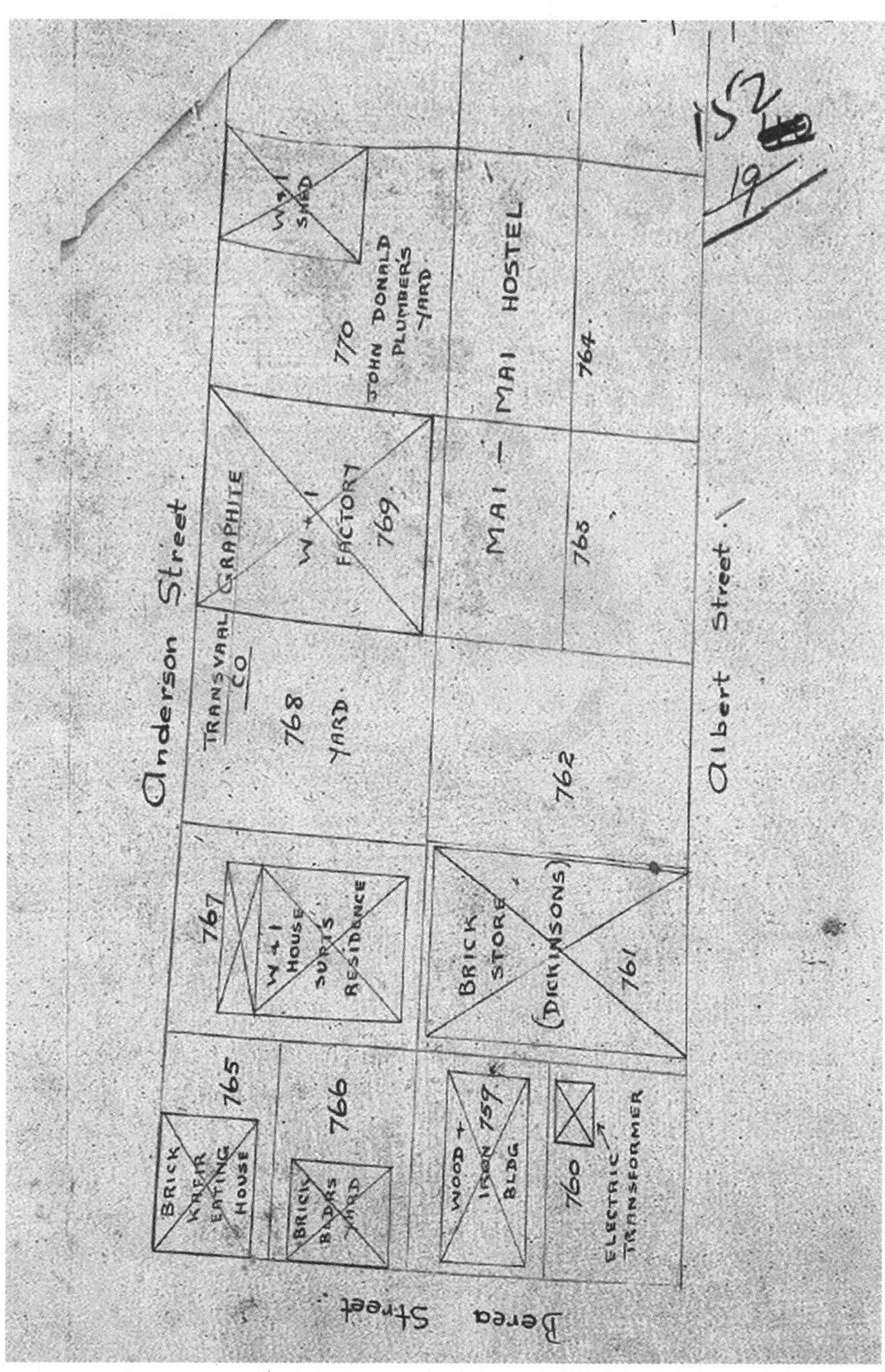


*Stands for expropriation, circa 1945 (Source: City of Johannesburg Town Clerk Department)*

## Maye! Maye! The name and its origin

It was when the compound was still in its original location that it got the name 'Maye Maye' or, as it is better known, 'Mai Mai'. A mine manager at the Salisbury and Jubilee Gold Mining companies, Mr Saul Msane, who hailed from Natal, became known for his signature exclamation and cry of 'Maye Maye' whenever a mineworker who had been injured underground was being brought to the surface. Msane, a founding member in 1901 of the Natal Native Congress (NNC), an organisation that advocated awareness training for Africans about their rights, had come to the Transvaal from Natal in about 1907 and found a job as compound manager at the Salisbury and Jubilee compound. Later he become an agent recruiting Africans for jobs on the mines, for which he received a good salary.

A man of political and social standing, Saul Msane played a key role in wooing Africans from the villages. Ironically, however, he would later be branded *isita sa Bantu* (enemy of the people) for not siding with African labourers when they embarked on a strike, demanding better pay and improved conditions on the mines.

It is reported that when black mineworkers embarked on a general strike across the Witwatersrand following a strike in Johannesburg by black sanitary workers (1918), Msane played an important role in diffusing the anger of the belligerent mineworkers. In fact, Msane not only discouraged the strikers from voicing their grievances, but also reportedly issued a statement that denounced the strike as an unnecessary action, a statement that eventually found its way into leading Sunday newspapers. It was this action that fuelled negative sentiment about Msane and led to his being labelled an enemy of the people.[18] Because of this stigma, he became isolated from the African labourers and went on to live life as an outcast in Bree Street, Johannesburg. He died in 1919.

When he assumed his high-level management position in the mine, Msane underwent a character change – which resulted in behaviour that was in stark contrast to how he had conducted himself during his political career. Besides being a founding member of the NNC, he had been a member of the Transvaal Native Congress (TNC) and one of the founding members of the South African Native National Congress – a precursor of the African National Congress (ANC). Always destined for leadership positions, he had played a prominent role in the struggle for the liberation of African people in South Africa, which had also included becoming Secretary General of the ANC in 1917.

## The rise of the market

Right from the beginning, the Mai Mai hostel and bazaar operated as a trade zone and became a go-to place for those looking for traditional items and other necessities. Those who came to the city to seek employment, but were unsuccessful, turned into self-employed migrant workers making and selling a variety of essential goods and other paraphernalia. These job seekers-turned-traditional entrepreneurs included 'skin workers, bangle makers, carpenters, snuff makers, sjambok makers and a number of well-known herbalists, whose small shops were a veritable cornucopia of remedies such as herbs, animal extracts, snake skins and dried snake venom'.[19]

Calling it the 'strangest of the shopping centres', Knox and Gutche (1947:77) acknowledged that this part of the city and the market had been claimed by the Bantu as their 'own Johannesburg'. Knox and Gutche (1947) also noted that, since the move to the new site, the market had lost its original character even if it now had the advantage of being a much cleaner and more hygienic environment. However, the market was still popular among those looking to quench their thirst, either at the gate where coffee was sold or inside the Kwa Mai Mai beer hall where traditional beer – also called Mai Mai or kaffir beer – was sold. In the 1940s (see photograph on p. 56), as Knox and Gutche (1947:77) noted, the profusion of herbal shops was the most noticeable feature of the market: 'In grim confusion can be found baboon's skulls, hare's feet, monkey's paws and teeth, lizard, python, armadillo, crocodiles, chameleon, and liguana skins, snail and seashells, porcupine quills, snake's fangs, eagle's heads, and ostrich eggs.'

Everything in the above-mentioned collection had a particular purpose – among them rekindling love relationships or repelling bad spells perceived to have been cast by enemies. Each herb sold at Kwa Mai Mai fixed something, and still fixes things today. Nothing has changed. What was found in the 1940s is still found today.

Cultural entertainment was a key feature of the mines and mineworkers used their free time to engage in all sorts of traditional competitions.

The Kwa Mai Mai market provided the much-needed traditional regalia used by the various dancers, who had teamed up in formidable dance groups, performing at competitions or showcasing their dance routines every weekend. All the dance groups needed traditional regalia and the market was a convenient source of traditional hides or beadwork and bangles. If the customers could not come to the market, the market went to the customers, with the traditional regalia makers visiting one mine compound after another selling their wares.

One of the most popular items bought by mineworkers who were returning home for a traditional wedding ceremony was the wooden kist, which they bought either for the sister or the daughter about to get married. This is one item that earned the returning migrant workers bragging rights. It symbolised young men transitioning into adulthood, as they were not considered to be men until they were able to provide for their siblings or parents. The wooden kist, which was 24 inches long, 18 inches high and 18 inches wide, had very distinctive features. It was not just a wooden box for storing clothes and other essential items; it was also beautifully carved and decorated with striking images, mirrors and other decorative elements. An interesting feature on the front of the kist – beside mirrors – was an image of Jesus Christ, which was gradually replacing traditional African images. This is explored in subsequent chapters that discuss woodworking activities at Kwa Mai Mai.

*The early days of the Kwa Mai Mai market, showing the daily visit by traditional healers to buy animal skins (Source and date unknown)*

The wooden kist was not to be used by men; rather, it was an important item that a bride who was leaving her father's home to get married would take as a personal item on the day of the wedding. The kist would store the newlywed's pricey possessions, including blankets. Therefore, the migrant workers returning home with this celebrated wooden kist would have bought it either for a sister who was about to get married, or for a daughter of marrying age. Men would not buy a kist for their fiancées, as it could only be bought by the brother or father of a sister or daughter getting married.

Besides the wooden kists men made at the compound was another popular item – sandals – produced by the Zulu traders and sold in large quantities. The base of the sandal was made of repurposed car tyres and there was a colourful strap on top that secured the foot. The strap was made of cowhide that had been tanned and softened to prevent it from cutting into the flesh. These sandals must have been a source of immense frustration to regular shoemakers and merchants who would have liked to increase their customer base, particularly as Africans were becoming increasingly urbanised. But for Africans (mainly Zulus), the sandal was a fashion statement, a symbol of defiance and also a convenient type of footwear.

It was a fashion statement because it stood out on special occasions when Zulu men dressed up in full Zulu regalia and its distinctive colours complemented their traditional attire. It was also a symbol of defiance as it sought to show Europeans that the tyres that propelled motor vehicles could be used by those who had to walk long distances in the absence of any other mode of transport. In other words, Zulu men used the same tyres to walk distances that Europeans could only cover when travelling in a motor vehicle.

These tyre sandals were economical footwear, as most Zulu men could not afford the modern shoes brought to these shores by Europeans. They also played an important part in the dance competitions that took place at various men's hostels. At these dance competitions, which attracted dance groups from various compounds, there was definitely no place for ballet or waltzes. These dances were fierce and sent shivers down the spines of the onlookers, stirring the long-hidden warrior spirit. As the dancers' feet rose up to the sky and then descended again, hitting the ground hard and shaking it to its core as if to awaken the ancestors, it was the sandals that cushioned the feet as they hit the solid ground. As the motor tyre sandal asserted its authority over the barren soil, with dust swirling, the sandal makers watched with satisfaction as this 4x4 of all footwear held firm.

These were the same sandals that the Zulus wore when, having braved the wild animals in the forests, they walked to the Witwatersrand from whatever remained of the Zulu Kingdom. The sandal was resilient, durable and impenetrable – even by the treacherous thorns of the *umnqawe* tree, ie, the *acacia nilotica*, which is better known as the scented-pod acacia.

The distinctive greeting in green letters, 'Welcome to Kwa Mai Mai', first appeared at the entrance to the market more than seven decades ago. Inside are third- or fourth-generation children and their parents, descendants of great-grandparents who were traders and residents of Kwa Mai Mai from as early as the 1920s, before the hostel and bazaar compound was moved to its current location in the late 1940s.

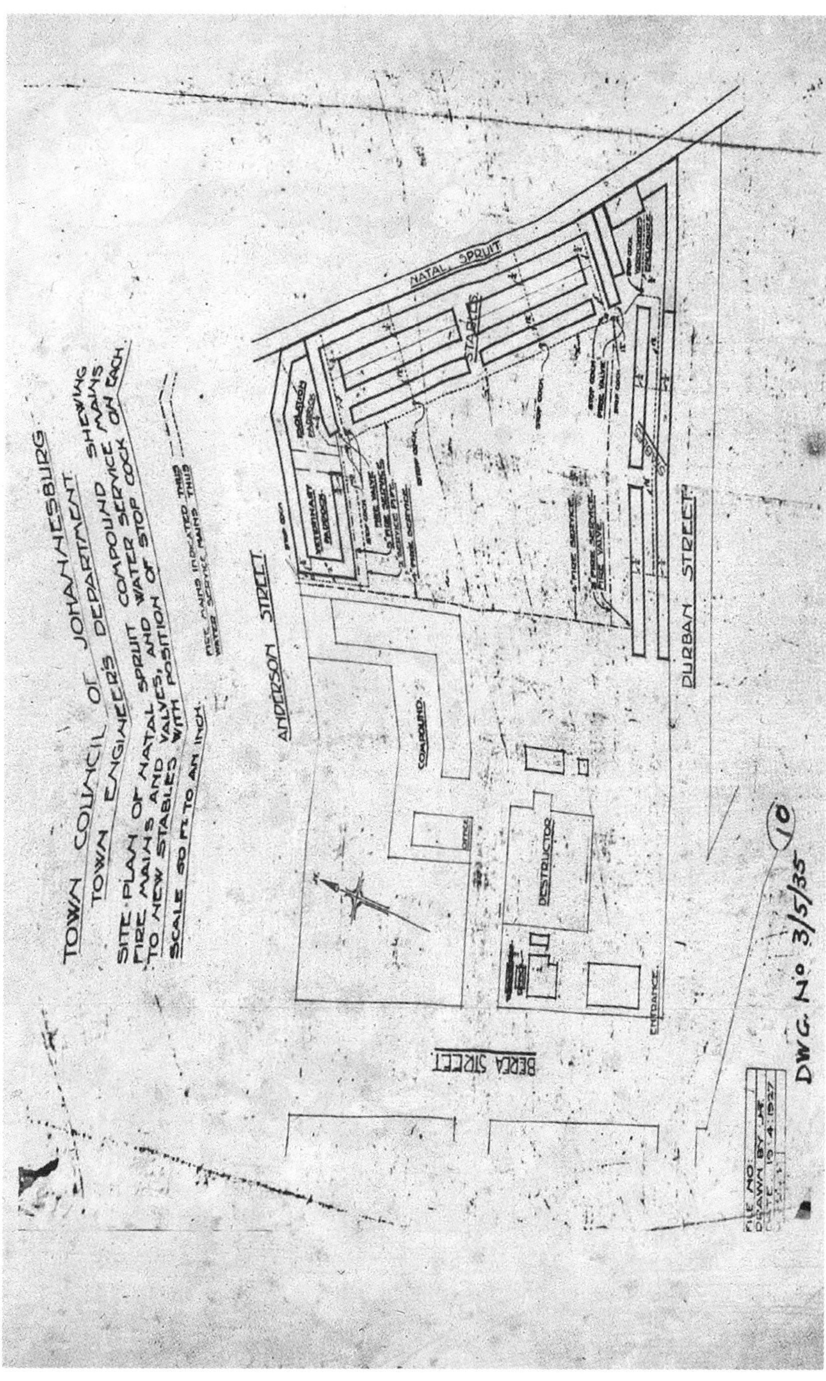

*Early Town Engineer's drawing of the planned relocation of the Kwa Mai Mai compound to the new site (Source: National Archives of South Africa)*

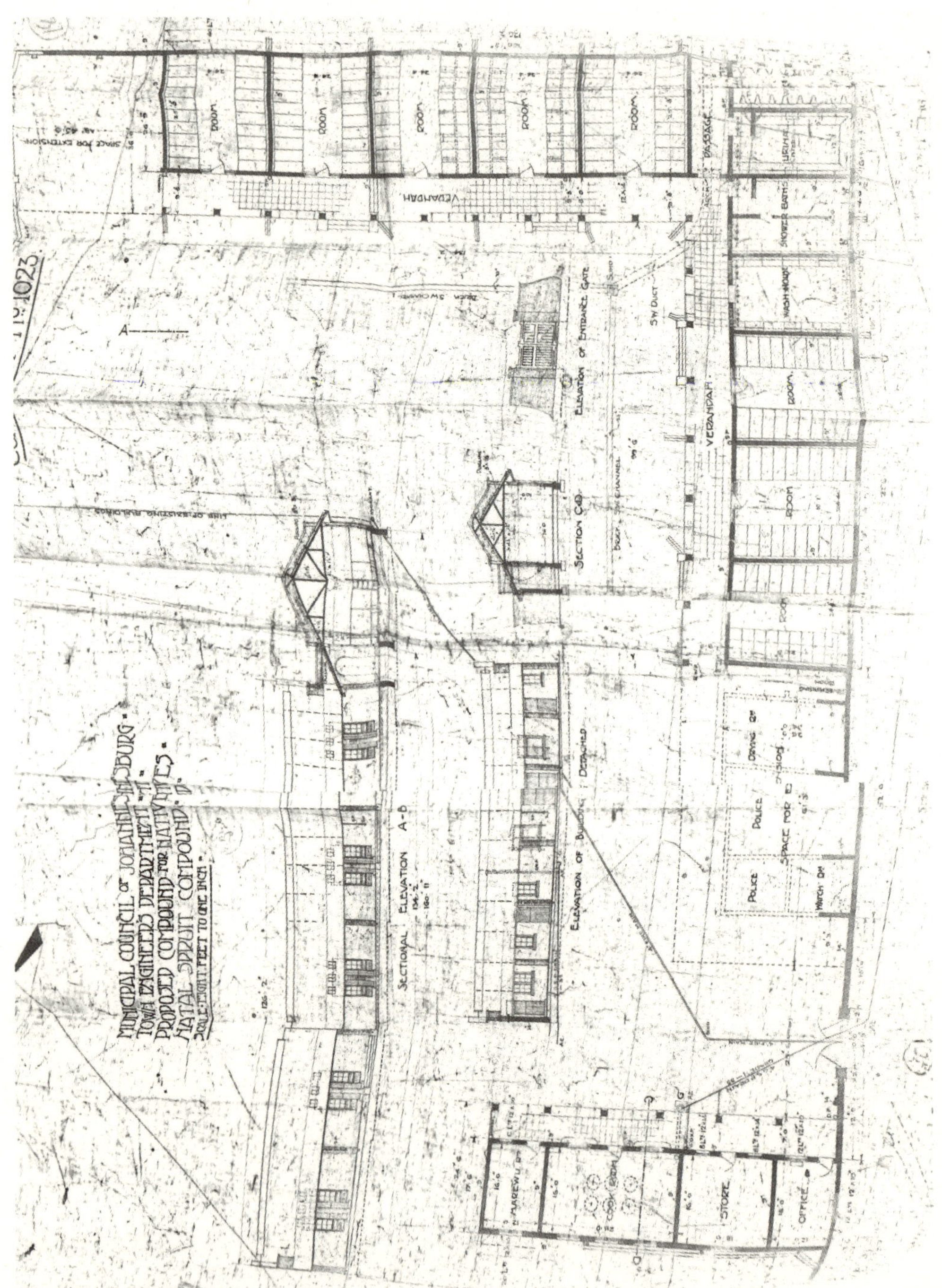

*Town Engineer's elevation drawing: conversion of stables to the Kwa Mai Mai compound (Source: National Archives of South Africa)*

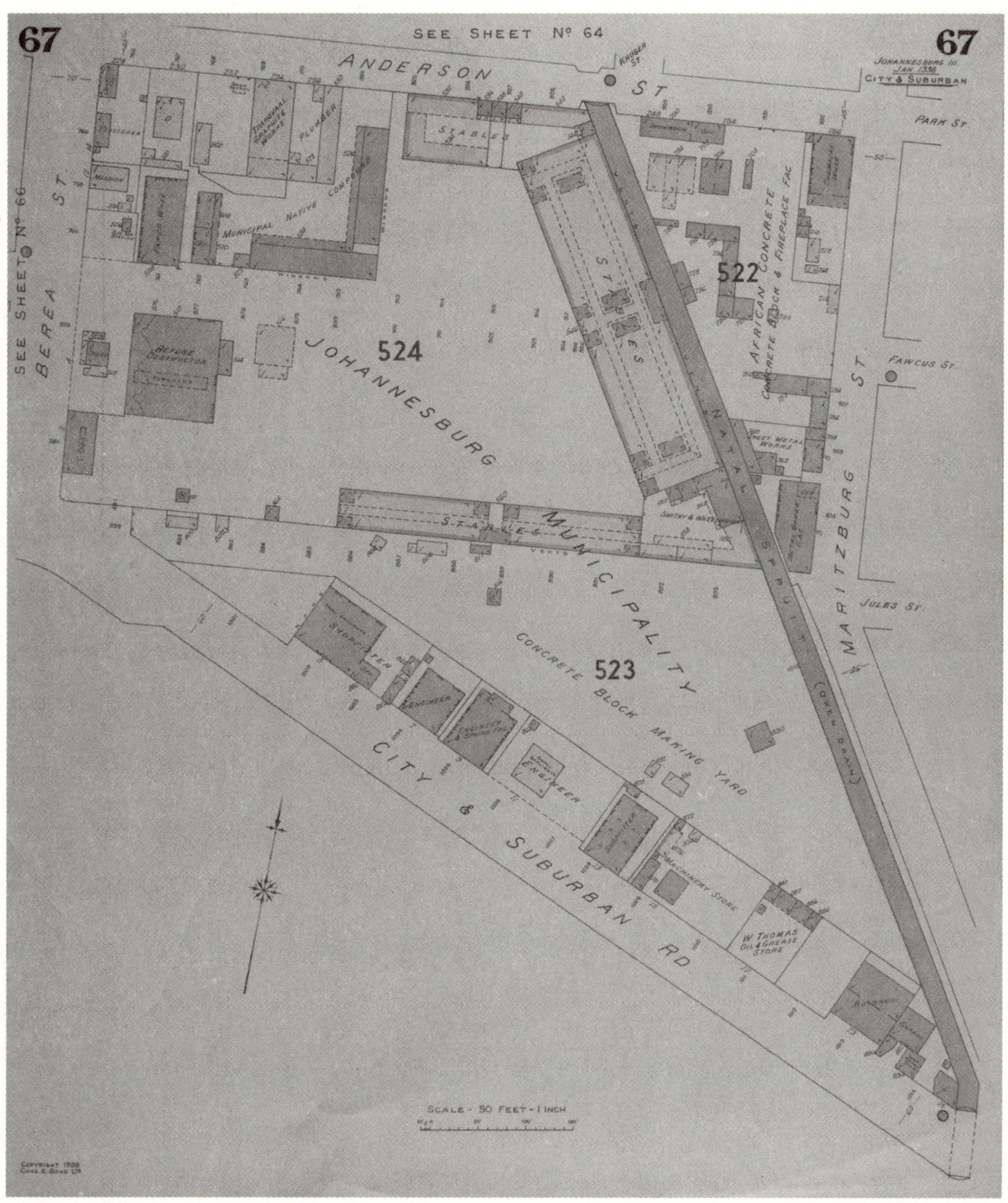


*Town Engineer's plan of the old stables before the conversion to the Kwa Mai Mai compound (Source: Chad E. Goad Ltd, Civil Engineer, 1938)*

# Four
# A Bantu affair

A drive down Albert Street gives the impression of a drive too far, urging a U-turn back into the hustle and bustle of the streets downtown. However, Albert Street in Johannesburg is anything but the end; it is the beginning of hope where there used to be despair.

Albert Street is one of five streets, the others being Commissioner, Troye, Ferreira and Cornelius, which were named in September 1886 when Kidger Tucker drew up a plan for a new residential area in Johannesburg,[20] which of course did not include the natives. Albert Street begins its imperial quest by unashamedly cutting through Joubert Street, a street named after General Piet Joubert, Commander General of the Boer forces and the runner-up in the 1893 presidential election, who lost by a narrow margin to Paul Kruger (Leyds 1964).

Whether the naming of Albert Street in 1886 was to immortalise Prince Albert, the husband of England's Queen Victoria who had died in 1861 or was sheer coincidence, the same street cuts into Phillip Street. Obviously, there is no association with Prince Philip who was only born in 1921, long after the establishment of Johannesburg. Nevertheless, both street names and many others, for that matter, are an indication of colonial expansion, where symbols of imperial conquest were engraved on every significant location or site.

Today, Albert Street traverses a part of Johannesburg to which the privileged and favoured are oblivious, each side of the street being the epitome of dejection and rejection; yet, strangely, it beckons you. Just when you think you have reached the furthest point beyond which downtown Johannesburg ceases to exist, Albert Street – with its rather curious character that is reminiscent of its colonial past – pierces through End Street, determined to present what remains of its former imperialist glory.

History tells us that End Street signalled the end of town, beyond which was a six-mile stretch to the eastern part of a farm owned and occupied by a Mr Barend Bezuidenhout (Leyds 1964). The farm, which he bought in 1877 for a span of oxen, stretched from Doornfontein to Bedfordview. Until the early part of the 20th century, Mr Bezuidenhout's farm, including End Street Park, was a beautiful product of nature. But by the middle of the 20th century, the area had become a shadow of its former self.

It was in End Street that a Mrs J Dale Lace, the wife of an executive at Lace Diamond Mines, owned a house that became a showstopper for overseas visitors and the city's aristocrats. Mrs Lace's house was frequented by mining magnates, property owners, farmers and city planners, as well as high-ranking government officials. Not far from the mansion was the End Street Park, where weekly gatherings of high-society ladies who showcased their opulent fashions (from tight corsets to gigantic hoop skirts and outrageous bustles) were held. Propriety and respectability dictated what women and men should wear, regardless of the occasion. For men, for example, stovepipe pants with tightly fitted frock coats and waistcoats were the order of the day. It was also at these high-fashion engagements that men and women occasionally gathered to play or watch cricket while enjoying tea served by a white butler. Blacks were employed as gardeners, responsible for the upkeep of End Street Park and the sprawling lawns at Mr and Mrs Dale's manor house and possibly Mr Bezuidenhout's farm.

Leyds (1964:184) painfully observed: 'Until and during the First World War, the End Street Parks were gems of the gardener's care, the lawns always beautifully kept, and the borders full of flowers. That was years before the "Meth Gang" and the hoboes took over, and the fences and hedges fell into disrepair and a general air of desolation came over the once charming scene.'

It is safe to assume that there were no African hoboes or drug addicts during the period referred to above. African labourers would have been confined to the compounds or the premises of their masters, where they worked as domestic servants or gardeners. In any case, Africans would not have been allowed to linger in town, as hoboes or otherwise, lest they got arrested for vagrancy or sent back to the villages for being in the city illegally.

Albert Street had its own vivid history. In fact, if this street could tell the tale of the city, it would reveal the secrets of how those who were considered urban outcasts suffered ill treatment and denigration at the hands of Europe's finest gentlemen and ladies, who saw themselves as civilised to the exclusion of everyone else. Yet, it was these supposedly civilised people who displayed a complete lack of civility towards those who had unwillingly come to the city to seek employment. It was James Ball, writing in the *Heritage Portal*, who referred to Albert Street as the 'nerve centre for controlling black lives during the early stages of Apartheid'.[21]


## The pass laws

The defeat of General Jan Smuts's United Party by Hendrik Verwoerd's National Party redefined race relations and urban migration in this country. Even though the migrant labour system had been in existence before the advent of apartheid, the 1948 elections scuppered General Smuts's attempts to allow different races to live side by side in towns, which would have meant the relaxation of some of the pass laws.

With the National Party having triumphed, Hendrik Verwoerd planned to control the movement of blacks and where they could reside in the cities. To control the movement of blacks in the urban areas, particularly the cities, Verwoerd introduced the *dompas* (pass book), which every adult African had to carry and which controlled where they could reside if allowed to come to the cities. Whereas the Labour Party had hoped to see a relaxation of the pass laws and restrictions on Africans coming into and living in the cities, these restrictions were intensified when the National Party came to power in 1948.

Up until then, a fair number of Africans had been found to have contravened urban migration rules, but numbers spiked dramatically between 1950 and 1959 (Bank et al. 2020), as shown in Table 1 below:

Table 1: Pass law contraventions, 1921–1975

| Decade | Average annual number of contraventions (thousands) |
|---|---|
| 1921–29 | 54.7 |
| 1930–39 | 110.8 |
| 1940–49 | 157.7 |
| 1950–59 | 318.7 |
| 1960–69 | 469.1 |
| 1970–75 | 541.5 |

Source: Wilson 1972:75

Note: Until and including 1962, the figures were for convictions – which were slightly lower than those for prosecutions.

These pass laws, which came into effect in the 19th century and were further entrenched with the introduction of apartheid laws from 1948 until 1986 when the pass laws were finally abolished, would not have been effective had it not been for the dedication of their enforcers in the now-derelict building at 80 Albert Street, Johannesburg.

## The Pass Office

A building at 80 Albert Street had become the port of entry and the control point for natives coming to the city. The building was also the head office of the Johannesburg Non-European Affairs Department (JNEAD). For more than 30 years, it had housed the Pass Office where 'Bantu affairs' were handled in the most inhumane manner imaginable. This was where the fate of black people arriving from the villages was decided with a single, often arbitrary stamp: they would be allowed to stay in Johannesburg or they would be deported back to the villages.

When the JNEAD was first established in 1927, it just had a manager, four clerks and a typist, but by the 1970s its staff complement had grown to an estimated 3 500 people. The Pass Office had its hands full controlling the influx of natives; hence the sharp increase in the number of JNEAD staff. It had become a huge human engine overseeing almost every aspect of urban African life.

In July 1953, the City Council took over the responsibility of employment contracts and the administration of what was referred to as 'the male labour bureau' from central government, and established a registration branch. Between August and December 1953, over 280 000 'reference books' were issued. As the number of Africans arriving in Johannesburg to seek employment or to work in the mines kept growing, the City Council approved further extensions and renovations to 80 Albert Street. This was to provide more space and accommodate more staff to process permits and evaluate the suitability of those wishing to remain in the city. In June 1954, Councillor Leslie V Hurd, the chairman of the Non-European Affairs Committee, laid the stone at the newly completed building, marking the official opening of the JNEAD at 80 Albert Street. It was also the home of the Pass Office.

Those seeking employment and those wanting to employ Africans needed to come to the local labour bureau in Albert Street. It was in this street that blacks experienced apartheid laws first hand, diligently enforced by Afrikaner civil servants tasked with tightly controlling the movement of black people in and out of Johannesburg and in the surrounding metropolis.

It was illegal for Africans to be without a pass, which contained their photo, place of birth, employer (including evidence of tax compliance) and even their criminal record, if applicable. Being found without a pass in a restricted area could lead to a fine or even imprisonment. This all required a massive administrative machinery. Not surprisingly, the mandatory pass became known as the 'hate law'.

*No. 80 Albert Street, the nerve centre for influx control (Photo: The author)*

*Foundation stone of expanded Johannesburg Non–European Affairs Department, 1954 (Source: The Heritage Portal)*

*The Bantu Affairs Office at 80 Albert Street was always packed with Africans seeking permits that allowed them to be in the city (Source and date unknown)*

*Mtutuzeli Matshoba (Photo: Siphiwe Mhlambi)*

Mtutuzeli Matshoba, the author of 'To kill a man's pride', whom I interviewed, offers a clear view of what 80 Albert Street meant to Africans who wished to stay in the city:

80 Albert Street was where you applied for a pass or special permit to be in the area of Johannesburg for 2 months, 3 months or the time they (officials) decide to give to you. Humiliation was very profound there because there was a place called *Esibayeni* (the Kraal), where they would crowd you like cows going to the dip. There you would zigzag till you get to a section where you would get a stamp saying 'cross the street' to 80 Albert Street. Once you cross to 80 Albert Street, you form a single line and stripped naked. Whether you were 16 years old to apply for your first pass, you will be stripped together with a man old enough to be your father; he also would [be] stark naked. Naked, you would walk past a fat guy, who resembled a frog, and his job was [to] look at your private parts as you show him. Once you pass his examination, you will then be directed to another section where you get a huge injection.

So, this is where there was this long queue of people stripped naked under the pretence of being examined for whatever disease

> Africans were purported to have. But there was no real examination
> happening there, except for humiliating black people. After that you
> would get a red stamp on your pass. That place really became a place
> that represented humiliation of a black person.[22]

The above testimony by Matshoba was corroborated in the article by
James Ball (see note 21). In his article, Ball also speaks about the 'invasive
medical examination' at 80 Albert Street, where no black person could
be certified for work unless declared medically fit. He also confirms
the lack of privacy during these medical examinations, which involved
'a general physical inspection, a chest X-ray to test for tuberculosis,
vaccinations against smallpox and in some cases blood tests for typhoid
and venereal disease'. In 1960, approximately 100 000 examinations
were performed by the man Matshoba called an ugly frog.

After receiving a special permit from 80 Albert Street that allowed
them to look for piece work, job seekers would stand outside the building
hoping for a bakkie to stop by and pick them up. Matshoba (1980:5)
describes this process in an excerpt from 'To kill a man's pride':

> The street would be full of wretched men with defeated eyes, sitting
> along the gutters on both sides of Albert Street, the whole pass
> office block, others grouped where the sun's rays leaked through the
> skyscrapers and the rest milling about. When a car driven by a white
> man went up the street, pandemonium broke loose as men, I mean
> dirty slovenly men, trotted behind it and fought to give their passes
> first. If the white person had not come for that purpose, they cursed
> him until he went out of sight. Occasionally a truck or van would
> come to pick up labourers for a piece job.

It was also in the building at 80 Albert Street that the JNEAD had
diversified its operations, establishing a lucrative business aimed at
a black clientele living in the labour compounds. Men living in the
compounds had ventured into the illicit brewing of traditional or
native beer, far from the gaze of the authorities. This had become a
lucrative venture for those engaged in its production and sale. But the
department, seeing how illicit beer brewing had become big business in
the compounds, decided to enter this terrain and establish its own beer-

brewing enterprise, selling to the same native clientele who resided in the compounds.

On 10 October 1916, the Council passed a motion for the establishment of so-called kaffir beer canteens (beer halls) within the compounds, which stated that the government would grant the city the requisite authority to bring this into effect. The matter was raised again at subsequent sittings of the Council, both at its conference on 25 January 2017 and at its meeting on 29 May 1917.

In December 1937, by exercising its powers under the Natives (Urban Areas) Act of 1923, the JNEAD officially became a brewer of African beer. And what better place to sell this alcoholic concoction than at men's hostels to which African men were confined after work? The construction of beer halls in hostels and other strategic locations began in earnest. By the 1960s, the production, distribution and sale of African beer to designated beer halls inside the single men's hostels was already generating almost 100 million rand in profit annually. This constituted much-needed revenue for the City Council. Locking migrant labourers behind the walls of the compound and getting them drunk by selling them beer was justified on the grounds that it filled the Council's coffers, which helped to fund some of its programmes. Ironically, 'kaffir beer', as the officials called it, was becoming the conduit to the financial prosperity of the City Council. However, one of the critical challenges faced by the Council was providing housing for Africans, as well as services to improve the social or recreational amenities in African-designated areas.

As 80 Albert Street was a few blocks away from the new Kwa Mai Mai, the compound was not spared from the Council's opportunistic commercial venture. When the Council relocated the old Mai Mai mining compound from Wemmer and Jubilee, it made sure that a beer hall was also constructed in the new Kwa Mai Mai compound.

## Mai Mai! The traditional beer debate

Matshoba spoke about the entertainment that Kwa Mai Mai offered to Africans working in nearby factories, such as in Doornfontein. After they knocked off for the day, Kwa Mai Mai became the boys' afternoon out, so to speak. There was a long and established tradition of natives spending their evenings at the beer hall inside the Kwa Mai Mai compound. According to Matshoba, this Kwa Mai Mai tradition could be traced back to the Salisbury and Jubilee compound, where natives had employed their entrepreneurial skills by illegally brewing African beer, known as *skokian* or 'kill-me-quick'. This beer brewing by Africans inside the compounds dated as far back as the early 1900s when Kwa Mai Mai was still called the Salisbury and Jubilee compound.

From the various exchanges of letters between compound managers and City Council officials, it appears that the illicit brewing of the so-called 'kill-me-quick' traditional beer soon became a real nightmare for the Council. In one letter, dated 26 July 1922 and addressed to the Director of Native Labour, CG Davison (Special Justice of the Peace in Johannesburg) attributes the high number of reported cases of assault to the illicit liquor supplied at the Salisbury and Jubilee compound. Davison wrote that the compound had become a menace: 'Instead of serving a very useful purpose as a residential compound for respectable employed natives who cannot be supplied with quarters by their employers, it would appear to be the resort of unemployed vagrants, and no doubt natives of a criminal type, in fact a place to which respectable natives would be ill-advised to go.'

## Crime in a compound

Johannesburg's newspaper journalists were having a field day over what was going on at the compound. An article in the *Rand Daily Mail*, dated 11 January 1922, revealed what had become a source of frustration for one magistrate, who complained that his court was being overrun with assault cases emanating from the Salisbury and Jubilee compound. Voicing his frustration and even instructing the prosecutor to write to the municipal authorities, Magistrate TM Doran observed that the natives at the compound did nothing but assault each other: 'These cases of assault are of daily occurrence, and it seems as if assaulting each other is the only thing the natives in the compound have got to do. But this sort of thing has got to stop. The Salisbury and Jubilee compound is solely under the supervision of the municipality, and it seems to me that there is a lack of discipline there.'[23]

# CRIME IN A COMPOUND

## CONDITIONS AT SALISBURY AND JUBILEE

## STRICTURES FROM THE BENCH

The number of assaults and contraventions of the Liquor Ordinance emanating from the Jubilee and Salisbury compound within the last few days called forth some strong remarks from Mr. T. M. Doran in the Magistrate's Court yesterday.

"These cases of assault are of daily occurrence," he said, "and it seems as if assaulting each other is the only thing the natives in the compound have got to do. But this sort of thing has got to stop. The Jubilee and Salisbury compound is solely under the supervision of the municipality, and it seems to me that there is a lack of discipline there. These cases indicate a lack of control. It is positively scandalous that this court should be occupied all day with cases from this compound."

The prosecutor, Mr. H. Jackson, was requested to write to the municipal authorities and draw their attention to the existing state of affairs.

Rand Daily Mail *article, 11 January 1922*

One irate Thos G Jones penned a letter to the editor of the *Rand Daily Mail*, furiously objecting to the coverage and publication of what had transpired in the court of Magistrate Doran. Writing as a member of the Johannesburg City Council, Jones appeared to take exception to the newspaper headline, 'Crime in a compound'. He found the headline to be totally unjustified and demanded that the paper conduct a proper enquiry that would prove the claim to be baseless. Jones stated, 'Unless [this] is done, a grave injustice may be done to the Municipality's most trusted officials. The police and the Native Affairs Department will, I venture to say, express an opinion very different from that of Mr Doran. Enquiries might also be made amongst the residents in the vicinity of the compound.'

Jones argued, contrary to what he believed was the magistrate's unfounded view, that there had been only three cases of assault during that period. He went on to say that in a police raid on the compound in the early hours of Dingaan's Day,[24] the police had not found even 'a teaspoon of liquor'.[25]

A Mr Brooks, Chairman of the Parks and Estates Committee of the Council, which oversaw the compound, also joined the fray and attacked the magistrate for his ill-advised utterances. Mr Brooks took serious exception to the magistrate attributing all crimes committed at the compound to compound dwellers. He pointed out that only 881 workers resided in the main compound, whereas 2 271 were 'casuals' housed outside the main compound. He argued that most 'natives' arrested for various crimes used the compound as their address, which was misleading. About 35 000 to 45 000 Africans passed through the compound every year and most of them, according to Mr Brooks, were criminals.

It is interesting that the reference to the Salisbury and Jubilee compound as 'Mai Mai' was first seen in an article appearing in *The Star*, in which Mr Brooks was quoted as saying: 'The neighbourhood round here has a lot of shanties, where natives reside and where liquor is obtainable, and when assaults take place at any of these places they naturally quote "*Mai Mai*" as their place of residence.'[26]

Reacting to the newspaper reports, some members of the public similarly felt that there was an urgent need to address what was becoming a scourge and argued that steps should be taken to cleanse the town of what they regarded as dangerous elements plaguing the city. Some even suggested that natives convicted of being in possession of large quantities of the 'kill-me-quick' alcoholic concoction should be barred from living in the compound. Others called for the dismissal of native *indunas* and police boys for their inability to maintain law and order. So concerned were the City Council and law enforcement officials that they even started to monitor some of the items, including paraffin tins and other containers, coming into the compound and which they suspected were being used as receptacles for illegal alcohol.

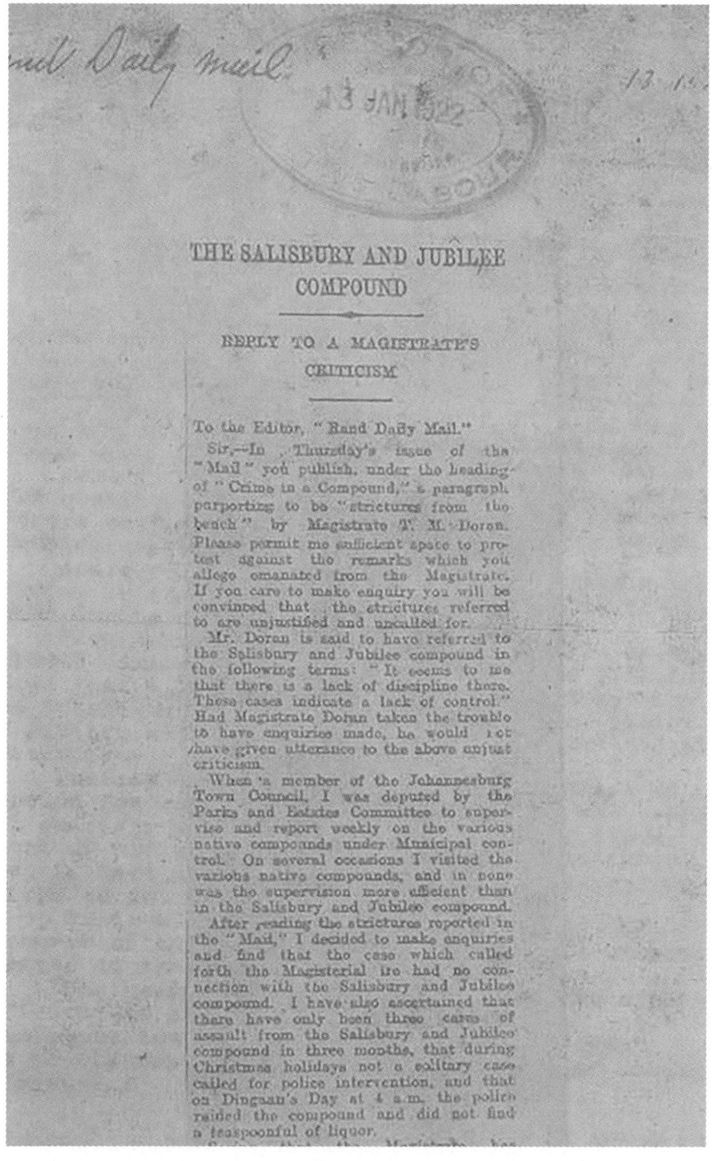

*Thos G Jones' letter to the* Rand Daily Mail, *13 January 1922*

In its issue of 25 July 1922, the *Rand Daily Mail* ran the story, 'Black brewers, big bank balances', attributing this headline to what had become a lucrative business under the full control of the natives in the compound. The same article referred to '1 000 natives drunk before 10 am'. This caption was the work of City Council officials who disliked the idea of any native selling alcohol, illegally or otherwise. The paper reported that during one raid the police had confiscated the books of one native brewer who, over a few months, had banked £240, in sums of £90 at a time. It was unfathomable that natives, who earned just shillings as labourers, could be accumulating so much money from alcohol sales. Action had to be taken to curb this scourge. Even fines, ranging between £1 and £2, for those found guilty of brewing this *skokian* were never going to be a deterrent for those engaged in such a lucrative business operation.

The fact that the natives had become so entrepreneurial and had created an economy that the municipality could not tap into to inflate its revenue was the key frustration for some City Council officials. A thriving business that contributed nothing to the City Council's coffers had to be extinguished in its developmental phase. The compound became the place where the police would regularly go and flex their muscles. In trying to crack down on the illicit brewing of traditional beer (*skokian* or 'kill-me-quick'), compound managers, assisted by the police, embarked on a series of raids.

Thousands of gallons of beer were destroyed during these raids and hundreds of beer brewers and their captive customers (who used to drink themselves into a stupor) were arrested. Regarding one particular raid, the *Rand Daily Mail* reported that some 80 mounted police, both black and white, and under a commissioned officer, had descended on the compound to conduct a search: '[T]he raiders found some 6 200 gallons in the morning raid. The liquor was concealed in great iron cases, and in paraffin tins in wooden boxes. On entering the police simply perforated the tins with picks and allowed liquor to escape down the compound gutters and drains.'[27]

No sooner had the police left the premises than the brewers produced more gallons, which had gone undetected by the law enforcement officials in the morning raid. Indeed, it was not uncommon for the police to conduct raids twice or even three times a day, each time discovering more gallons of the intoxicating brew. Yet there was always more that remained undetected, hidden in unimaginable places.

## *A little bit of public flogging*

One deputy police commissioner accused the compound management of gross negligence for ostensibly failing to detect and prevent the brewing of large quantities of alcohol on the premises. He also scolded them for failing to notify the police when they clearly knew about the brewing of kaffir beer under their noses. Clearly frustrated by the failure of the police to quash the ongoing production of beer, the deputy police commissioner went so far as to suggest in a letter to the Director of Native Affairs in Johannesburg on 25 September 1919 that 'a little public flogging would have a good effect'.

It is interesting that this law enforcement officer, who was obviously white, advocated flogging, a practice that was common at the height of the Roman Empire and administered at the crucifixion of Jesus. Flogging had been part of the political and social landscape of colonial South Africa for a long time. The practice was a key institution at the Cape, first under the rule of the Dutch East India Company between 1652 and 1795, then under both the Dutch and the British administrations between 1795 and the emancipation of slaves from 1834. Slaves were frequently flogged as a type of punishment for a variety of perceived infringements, with the practice forming part of what Sacks (1973) referred to as 'extraordinarily barbarous punishments'. Peté (2019), looking at documents for colonial Natal in the period 1876–1906, refers to 'the near obsession with flogging of Africans' by white settlers. Sacks (1973) recorded in detail how flogging (eventually replaced by caning) within the prison system became an increasingly frequent method – over several decades – of disciplining (predominantly African and coloured) inmates following the formation of the Union of South Africa in 1910. As a disciplinary measure, flogging would clearly have been within the mind-set of many white law enforcement officials who considered natives to be inferior to them, or even less than human.

One report to the municipality revealed that in the period January to March 1921, 3 532 gallons of illicit alcohol were destroyed, which was only 10 per cent of the quantity consumed in the compound. By July 1921, 11 874 gallons had been destroyed and 197 natives arrested for offences that contravened the liquor and pass laws. It was clear that no amount of policing and arrests would prevent the illegal brewing of alcohol in the compound. New economic measures were therefore required.

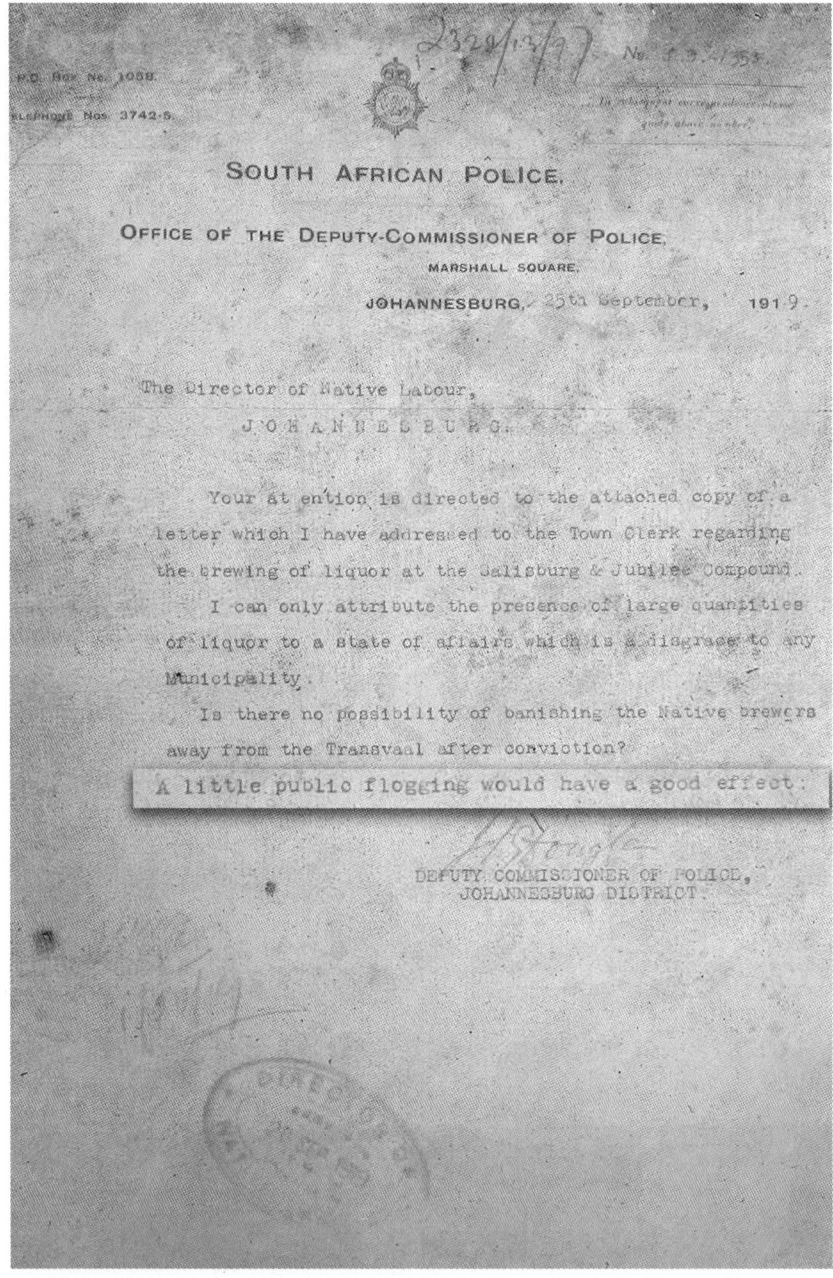

SOUTH AFRICAN POLICE,

OFFICE OF THE DEPUTY-COMMISSIONER OF POLICE,

MARSHALL SQUARE,

JOHANNESBURG, 25th September, 1919.

The Director of Native Labour,

JOHANNESBURG.

Your attention is directed to the attached copy of a letter which I have addressed to the Town Clerk regarding the brewing of liquor at the Salisburg & Jubilee Compound.

I can only attribute the presence of large quantities of liquor to a state of affairs which is a disgrace to any Municipality.

Is there no possibility of banishing the Native brewers away from the Transvaal after conviction?

A little public flogging would have a good effect.

DEPUTY COMMISSIONER OF POLICE,
JOHANNESBURG DISTRICT.

*Letter from the Deputy Police Commissioner to the Director of Native Labour (Johannesburg) regarding the brewing of beer at the Salisbury and Jubilee compound, 25 September 1919 (Source: National Archives of South Africa)*

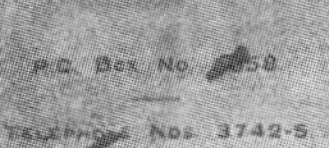

P.O. Box No. 2058   A.B.   No. J.D.4/356
Telephone Nos. 3742-5

SOUTH AFRICAN POLICE.

OFFICE OF THE DEPUTY-COMMISSIONER OF POLICE,
MARSHALL SQUARE.

JOHANNESBURG, 25th September, 1919.

The Town Clerk,

 P.O. Box 1049,

  JOHANNESBURG.

Sir,

 I beg to call the attention of the Municipal Council to the disgraceful condition of the Salisbury & Jubilee Compound as discovered on Sunday last, the 21st instant.

 Some 4000 to 5000 gallons of native liquor was found in the location.

 I have recently had to increase the number of police patrols in this locality on Sundays.

 Surely the existence of liquor must be known to the Compound Officials, and I can only attribute the presence of the liquor to negligence.

 The Police have the authority to search for liquor at any time should they have reasonable grounds to know liquor is in the possession of natives, and all we ask is that the location authorities should notify us when they know liquor is being brewed: They must know it and liquor could not be brewed in such large quantities without their knowledge.

  I have the honour to be,
   Sir,
  Your obedient servant,

   DEPUTY COMMISSIONER OF POLICE,
   JOHANNESBURG DISTRICT.

*Letter from the Deputy Police Commissioner to the Town Clerk of Johannesburg regarding the brewing of beer at the Salisbury and Jubilee compound, 25 September 1919 (Source: National Archives of South Africa)*

A report was tabled, suggesting that the municipality should consider making kaffir beer legally available for consumption on the premises to discourage the brewing of what the officials called 'vile stuff' – the 'kill-me-quick' beer.

When the Salisbury and Jubilee compound was relocated to the new site along Albert Street, its beer hall moved with it. Mai Mai was the name of the compound and the beer produced at its beer hall also became known as 'Mai Mai'.

At an ordinary meeting on 31 August 1962, the City Council moved swiftly to register and trademark the name 'Mai Mai' for the Bantu beer that had been legalised, with brewing activities now falling under the control of the city. The minutes of this Council meeting revealed the deliberations of the Council and the need to hastily secure the trademark 'Mai Mai' as the official name for kaffir beer: 'It is of vital importance to the Non-European Affairs Department that no unnecessary delay should be permitted. Inquiries are pouring in from all over the City for Bantu beer, and on Tuesday, 21st August 1962 more than forty inquiries were received for several thousand gallons in all.'[28]

In view of the urgency of the matter, the Council resolved that the Town Clerk be authorised to have the name 'Mai Mai' and the label registered as a trademark. The instruction to Messrs DM Kisch & Co. to register the trademark was subsequently confirmed by the Council.

## Still hustling

There is something in the name Mai Mai that has become a rallying point for those determined to make it in Johannesburg so that they can go home to the villages with a great sense of achievement. Mai Mai or Kwa Mai Mai is where hustlers and onlookers converge and often find themselves transfixed, for a variety of reasons.

Today, Albert Street is the antithesis of royal panache, although it still bears some remnants of its colonial past. The street also epitomises a sense of hustle – from the top all the way to the gates of Kwa Mai Mai. Albert Street's filth and general unattractiveness give the impression that it has been condemned by those whose task is to keep the city clean to lure motorists, pedestrians and traders to it.

*Relaxing with friends over generous beer servings (Source: Ezra Eliovson & Sima Eliovson.* Johannesburg: The Fabulous City. Howard Timmins, 1956)

However, Albert Street is far from forlorn or forgotten at the end of town. It is alive with all sorts of street hustlers wanting to make a quick buck. On each side of the street there are minibus taxis – the preferred mode of transport for multitudes of people commuting into the city from surrounding townships and other locations. After the morning rush into the city, the drivers take their minibus taxis for a quick wash by enthusiastic and otherwise unemployed young men, who have turned the street into a car wash emporium. Just as most of the minibus taxi drivers hail from one particular region in KwaZulu-Natal, uMsinga, so, too, do the car wash hustlers. Most of the young men who wash vehicles are either sons or relatives of hostel residents who live in the Jeppe, Denver (Wolhuter), George Koch and Murray & Roberts hostels, among others.

It is easy to pick up where most of these car washers come from, just from the conversations between them. Surreptitious eavesdropping on their conversations reveals frequent references to life in the villages. They talk about dance, *isicathamiya* (singing) competitions, maskandi artists and traditional ceremonies occurring back home. But the brutal reality of the city is not far from their minds as they exchange stories about violent incidents experienced in the compound. In this part of town, grievances and disputes are not resolved through polite conversations. Shots are often fired; people sometimes die. Therefore, talk also revolves around funerals of friends who succumbed to violence in the streets of Johannesburg. While their language is often laced with machismo, words are carefully chosen to avoid saying anything that could be construed as offensive, as this alone could end up in an exchange of blows which, in this part of the world, is neither a fist fight nor a stick fight: it is a gun battle.

How these street hustlers manage to negotiate the constant supply of water that is needed to wash the vehicles remains a mystery. There is a water tap protruding from the pavement on one side of the road. High-pressure water-dispensing devices, vacuum cleaners and other equipment do not feature here; instead, a bucket filled with water, washing liquid and a cloth are the tools of the trade for the car washers. For the tyres, natural science prevails – Coca-Cola is simply applied to the rubber to give it that shiny, black finish – a previously unheard-of solution.

# A red–light district on Albert Street?

Albert Street has numerous other offerings. Vendors sell anything from sunglasses to belts, and pavement hair salons and barber shops give quick haircuts or construct Brazilian weaves for the 'white wannabes'. Albert Street also boasts small-time mechanics who repair or panel beat motor vehicles, giving them a facelift or another shot at life when they would have been condemned by wealthy car owners. On each side of the street there are people who, in the country's unpalatable past, would have been classified as vagrants and subjected to humiliating treatment by policemen and protectors of a despotic system designed to rid the City of Gold of unwanted elements.

For those with an inquisitive eye, driving down Albert Street will offer a glimpse of women who have lost hope of finding formal employment and have opted to enter the sex trade, their earnings dependent on how quick the encounter is and what services are being rendered. Women of all shapes and sizes, either dressed to impress or scantily clad, strut their stuff to catch the wandering eye of those driving down the street. Even when the odds are stacked against them, they fight for their survival – a testimony of the strength of the human spirit in dire circumstances.

The blatant visibility and yet obscurity of the sex trade is an enigma for those who are not active participants in it. Much as these sex workers openly advertise their services and go all out to clinch the deal, where and how the deal is concluded remains a mystery. Day after day, rain or shine, these women are on the streets, hoping to secure enough business before the day ends. Unfortunately, this is not the kind of street where transactions can take place in the dead of night, as streetlights probably last worked during the Victorian era when the privileged classes mixed and mingled under the star-studded African sky. Therefore, the sex workers of Albert Street need to engage in brisk trade during daylight. Unlike in the red-light district in Amsterdam in Holland, there appear to be no obvious locations where favours are exchanged once a deal is clinched, unless the daylight displays are just promotional campaigns for the real encounters that take place later in the evening, at spots agreed to during the day.

This colourful cross-section of activities is evident during a quick drive down Albert Street, a street that means business, whatever it may be – from sexual favours to car washes and vehicle repairs. The fascinating trip down the street comes to an abrupt stop when you reach the gates and the sign welcoming you to Kwa Mai Mai. This is the trade zone and alternative economic hub for many migrants from the villages, who would otherwise be tending to their cattle or collecting firewood

*Aerial view of Kwa Mai Mai (Photo: Drone shot taken by the author)*

or fetching water from rivers that have long since run dry. In contrast to the hustle and bustle of Albert Street, Kwa Mai Mai is a separate enclave where the dispossessed and marginalised have reimagined economic opportunities in the post-colonial, post-apartheid era.

# Five
# Kwa Mai Mai: Not your usual hostel

A sign above the gate saying 'Welcome to Kwa Mai-Mai' can mean different things to different people, depending on their cultural persuasion and emotional triggers.

*The entrance to Kwa Mai Mai (Photo: The author)*

In Zulu, *kwa* means 'at' or 'place of', which can be used in an associative or possessive sense without attaching it to the full noun. When *kwa* is used together with *Mai Mai*, the name starts to become interesting. Because the name is used colloquially and not in a formal sense, it is easy to get 'lost in translation'. Yet when it is applied properly and pronounced as *Kwa Maye Maye*, there is a spike in interest, especially among those who understand the language. Inevitable questions are posed: What really happened here? Why was this place given this name?

Imagine a place called *Kwa Mshaye Azafe*, which means a place where one is beaten to death. There are place names that denote some form of activity or inherent significance, as when Johannesburg is referred to as *Kwa ndonga ziyaduma* (walls that thunder) *or Kwa nyama ayipheli kuphela amazinyo endoda* (a place where meat is in abundance and only teeth wear out from eating it).

In Nguni, *maye maye* is an expression of shock, disbelief or exasperation, which will inevitably induce some awkwardness and discomfort in those who pass through the gate for the first time. Hearing someone down the street or a next-door neighbour screaming *'Maye Maye'* or *'Mai Mai'* could easily persuade you to call the emergency number. It can only mean that something is very wrong and needs the urgent attention of whoever must come to the rescue. As previously explained, it was popularly believed that 'Maye Maye' was the signature scream of a particular mine manager whenever there was an accident in the mine. The Salisbury and Jubilee mining compound could not rid itself of this name, and so, when the compound relocated to the current site, the name persisted.

Today, the new Kwa Mai Mai is sandwiched between Anderson Street, one of the nine oldest streets in Johannesburg, and Durban Street, which has no particular link to the city of Durban (located more than 500 km from Johannesburg). With everything under one roof, Kwa Mai Mai is a place where village migrants-turned-ethnic entrepreneurs have converged to supply products and services to clients, who include both tourists looking for souvenirs to take back to their cities or countries and those making a deliberate trip to look for items that only Kwa Mai Mai supplies.

Tucked under a bridge in downtown Johannesburg, and far from the gaze of economic hitmen and venture capitalists, is a place where culture, heritage and tradition (as championed by its residents) converge and find expression in the creative pursuits and cultural narrative of migrant workers who, once on the margins of society, have become ethnic entrepreneurs. The story of Kwa Mai Mai conjures up Marx's notion of 'man as a producer', in that a migrant class has succeeded in elevating itself, through a major reorganisation, from a position of subordination to one in which it owns and controls the means of production.

Beyond the gate is a busy cultural economy, built from the ground up by those from the edges of society who were rejected by the formal employment system. Not willing to go home and face the prospect of mockery and rejection in the villages as *abashaywe iGoli* (those who failed to make it in Johannesburg), they have created an economy based largely on a social system woven from their combined beliefs and traditions. It is a place that has become a refuge for those who left their villages to look for formal employment but soon abandoned the search when it became clear that such opportunities did not favour them. A determined group of ex-migrant workers took over a space that initially was the preserve of an elite, capitalist class, that is, a stable for the horses belonging to those who enjoyed privileged positions in society. With vision and ingenuity, a single-purpose stable was transformed into a thriving cultural hub.

There is something intriguing about the way in which Kwa Mai Mai has managed to survive and resist property developers who have combed most of Johannesburg in search of areas in which to establish upmarket trade zones, which would be partitioned off and rented back to traders at a premium. Refusing to succumb to the challenges of unemployment, poverty and inequality, this cultural market has also refused to be swallowed up by property developers eager to turn traditional African marketplaces into shopping malls, which would eventually disparage the very people whom these trade zones were designed to serve in the first place.

There is much more to Kwa Mai Mai's socio-economic character than meets the eye. Unlike 'Chinatown' or a market named after a homogeneous ethnic or racial group, Kwa Mai Mai constitutes a multi-ethnic group of South Africans bound together by the spirit of entrepreneurship and creative innovation, and embodies a community at work that has embraced the concept of *vukuzenzele* (self-help) and created an industry that has stood the test of time.

Kwa Mai Mai may not be a gated community such as those that characterise the lifestyle of so many in the northern suburbs of Johannesburg. There is no intercom for visitors to press or register to sign to be admitted through the gate. However, not a single visitor goes in or out unnoticed. Whether or not there are barriers to trading is determined by one's ability to assimilate and accept the traditional leadership structures that have been in place at the hostels for decades. Some visitors come to Kwa Mai Mai not just to buy cultural goods; they are interested in the social structure or make-up of the place. However, unless one is coming to buy cultural goods or to consult with traditional healers or diviners, it may be necessary to seek permission for the visit from the *induna* (the headman). After satisfying himself and having consulted with *isigungu* (a committee that looks after the affairs of Kwa Mai Mai), the *induna* will either grant or deny access to a prospective visitor, depending on the nature of the permission being sought.

Kwa Mai Mai may not bask in the same light as other emerging collaborative hubs where culture meets business and entertainment is the tie that binds. It may not be in the same league as the creative enclaves of the privileged few, which are located uptown or downtown in places such as Maboneng or Braamfontein. It should also not be forgotten that these other cultural precincts have had their fair share of economic challenges. Precincts such as Maboneng, the Market Theatre and Braamfontein have experienced mixed success and have been subjected to severe economic buffeting. Because of urban decay and security concerns in downtown Johannesburg, all these precincts, despite their best efforts, have proved to be hard to sustain, within what is largely a problem of 'location'.

What makes Kwa Mai Mai distinctive, despite its urban setting, is its all-encompassing character, which sees it alienating neither the marginalised nor the prosperous. In other words, it does not distinguish between the 'haves' and the 'have-nots'. Having endured all sorts of socio-economic challenges, Kwa Mai Mai has been around for seven decades – at least in its new location.

*Tourists visiting Kwa Mai Mai in search of African artefacts and crafts (Photo: The author)*

Fortunately, none of the traders and cultural entrepreneurs in Kwa Mai Mai are subjected – as they were in the past – to the long queues at the Bantu Affairs Department, originally a few blocks up the road, to obtain a permit legitimising their presence in the city. They are no longer the so-called natives seeking permission to enter, leave and work in Johannesburg. As Ngcobo (1999:11) remarks in her book *And They Didn't Die*, the residents and traders of Kwa Mai Mai have survived what she calls 'the burial ground of all human dignity'.

Today, the residents and traders of Kwa Mai Mai are spared indignity and humiliation – at least at the hands of Europeans. Even those who frequent Albert Street to ply their trade as car washers and parking attendants for the more well-heeled (who typically reward these entrepreneurs with a paltry collection of coins), do not need to produce a permit.

*During apartheid, Africans had to obtain a permit to seek employment in the cities (Source: Flashback.com)*

Inside the Kwa Mai Mai compound is a group of proud villagers who have dug deep into their tradition and heritage to unearth the long-hidden treasures that make them truly unique and distinguishable from other urban dwellers. In the process they have discovered what in the villages was often taken for granted – the everyday life of a rural community who followed a daily routine and practised ancient rituals through the medium of dance and song, adorned in traditional garb and using simple, inexpensive artefacts to add to the display.

Determined to reimagine a new life for themselves in the post-colonial era, these villagers-turned–city dwellers have managed to build businesses on the strength of their belief in the economic value of a culture that for many years had been exoticised for the amusement of spectators. Escaping the margins of society, these urban villagers have entered a space traditionally reserved for merchants and traders of other races, who would typically operate as middlemen, employing migrant workers to produce cultural artefacts which they would then sell for a considerable mark–up, leaving the migrant workers out of the profit loop.

*Kwa Mai Mai is now a family compound (Photo: Siphiwe Mhlambi)*

Kwa Mai Mai is unlike the popular road-side spots where street vendors crowd the city's pavements, selling anything from sunglasses, belts and *amagwinya* (fat cookies) to cell phone chargers, fruit and vegetables. Rather, the thriving economy of Kwa Mai Mai has thwarted attempts to turn black city traders into small-time vendors of basic essentials. Kwa Mai Mai today is not only what, on the surface, looks like a trade zone for crafts, *shisanyama*, traditional medicine and herbs; it is also the epitome of how people, driven by a desire to beat the odds, have risen to the occasion and taken control of their own destiny.

Kwa Mai Mai has always been known for its herbal medicine, for the craftsmen who produce wedding kists and boxes for mineworkers to store their personal clothing and other items, for traditional garments made of skin or fabric, and for traditional fighting sticks and shields decorated with cow hide. As mentioned earlier, one of the items produced in Kwa Mai Mai is the wedding kist, which is still very popular among migrants returning home for a visit or among mineworkers whose contracts have expired. For many years, returning migrants would not dream of going home without a wooden kist – lavishly decorated with mirrors on the lid and/or the sides and with an African motif worked artistically into the surface of the wood in the form of a wood cut or through a burning process.

Kwa Mai Mai has also long been a convenient location for an interesting cross-section of self-employed village migrants, such as skin/hide workers, carpenters, snuff producers, sjambok and spear makers, and bangle makers. The bangle makers are very skilled at intricate designs, which are often applied to beautifully crafted, ornamental 'dancing sticks' and purses. The compound is also home to healers and several well-known herbalists, whose shops are veritable cornucopias of remedies comprising herbs, animal extracts, snake skins and dried snake venom. Traditional medicine is a major industry today; and some shops are very large indeed.

There is a high demand for traditional regalia and assorted ornaments among the mineworker dance teams: weekend entertainment is popular at the mines and has translated into a thriving trade for those skilled in producing cultural goods. If it so happens that customers do not visit the compound, craftsmen sometimes travel across the reef, laden with goods they have made, visiting one mine compound after another.

Of course, villagers are known for their ability to travel long distances on foot, travelling from one village to the next or even across different *izigodi* (wards). With the discovery of diamonds and gold during the middle and latter part of the 19th century, Africans used to practically walk the length and breadth of the country to join the labour force. It was not uncommon, for example, for job seekers to walk for a week or more, or even a month, to get to Kimberley or Johannesburg, the country's diamond and gold mining hubs. On these long journeys, they wore handmade sandals known as *izimbadada* or *izingxabulela*, which have become ubiquitous and are highly sought after from the skilled craftsmen at Kwa Mai Mai.

The sandals are multi-purpose footwear, used mainly by Zulus, who wear them both during their traditional dance routines and for their day-to-day movements in and around the city. Though simple in design, they are particularly sturdy and have withstood competition from many other (including foreign) footwear designs, even coexisting with leather sandals and flip flops, which were unknown to Africans. Today, these sandals are popular among various traditional dance groups, such as those who dance *umzansi* from Bergville, *ushiyamen* from the KwaZulu-Natal Midlands and *isibhaca* from the south coast of KwaZulu-Natal, and those from Nongoma, the heartland of the Zulu Kingdom.

The snuff makers import a wide variety of very crude and harsh tobacco from the Transkei and mix it with aloes and other vegetable matter, after which they dry it and pound it into fine powder using a large mortar and pestle. In this way, they make sure that inveterate smokers get their fix. Among others, *izinyanga* (traditional doctors) and *izangoma* (diviners) use snuff, which has always been regarded as the conduit to the ancestors when the living wish to appeal to the departed for the well-being of the earth. Using snuff and burning incense are prerequisites if the ritual of communicating with the departed is to deliver the intended results.

## Covid-19 and traditional medicine

According to Whiting et al. (2011:84), 'In South Africa, animals and plants are commonly used as traditional medicine for both the healing of ailments and for symbolic purposes such as improving relationships and attaining good fortune.' Traditional medicines in southern Africa fall into two categories: those used to treat medical afflictions ('white medicine') and those used to deal with ancestral conflict ('black medicine') (Bye and Dutton 1991). A significant proportion of traditional healing makes use of the 'magical' properties of plants or animal parts (Whiting et al. 2011:85).

Belief in the value of traditional healing and medicine, and the importance attached to Kwa Mai Mai as a place of healing, surged when the Covid-19 pandemic swept through the country. Those who believed in traditional medicine and rituals suddenly remembered a place hidden under a motorway bridge at the far end of town. Kwa Mai Mai must not be confused with Faraday Muthi Market, which is still the largest informal wholesale and retail market for traditional medicine in Gauteng province. The difference between the two markets is that Kwa Mai Mai is not a wholesale market; instead, it allows for more individual consultations with traditional healers. Faraday is where traditional medicine and herbs are sold to healers.

The role of traditional medicine and herbs became critical at the height of the Covid-19 pandemic. Diviners and healers alike suddenly had to scramble for their last remaining stock of whatever herbs were needed to curb the pandemic's spread and impact. Unfortunately, as they were barred from going out, they had to ration their limited stocks of herbs, such as *umhlonyana* (*artemisia afra* or the African wormwood) and snuff.

Even those who had heard of Kwa Mai Mai but had never been there were calling whoever they knew to help them with directions and, importantly, to find out if the place was open during the hard lockdown. What they did not know is that Kwa Mai Mai is both a place of residence and a trade zone. The same herbalists who could sell them *umhlonyana* and snuff lived in the very same place where these herbs were found. Shutting down the businesses would have meant shutting the compound and ordering everyone to go back to their villages. This was a tough call for City Council officials. Well hidden from the close scrutiny of the government, Kwa Mai Mai remained open to the public. With Kwa Mai Mai open, those who resorted to selling *umhlonyana* as a life-saving measure stood a chance of seeing another day, another week, another month and possibly another year.

In trying to limit the spread of Covid-19, the government issued a clear message: 'Wear your mask, wash your hands, social distance, and stay indoors.' However, people also needed to steam – but definitely not with the popular Western medicine, eucalyptus oil, made from the eucalyptus tree that is native to Australia. Those who believed in Western medicine and could afford eucalyptus oil soon emptied the shelves of this product at pharmacies around the country. Eucalyptus oil had gained prominence as the recommended oil for steaming and was also said to be good for treating various common diseases and conditions that presented as symptoms of Covid-19.

However, to most Africans and those who believed in traditional medicine for treatment and prevention, one of the herbs in great demand was *umhlonyana*. This herb is known in traditional communities as being effective in treating a wide range of ailments, including respiratory problems and asthma. With the rush for *umhlonyana*, Kwa Mai Mai soon ran out of the herb, and it was not until about May 2020 that Kwa Mai Mai herbalists were able to restock. One compound, though, at No. 150, was said to have enough of it to supply those who wished to use it for steaming. Kwa Mai Mai had thus come to the rescue and lived up to its reputation as 'a place of healers'.

## Snubbing the snuff

The imposition of Covid-19 restrictions had unintended consequences. In an unexpected move, the government banned the sale of cigarettes, including snuff. These tough measures, which were introduced during the hard lockdown, meant that traditional healers and diviners could not stock and use what to them was essential for communicating with the ancestors. These healers and diviners voiced their extreme dissatisfaction over the government's decision to include snuff as a banned product along with tobacco.

As Simelane (cited in Whiting et al. 2011:84) attests, 'Traditional healers in southern Africa view health and welfare issues as being tightly linked to supernatural forces, social relationships and an individual's relationship with their ancestors.' Thus, with the banning of snuff, the work of traditional healers was severely hampered. Their outcry was based on the belief that their communication with the ancestors during this difficult time had been thwarted, which meant that they were no longer able to get the attention of the departed to plead for guidance and protection against the dreaded disease.

One of the popular and widely read Sunday papers, *City Press*, ran the following headline on 12 August 2020: 'Snuff is existentially essential to many South Africans.' The author of the article, Anna Trapido, observed with trepidation: 'There has been no consideration of ancestral requirements. Snuff is a tobacco product without which the channels of communication between the living and the ancestors are often blocked. But it has also been banned, along with cigarettes.'

Yet, pandemic or no pandemic, nothing was going to stop the Kwa Mai Mai trade zone; its resilience was unparalleled. This market had survived outside of the mainstream, bolstered by longstanding traditions that had ensured its survival long before it was relocated to the current site. Even with the passage of time, which saw the old Salisbury and Jubilee compound fall into disrepair and become the victim of a bad fire in the 1940s, Kwa Mai Mai has maintained its character and status as the only African market and trade zone owned by Africans. There is not a single Indian, Pakistani or Chinese person trading in African goods and services in this compound, as has become the norm in the townships and in other black human settlements.

## A one-stop shop

The Kwa Mai Mai bazaar is today a one-stop shop for anyone who prefers not to negotiate the streets and pavements of downtown Johannesburg, going in and out of the many shops looking for wanted items while also trying to avoid muggers and thieves. Kwa Mai Mai offers a wide range of goods and services spread over more than 100 retail outlets. There is even a daycare centre for children in the compound and a famous *shisanyama* lifestyle spot just next to the Shembe Church under the bridge. Many of those who visit the compound are surprised that the shops, which typically measure 3 m x 6 m, double up as living quarters for the traders.

Table 2 shows the type and number of offerings that Kwa Mai Mai provides to those who brave the hustle and bustle of downtown Johannesburg to explore this multidimensional market.

Table 2: Kwa Mai Mai's product and service offerings

| Category | Items | Number |
|---|---|---|
| Carpenters | Wedding kists and coffins | 8 |
| Traditional attire | Clothing and beaded attire | 28 |
| Traditional attire | Animal skins/hides | 11 |
| Traditional healers | Herbs | 12 |
| Sangomas | Divining services | 7 |
| African pharmacies | African medicine | 20 |
| Upholstery | Couches/car seats | 1 |
| Convenience shops | Grocery/bakery items | 9 |
| Vendors | Fruit/vegetables | 2 |
| Shisanyama | Braai/barbecue offerings | 13 |
| Pillow manufacturers | Bedding | 13 |
| Panel beaters | Vehicle repair services | 3 |
| Community hall | Meetings | 1 |
| Amphitheatre | Cultural activities | 1 |
| Crèche | Childcare | 1 |
|  |  | 130 |

*Source: Author's records*

Figure 1 shows the most popular products and services in the market. In the lead is traditional attire, followed by traditional medicine and traditional healers, which include diviners and herbalists. The relative contribution of each product or service is determined by the number of store outlets or, in the case of *shisanyama*, tables and outside spots just before the entrance gate.

Figure 1: Contribution of different products and services at Kwa Mai Mai

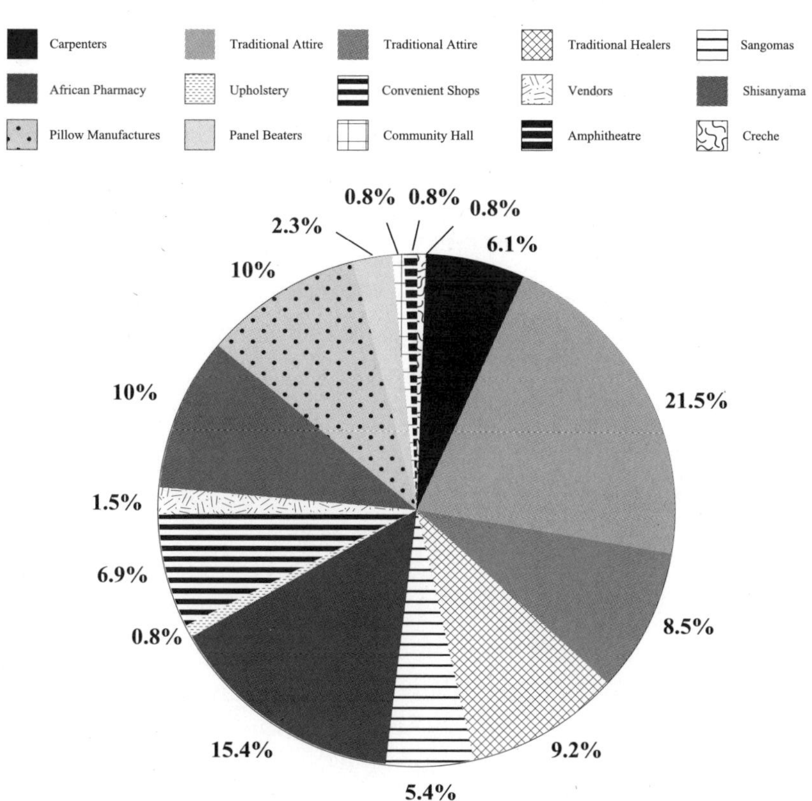


Source: Author's compilation from field visits

Table 3 makes various assumptions about the sales performance of each traditional attire shop. It surmises that 28 shops would sell three of each item per month at an average price of R195. This would generate a total monthly income of R236 320 for the 28 shops, with an average monthly income per shop of R8 400. Excluding material input costs and labour, the average income per shop per month would be way above the country's minimum wage (R3 500), especially considering that these shops are individually run and the owner is also the producer of the items or services on offer. In determining the monthly financial performance of these shops, the model further assumes that only 60 per cent of the shops would sell three of each item per month, which means that the average monthly income per shop would be reduced to just R1 778.93.

Considering the number of traders offering the same goods and services, who therefore compete for the same clientele, it is intriguing that each individual business remains profitable or sustainable. When asked about the profitability of their enterprises, some traders said that they just have an emotional attachment to their business and are keeping it going for sentimental reasons because it is all they know. As long as they are able to put bread on the table and send some money home, they will continue to trade at Kwa Mai Mai – despite their profitability being negatively affected by the large number of traders dealing in similiar traditional attire, weapons and beadwork. Niche businesses, such as carpentry, upholstery and auto repair, do not face this problem.

Traditional healers and suppliers of herbal medicine fall into a unique category. There is a popular Zulu saying, *awumbiwa ndawonye*, which, loosely translated, means that healers do not collect their herbs from the same place and that the strength of their *muthi* (herb concoctions) and the nature of their clientele differ from one healer to the next. Everyone has their own clients but some may have more than others, which influences the profitability of their business. While one traditional healer might have longs queues every day, others might have just a few people coming for consultations. However, all the healers seem to be doing well, judging from the number of years they have occupied their respective spots.

It comes as no surprise that the herbal medicine trade is probably the most successful business at Kwa Mai Mai, as it accounts for about 20 per cent of the shops inside the precinct. A key success factor is its ability to sell hope and foster the belief that those who use it for different reasons will see their fortunes turn around and strike 'gold' one day.

## Table 3: Value of items at traditional attire shops

| Item | Price (Rand) | Target market | No. of shops selling | Average items sold per month per shop | Total no. of items sold per month | Rand value of items sold per month | 60% of shops sel-ling items | Revised Rand value of items sold |
|---|---|---|---|---|---|---|---|---|
| Skirt | 250 | Girls | 28 | 3 | 84 | 21 000 | 17 | 4 250 |
| Belt | 150 | Girls | 28 | 3 | 84 | 12 600 | 17 | 2 550 |
| Necklace | 150 | Girls | 28 | 3 | 84 | 12 600 | 17 | 2 550 |
| Bangles | 50 | Girls | 28 | 3 | 84 | 4 200 | 17 | 850 |
| Anklets | 50 | Girls | 28 | 3 | 84 | 4 200 | 17 | 850 |
| Head gear | 100 | Girls | 28 | 3 | 84 | 8 400 | 17 | 1 700 |
| Vest | 30 | Girls | 28 | 3 | 84 | 2 520 | 17 | 510 |
| Skirt (Sdwaba) | 550 | Women | 28 | 3 | 84 | 46 200 | 17 | 9 350 |
| Apron/ Itete | 300 | Women | 28 | 3 | 84 | 25 200 | 17 | 5 100 |
| Head gear (ischolo) | 550 | Women | 28 | 3 | 84 | 46 200 | 17 | 9 350 |
| Ibhayi | 150 | Women | 28 | 3 | 84 | 12 600 | 17 | 2 550 |
| Amadavath | 50 | Women | 28 | 3 | 84 | 4 200 | 17 | 850 |
| Vest | 150 | Women | 28 | 3 | 84 | 12 600 | 17 | 2 550 |
| Earring | 50 | Women | 28 | 3 | 84 | 4 200 | 17 | 850 |
| Mbadada sandals | 350 | Men | 28 | 2 | 56 | 19 600 | 17 | 5 950 |
|  |  |  |  | 44 | 1 232 | 236 320 | 255 | 49 810 |
|  |  |  |  |  |  |  |  |  |
| Average price | 195.33 | Average income per shop | | | | 8 440 | | 1 778.93 |
| Median price | 150 |  |  |  |  |  |  |  |

*Source: Author's compilation from field visits*

Table 4 presents the traditional items available at Kwa Mai Mai for men of all ages and uses the same model and assumptions as those used in Table 3. This is a one-stop shop for men seeking traditional attire for ceremonies back home, where customers can be dressed from head to toe, inclusive of traditional sandals and head gear. Kwa Mai Mai has it all.

Table 4: Value of items at men's traditional attire shops

| Item | Price (Rand) | No. of shops selling | Average items sold per month per shop | Total no. of items sold per month | Rand value of items sold per month | 60% of shops selling items | Revised Rand value of items sold |
|---|---|---|---|---|---|---|---|
| Bheshu | 800 | 11 | 2 | 22 | 17 600 | 7 | 5 600 |
| Snene | 700 | 11 | 2 | 22 | 15 400 | 7 | 4 900 |
| Umginqo | 800 | 11 | 2 | 22 | 17 600 | 7 | 5 600 |
| Shoulder inyamane | 700 | 11 | 2 | 22 | 15 400 | 7 | 4 900 |
| Ingwe | 4 500 | 11 | 1 | 11 | 49 500 | 7 | 31 500 |
| Izikhono/ Arm bands | 350 | 11 | 2 | 22 | 7 700 | 7 | 2 450 |
| Head gear/ Inyamazane | 150 | 11 | 2 | 22 | 3 300 | 7 | 1 050 |
| Leopard | 400 | 11 | 1 | 11 | 4 400 | 7 | 2 800 |
| Mbadada sandals | 350 | 28 | 2 | 56 | 19 600 | 17 | 5 950 |
| Indlaka (with Snene) | 3 500 | 11 | 1 | 11 | 38 500 | 7 | 24 500 |
| Total | | | | | 189 000 | 80 | 89 250 |
| Average price | 1 225 | | | | | | |
| Median price | 700 | | | | | | |

*Source: Author's compilation from field visits*

## *Not your usual men's hostel*

Kwa Mai Mai is not a hostel or a halfway house for job seekers; nor is it a place to crash with a family for the night. It is a place for those who are willing and able to slog it out well into the evening, producing goods that will never be included in the calculation of the producer price index. The work that is done is below the radar – not by chance but by design, as this allows it to escape the attention of 'the system', which would necessitate the creation of a formal distribution pipeline to get goods into the wholesale market. This is a trade zone that has over the years managed to create its own informal economy, far from the wandering eye of venture capitalists and other economic hitmen.

Contrary to its stated entrepreneurial spirit and commercial sensibility, Kwa Mai Mai is often loosely described as a traditional herb market and a tourist destination for those eager to interact with its cultural milieu. However, it is much more than that.

## *A village transport hub*

Some of the items produced in Kwa Mai Mai, such as wedding kists, can no longer be transported to the villages in the Pullman or *uLoliwe* (the railway bus), as was possible until the 1980s. Today, these items often find their way back home either in the back of a bakkie or in a trailer pulled by the now-famous and convenient minibus taxis.

A few decades ago, private taxis used to pass by Kwa Mai Mai to pick up a passenger or two leaving for their village. Today an informal taxi transport hub, just outside the Kwa Mai Mai gate, provides a convenient transport service to those who are not able to travel back home but need to send goods to their families. This taxi transport hub is also used as a post office or courier to send letters to loved ones back home. It is not uncommon to hear people shouting at the top of their voices as a taxi drives off: *'Utshele uMa-Dlamini ukuthi athathe leyombuzi eyabuya eBathenjini ayidayise, imali ayiphathise uBheseni ngama Easter'*, which means: 'Tell Ma-Dlamini to sell the goat that came from the Tembus and give the money to Bheseni when he returns to Joburg after Easter holidays.'

The taxi rank outside Kwa Mai Mai might look very small in comparison with the minibus taxi ranks spread across the city, such as the Bree Taxi Rank, MTN Taxi Rank, Wanderers Taxi Rank and others, but it performs a key function in relaying goods purchased at the Kwa Mai Mai market to other destinations. The Kwa Mai Mai taxi rank also plays an important role in providing long-distance transport services to those returning home to the villages. The minibus taxis stationed outside Kwa Mai Mai are part of an estimated network of 150 000 minibus taxi owners in the country, with over 300 000 drivers, who together generate between R60 bn and R90 bn in annual turnover.[29]

Notably, the regular shipments of wedding kists and other essentials purchased from Kwa Mai Mai for delivery to the villages have given rise to an informal freight logistics service. Taxi drivers are given small, medium and even large parcels to transport. Depending on the size of the parcel, it may be allocated a seat in the minibus and charged as if it were a passenger. However, the cost does not deter those needing such a service, especially if they are personally unable to travel for the foreseeable future.

A minibus taxi arriving from Kwa Mai Mai at people's homes in a village can attract a lot of attention among the ever-inquisitive residents who are eager to see who is returning from the city and what is being offloaded. For the children in the village, it often means sweets and other goodies, brand new clothes and other treats. Legend has it that a husband once returned to his village from the city after several years of being away. When his children saw him walking towards the house, they jumped up and came running towards him, excitedly shouting, '*nangu uBaba, sodl'izifebe*', meaning 'Here comes Dad, we're going to eat prostitutes.' This was very embarrassing for the father, who did not expect such a greeting but knew exactly what the words meant.

This and other stories are the result of women in the villages growing increasingly suspicious of husbands who might be philandering. Children eavesdrop on mothers' conversations alleging that their husbands are not returning home as they are busy spending money on 'city women', leaving their families to starve back home. Village wives may pass comments such as '*Balibele ukudlana nezifebe*', meaning 'They are busy eating prostitutes' – in other words, sleeping with prostitutes. To innocent, unsuspecting children, *ukudla* is eating and *izifebe* is food, so when the father returns home from the city, it can only mean eating a lot of *izifebe*.


## *A place of jive and defiance?*

In an act of defiance, some of the young people from Johannesburg and surrounds have abandoned the more upmarket, classy youth hangouts in favour of Kwa Mai Mai's popular *shisanyama* lifestyle spot, which is located just before the entrance to the main trade market. This is where the who's who, the want-to-be-noticed, the slay queens and the well-connected come to dine. A thriving, daytime, open-air eating spot, it attracts hordes of people, including those who work nearby, minibus taxi drivers, urbanites and those wanting to say that they have been to Kwa Mai Mai – although they have not actually been inside the trade zone.

Popular for its steaming plate of *shisanyama* (grilled meat) and *mealiepap* (corn porridge), prepared right in front of patrons, the eating place at Kwa Mai Mai doubles up as a sociable, outdoor gathering point for the cultured. It offers a day-time fiesta for those who wish to combine eating and culture, treating visitors to cultural performances on a makeshift stage with easy access to the eatery.

Because of the centrality of Kwa Mai Mai and the nearby men's hostels, the eatery has become the go-to place for maskandi musicians who release new albums to legions of fans. A quick internet search reveals several listings of prominent maskandi musicians who have used the place to either sell or launch their new albums.

In November 2019, a prominent maskandi artist, Khuzani Mpungose (otherwise known as Khuba or Indlamlenze), launched his much-anticipated album, *Inhloko Nes'xhanti*, at the lifestyle spot. Truckloads of CDs were delivered for collection by distributors from KwaZulu-Natal, Mpumalanga, Gauteng and the Western Cape. These are not the mainstream music distributors or retailers in the regular music value chain. With a huge following, Khuzani has established 59 fan club branches across five provinces, which now act as a distribution network for his music. These distributors buy hundreds of boxes of CDs at a time and publicise their telephone numbers on Khuzani's social media platforms. Those who wish to buy CDs then contact these informal, though well-connected, distributors.

The distributors are either traditional leaders or just staunch and loyal fans of Khuzani, who have all volunteered to be the ground forces for this informal and lucrative distribution of music.

Through his innovative idea of establishing fan-based distribution networks, Khuzani has successfully displaced established music distribution platforms and retail networks. By forming strategic alliances with his fans and then identifying an existing marketplace (Kwa Mai Mai) as a product showcase venue, Khuzani has created new channels through which to push his product.

*Shisanyama being prepared in front of patrons (Photo: The author)*

Even ethno-soul artists, such as BET (Black Entertainment Television) Award winner, Sjava, and prominent vernacular and leading hip-hop artist, Big Zulu, have adopted Kwa Mai Mai as their alternative entertainment hangout precinct. As a result, Kwa Mai Mai has become the coolest place for young people to be seen at. Frequenting and posting about being at Kwa Mai Mai at weekends is no different from posting about being at the most popular lifestyle venues, for instance Kwa Max Lifestyle or Eyadini at uMlazi Township in Durban, and even Dubai. However, what makes Kwa Mai Mai different from these other posh places is that it has fused culture and tradition into a unique selling point, creating an appealing tourist attraction.

The Kwa Mai Mai eating place and the informal music distribution network are intriguing. They are a living example of what, in terms of business theory, Christensen et al. (2015:4) call 'disruptive innovation'. These authors argue that traders, drawing on their innovative, lived imagination, can create new market channels with value networks that successfully disrupt existing ones.

The new lifestyle spot, frequented by urbanites and migrants alike, has made Kwa Mai Mai a captive market for consumers of cultural goods and services, including entertainment. Even cultural practitioners and television programme producers are seeing the potential of the place for content creation – all because Kwa Mai Mai is alive with stories from the village.

Below is an important post from an artist returning from a tour of North America and Europe, which conveys how Kwa Mai Mai has become a place of convergence and remembrance.

# Six
# Meet the cultural entrepreneurs

**T**his chapter focuses on the traders whose wares bring colour to Kwa Mai Mai, while providing some historical titbits that convey migrants' struggle to survive in a city that still pretends they do not exist. The chapter also exposes the resilience of a community who sees this place as a market that they have inherited from their forefathers and which they can never abandon.

Some traders have been in business from an early age, while others came and rented their space from the city, with no connection to the early traders. However, whatever the traders' particular specialities are, they will continue to open their stalls, even if they receive no visitors, in honour of the long departed whose sweat and toil made the place possible.

## From stables to saddles

It is no coincidence that a horse saddle repair shop is found inside Kwa Mai Mai. The explorers who flocked to the city from all over the world in search of fortune arrived on horseback or in horse-drawn carriages. Horse stables mushroomed in various locations in the city, with present-day Kwa Mai Mai being one of them. About 176 stables were built to accommodate hundreds of horses. In addition, all sorts of horse-riding accessories were required, including saddles, halters, bridles, harnesses, rings, bits and spurs.

Many men came from far-flung villages to take care of the horses, feed them, clean the stables and make sure that all the equipment needed to ride the horses or pull the carriages was in good working order. Some of the horse handlers received minimal training, including on how to fix broken items, and often had to learn through trial and error. Many handlers also learned how to make horse saddles, which they then sold. When automobiles and trams replaced horses as the main forms of transport, the horse handlers could either go back home to the villages or remain in the city and apply the skills they had acquired in the stables in other ways.

## Tholukhazi Sithole, the horse-saddle maker

At Kwa Mai Mai, Tholukhazi Sithole fixes and makes horse saddles, a business he inherited from his father, who was active in the old Kwa Mai Mai in the early 1920s. Tholukhazi, who claims to have arrived in Johannesburg in the early 1980s and has been at Kwa Mai Mai ever since, says that he learned the trade from his late father.

It is not just a coincidence that a Sithole specialises in making horse saddles, which are largely made of hide. Jobe, one of the founders of the Sithole clan and chieftaincy, is credited with having defeated and decimated the Mbhele tribe, who were *amazimuzimu* (cannibals) and were killing and eating people at iLenge. Sithole (not related to the author of this book) was sent by uShaka to annihilate the Mbhele cannibals and when he did so, Shaka gave Jobe an area to oversee as a chief on his behalf. It was a large area stretching from the uMzinyathi River to what is today uMsinga. Jobe became known for trading in skin hides, and he was also quite skilled at using hide to make *iziphuku* (a blanket made of hide) as well as other goods.

Tholukhazi, who uses hide to make saddles, also happens to come from the area that Jobe was responsible for overseeing, that is, uMsinga. Jobe had a son, Matshana, who later became chief of the area stretching from Mzinyathi to the present-day uMsinga. However, he was deposed by Theophilus Shepstone in 1858 and retreated to eQhudeni, where the Sithole clan came from. Tholukhazi's father would have been part of the Sithole clan that remained, since Tholukhazi comes from the Kwazenzele ward, an area that also fell under Matshana's chieftaincy before he was deposed. The Sitholes would have learned the skin/hide trade from Jobe, who in turn would have passed this skill on to his son, Matshana, and the rest of the Sitholes in the area.

It is not surprising, therefore, that Tholukhazi's father would have ventured into the business of making and trading horse saddles at Kwa Mai Mai. Sithole now occupies one of the shops that his father and grandfather occupied when they relocated from the old Kwa Mai Mai compound. As a horse-saddle maker and repair man, Sithole offers his services to villagers who still keep horses back home. Owning a horse is still a status symbol in some villages and, back in the day, would have been the preserve of prominent figures in the community, such as government inspectors, teachers (mainly principals), chiefs and even *indunas* (local headmen).

Tholukhazi mentions that his customers include horse owners from Matatiele in the Eastern Cape, from KwaZulu-Natal, particularly Bergville, and from Mpumalanga. An important market for Tholukhazi is Matatiele, a region that has designed its outdoor cultural events around horse racing. In Matatiele, one of the horse-racing competitions called Umtelebhelo has become a popular annual event during the heritage month of September. The meaning of the word *Umtelebhelo* is very interesting for those who are not well versed in the vernacular. The word denotes a horse's brisk walking style – a four-beat gait in which the horse's legs follow a particular sequence of left hind leg, left front leg, right hind leg and right front leg. It is a marvel to watch. This is the name that the people of Matatiele have given to their horse-racing event. Just before the start of the race, the riders make a grand entrance, showcasing their horses' ability to walk, trot, canter and gallop. It is this horse-racing community that Tholukhazi, his father and grandfather have served since the early 20th century.

An important market and customer base for Tholukhazi's horse-saddle business is at Emangwaneni in Bergville, a place founded by iNkosi uZikhali, where his forefathers had settled and which – being in *ezintabeni zokhohlamba* (the Drakensberg mountains) – was accessible only on horseback. Horse-riding trails and horse-racing competitions have become synonymous with Bergville and iSizwe saMaNgwane (the AmaNgwane Clan). Without the lavish display of 100 tribesmen on horseback, there would be no traditional ceremonies or heritage celebrations at Emangwaneni. Again, Kwa Mai Mai is the go-to place for those who cannot afford a brand-new horse saddle and would rather have their old ones revamped or repaired.

With the recent emergence of the Dundee July in the KwaZulu-Natal Midlands, an annual horse-racing competition-cum-fashion show, Tholukhazi's customer base is expanding. However, he complains about the lack of assistance from government in purchasing and acquiring the necessary machines and stools needed to service his clients. Today, he still stitches the horse saddles by hand (as his forefathers did), which he says is cumbersome and very time-consuming. His lack of efficiency-enhancing machinery has cost him a number of customers who have needed their saddles repaired within a very short space of time.

Tholukhazi who, along with others, desperately needs specialised equipment to enhance his output, was encouraged when he received a visit from Mr Saki Zamxaka, CEO of the Gauteng Enterprise Propeller, a government entity mandated to provide financial and business development support to help small businesses grow and become sustainable.

## Ndwandwe, the herbalist and his muthi

Had it not been for a near-fatal encounter in the suburb of Kensington, when a gun-toting white man threatened to shoot him and his friend as they were out looking for work, Ndwandwe would probably be doing something else today. Not wanting to go into detail about what led to a gun being pointed at him and his friend, Ndwandwe simply reveals that on that day he took a decision never to work for a white man again or seek any form of employment.

Kensington (one of Johannesburg's oldest suburbs, which was established by Max Langermann in 1897), is synonymous with jacaranda and leafy oak trees which have lined the streets since the roads were laid in 1902. Once a stylish, up-market area, Kensington has undergone massive change and is now a shadow of its former self. The only feelings of nostalgia that the place stirs in anyone are for its landmark monuments and sites of historical significance.

It would appear that gun toting is not foreign to Kensington. Luckily for Ndwandwe, he was not shot at during his scary encounter. But years later, the place was in the news again when a member of the criminal underworld shot and killed someone who had been linked to the earlier killing of a multimillionaire mining magnate. Kensington has all the markings of the criminal underworld in South Africa, including absolute impunity from the law.

Ndwandwe's escape to Kwa Mai Mai offered him the perfect solution, and he remains there to this day. He has been a resident of Kwa Mai Mai since 1986 and is a traditional healer and herbalist, having inherited his knowledge from his uncle, Ntshangase, who also was a traditional healer. Ndwandwe hails from Mahlabathini, a small town in KwaZulu-Natal that is said to have been established by the British colonial government in 1898, one year after Zululand became part of the British colony of Natal. Mahlabathini means 'country of white, sandy soil' and is in close proximity to what could be regarded as the heart of the Zulu Kingdom, Ulundi and Nongoma. This is the home of iNkosi uMangosuthu Buthelezi, the traditional Prime Minister of the Zulu nation and the founder of the Inkatha Freedom Party (IFP). Prince Buthelezi is the former chief minister of the KwaZulu homeland, a position he held before the country's democratic transition in 1994.

Had he been born during the reign of Shaka, Dingane, Mpande or Cetshwayo, Ndwandwe would have been on call by any of the kings to ensure the herbal strengthening of the regiments as they prepared to go to war. His original home is in close proximity to eMakhosini Valley (Valley of the Kings), which has all the markings of an imagined modern-day cultural hub for the Zulu people and a natural landscape that harks back to the time of King Shaka. It is the area in which the greatest Zulu kings who ever lived originated and it is where Nkosinkulu or Senzangakhona ka Jama (the father of Shaka, Dingane and Mpande) and King Dinizulu are buried.

As a traditional healer, Ndwandwe epitomises Zulu culture, heritage and tradition. It is no wonder that he gravitated, from his early days as a cattle herder in the veld, towards a profession in which he was able to put his knowledge of plants and herbs (accumulated from a young age out in the veld) to good use, by making various herbal concoctions for different needs and ailments.

His herbal shop in Kwa Mai Mai is like a small supermarket. With only 2 m x 2 m of shelving space, Ndwandwe has managed to ensure that every herb that his clientele requires is available in his humble shop. There is no concoction, whatever its purpose may be, that he is unable to make. Some shelves look like bookshelves, while others resemble postbox pigeon holes. All sorts of receptacles, from peanut butter jars to butter containers, as well as whiskey bottles and 5-litre buckets, are used to store different herbs, plants, bark from various trees, animal fat, skins of various wild animals, birds and even monkey skeletons.

On one of the many occasions when I have visited Ndwandwe, no fewer than five people walked into his shop during the space of an hour, looking for various types of herbs. Some of the walk-in customers appeared not to know who Ndwandwe was, having simply been referred to him by someone else. Judging from their facial expressions, some people were troubled and were obviously seeking respite from or a solution to their challenges. Women appeared to be more stressed than men, which is indicative of the uneven power relations between men and women in our society.

Some people request a private consultation with Ndwandwe; others come in and tell him the exact herb or traditional medicine that they want, given their specific circumstances. In such cases, Ndwandwe simply stands up, goes straight to the shelves and retrieves the exact herb(s) that the visitor is looking for. All that remains is a discussion on the quantity and how the medicine should be used. Some customers complain about how small the prepared herbal concoction is after Ndwandwe has wrapped it in a piece of paper.

Personal consultations are conducted behind a curtain, just behind the shelves, which suggests that, while visitors find themselves squashed in the small shop, there is another room dedicated to more private discussions. It is not difficult to see that when some customers emerge from their consultations, they have difficulty maintaining eye contact. One wonders, therefore, what prompted their visit. Were they interested in a love potion, a promotion at work, or something else? Whatever the reasons, Ndwandwe is never short of visitors.

On one occasion, a prominent Zulu maskandi musician, who was on his way to a festival on the East Rand, arrived for a consultation with Ndwandwe. The maskandi music scene is heavily contested and there is a strong reliance on traditional medicine to repel spells that might have been cast on an artist by a competitor in a bid to compromise their performance on stage. This is because of a prevalent belief in the use of black magic, equivalent to witchcraft, among maskandi musicians. This has been exacerbated by tensions between prominent maskandi musicians and further fuelled by fans who appear to enjoy witnessing feuds between artists. The famous maskandi musicians who pop in at Ndwandwe's herbal shop are not here by accident or because they come from Mahlabathini, like Ndwandwe. The musicians come for traditional medicine and herbs to strengthen their performance and hopefully cause *itwetwe* (fright) to any group who succeeds them once they have left the stage.

*Ndwandwe, the herbalist and traditional healer (Photo: Siphiwe Mhlambi)*

On the day in question, the musician purchased his traditional herbs from Ndwandwe and then rushed to the festival taking place to the east of Johannesburg, about 30 minutes from the city, arriving just in time for the back-stage call. No sooner had the musician left the shop than an elderly man arrived with two young men (*izinsizwa*) who had come for *ibhande*, the popular name for an arm belt that is fastened just below the shoulder on the upper arm. *Ibhande* is meant to protect the wearer from all manner of attacks or bad luck, either of a physical nature or the result of a sorcerer's spell. Unlike a flex arm belt, worn by body builders to strengthen their biceps and triceps, or an elliptical machine used to engage in dips, pilates or yoga, the *muthi* belt worn by Zulu men has been dipped into herbs and other ingredients to protect them from harm.

Whether he has been consulting, prescribing or selling herbs, or preparing *umuthi* belts, Ndwandwe has been steeped in this trade since the Kensington gun incident back in 1986. He has built a lucrative business from a customer base who truly believe in traditional medicine and the value of consulting diviners and herbalists. Ndwandwe reports that he has managed to support his two wives, who live back home in Mahlabathini. He hastens to add that he is already working on acquiring a third wife. He has also managed to support 15 of his living children (five are deceased), all of whom he has put through school from the income he has earned as a traditional healer and herbalist.

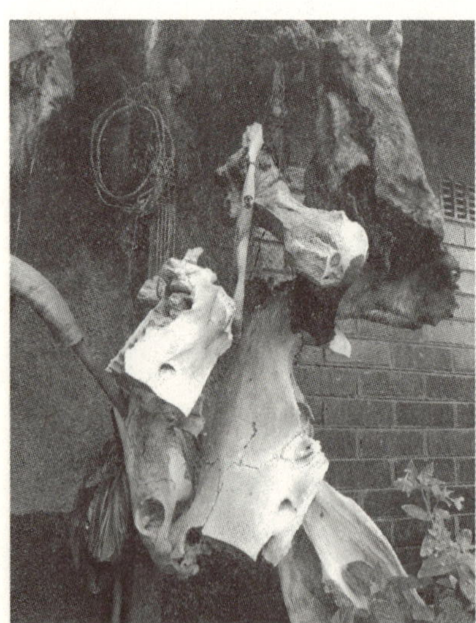

*Animal skulls and skins are among the items used in muthi and interventions by traditional healers (Photo: The author)*

It is not surprising that the herbal trade is arguably the most successful line of work at Kwa Mai Mai, accounting for about 20 per cent of the shops inside the precinct. One of the herbal traders' secret weapons is their ability to sell hope and to make customers believe that the remedies will have their desired effect.

While practising as a herbalist, Ndwandwe also doubles up as an *induna*, the headman for the Kwa Mai Mai hostel and bazaar. This is discussed in more detail in Chapter 8. Suffice to say at this stage, though, that Ndwandwe is one of the most consulted traditional healers at Kwa Mai Mai.

## Shongwe's traditional weapons and symbols of masculinity at Kwa Mai Mai

The making and selling of traditional weapons, such as sticks, *izagila namawisa* (knobkerries), assegais and shields, is one of the most important trades in the Kwa Mai Mai compound. In fact, Kwa Mai Mai could be classified as a cultural weapons arms cache. The carrying of traditional weapons is a common feature at cultural events and ceremonies. Whether it is a traditional wedding, *umemulo* (coming-of-age ceremony), *izimbizo* (a traditional gathering, normally called by traditional leaders) or a dance ceremony, including *umkhosi womhlanga* (the reed dance), cultural weapons are essential bodily accessories. In addition, they are a sign of masculinity and convey a sense of cultural identity, while also projecting a warrior-like persona, with which Zulus have historically been associated.

Sticks, knobkerries, spears and shields are longstanding features of the Zulu culture. For example, herdsmen carry sticks when shepherding cattle, while hunters carry knobkerries and spears when hunting *izagwaca namathendele*, including wild animals, even lions. Zulu men use these traditional weapons when they engage in *ukugiya*, a provocative performance in which a man breaks rank and rushes forward, leaping and stamping, while wielding his shield and spear in a threatening manner as if preparing for war with an enemy. The cycle of leaping and running towards imaginary warriors is repeated, while the performer's peers shout praises and proclaim the glorious deeds that took place in battle, much to the admiration of the onlookers.

It is in these exaggerated, war-like charges – as if they were regiments preparing to go to battle – and boastful displays of prowess and agility that these traditional weapons are on full display. Without these sticks, knobkerries, spears and shields, and *ubhoko* (the sharpened stick used to anchor the shield), the performers would not be able to take full advantage of the exciting custom of *Giya*. This is what would have happened during the march by IFP supporters to the ANC's headquarters at Shell House in Johannesburg in 1994, as the absence of their accessories would have greatly diminished the overall effect.

The range of sticks would not be complete without those used when attending *imigcagco* (traditional weddings) and used at *umgangela* (a staged stick fight between men). Before the advent of guns and gun battles, stick fighting was used to resolve internal disputes between male rivals, who sometimes ended up fighting over a woman. Even today, stick fighting remains an integral part of Zulu cultural tradition, while also serving an important teaching purpose. As such, for Zulu men, stick fighting is pivotal to the maintenance of a social system that delineates accepted roles and modes of behaviour.

Stick fighting has always been the preserve of men and boys, and it is not subject to any age restriction. Many boys engage in stick fighting from a young age, when looking after cattle, for example. It is not uncommon for adult men (*ingqwele*) to approach boys in the veld and ask to *qhata* them (ask them to fight). Mastering the act of stick fighting helps to prepare young boys for manhood. Hitting an opponent in the head must be avoided at all costs. Engaging in stick fighting allows adult men to showcase their talent, even at public ceremonies arranged by wards or at district competitions.

Stick fights are overseen by the headmen or the war captains, officially known as *induna yezinsizwa* or *umphathi wezinsizwa*. These overseers of stick fighting are always on the alert, just in case what was meant to be *izinsizwa* (young men) simply testing their strength gets out of hand. The stick-fighting culture and tradition go way back – according to some, to 1670, when Malandela, who preceded King Shaka, consolidated the Zulus into one nation. Shaka then formalised stick fighting, using it as a means to train his warriors for war and conquest. Even today, it is an indelible part of Zulu culture and tradition as it is seen to instil discipline and teach young boys and men that status within the Zulu social construct must be earned.

*Zulu man with so-called cultural weapons (Photo: Siphiwe Mhlambi)*

Kwa Mai Mai is a convenient source not only of sticks for those who wish to engage in stick fighting, but also of traditional medicine and herbs that prepare stick fighters for a particular fighting event, as does the traditional arm belt that Ndwandwe supplies.

## Sticks from the mystery forest

What is sometimes seen as a nation of blood-thirsty Zulus with a penchant for violence is actually the reflection of a well-entrenched social system that, through stick fighting, reinforces the importance of self-mastery and 'honour', both metaphors for manhood that have helped to bolster kinship obligations during periods of social turmoil.

The only place in Johannesburg that stocks and sells all the necessary items for stick fighting is Kwa Mai Mai. Many shops in the compound sell them, with one of the traders, Themba Shongwe, who hails from Nkandla in KwaZulu-Natal, under Chief Biyela, boasting an impressive collection.

Themba's shop is stocked with all sorts of sticks, which are used for different purposes. Some are artfully embellished with colourful masking tape and bird feathers at one end. One can see from the different makes of stick which region they relate to and their specific cultural significance. Those from northern Zululand are different from those from southern KwaZulu-Natal, for example, and they have different uses. For example, the straight and slim variety with different colours of masking tape is used by amaBhaca from uMzimkhulu for their signature dance, *isibhaca* or *ubhaca*, while the variety with colourful bird feathers and a sharp edge at the top is used by, for example, Nongoma, Hluhluwe and Mahlabathini from northern Zululand.

To acquire the raw materials from which he fashions a range of traditional weaponry, Shongwe makes regular trips to the Nkandla forest, where he chops down different types of trees. From the wood he then carves sticks in the desired sizes. The Zulus have had a long association with the forest, which is regarded as mystical and the home of supernatural beings. At one stage it was used by other tribes as a hideout, to avoid being conquered by Shaka. More recently, warriors under the leadership of Chief Bhambatha ka Mancinza, duly assisted by Chief Sigananda ka Zokufa Shezi, were holed up in this forest when they waged *impi yamakhanda* (the poll tax rebellion). In 1906, Bhambatha chose the Nkandla forest as a base from which to wage a guerrilla war against the British colonial soldiers. The British soldiers were armed with machine guns and cannons, while the so-called rebels were equipped only with *assegais* (spears), fighting sticks and knobkerries, and with cowhide shields, to withstand the fire power of the British.

Shongwe's main customers buy sticks for their cultural significance, for use during wedding ceremonies and other traditional events. A complete set of sticks would comprise one made of cowhide with *ubhoko* (a sharp stick used to hold the shield), *umgobo* (a short, sharpened stick that is inserted into the centre of the shield to keep it straight), a fighting stick and (sometimes) an *assegai*, depending on the occasion. A complete set would set a customer back no less than R3 000 – about US$160.

Whether his business revolves around 'cultural weapons' or 'weapons of Zulu masculinity', it is sufficiently lucrative to have enabled Shongwe to build a homestead back home in Nkandla, pay *lobola* for his wife and even buy a motor vehicle.


## Broken sticks and the Shell House massacre

It is unknown whether the formidable array of traditional weapons that about 20 000 IFP supporters were carrying on 28 March 1994, as they marched to the ANC headquarters in Shell House in Johannesburg, had come from Kwa Mai Mai. However, their imposing presence meant only one thing to the onlookers – war was threatening. The decision to march on Shell House was the culmination of a series of skirmishes between ANC supporters and the IFP in the run-up to the 1994 elections, which the IFP was intending to boycott.

The Shell House massacre (as it is now commonly called) was not an isolated incident signalling a fallout between the IFP and the ANC. It was the tipping point after years of slowly brewing tensions over what the IFP saw as the fight for the legitimacy and authority of traditional rule, and the power of Zulu chiefs. Central to the escalating tensions was the IFP's insistence that the Zulu Kingdom be restored and that the land lost in multiple colonial wars be returned. The ANC, however, was hellbent on dismantling all remnants of what it perceived to be the perpetuation of the apartheid system.[30]

The IFP, through its leader, Prince Mangosuthu Buthelezi, had refused to enter and contest the first democratic elections in 1994. What had started as a string of violent clashes between supporters of the ANC underground movement in the 1980s in KwaZulu-Natal had now spread to the Witwatersrand and the outskirts of Johannesburg. The hostels were the support base of the IFP, and could probably have assembled a standby Zulu regiment if circumstances warranted it. On this particular day, the hostels had been mobilising for the march to Shell House, with the Zulus intending to make a strong showing. With women ululating and showering the armed men with words of encouragement, the stage was set for an ugly encounter.

Writing for the *Daily Maverick*, Greg Marinovich recalls:

That seminal year of 1994 leaps into the mind's eye like it were just yesterday, yet infants born that year have since mysteriously developed into voting adults ... On 28 March 1994, journalists, police, military units and peace monitors began work long before dawn, traversing the black townships that punctuated the towns and cities along the reef of gold deep under the veld. Thousands of Zulu men poured out of hostels and shanty neighbourhoods, resplendent in their IFP regalia and a variety of militant, traditional or simply peculiar adornment. Civilians not savvy enough to have stayed in bed, ran from the stick- and spear-wielding men as they advanced.[31]

A throng of IFP supporters had gathered at Library Gardens that very same morning and were heading towards Shell House for a political standoff aimed at voicing their displeasure over how the democratic dispensation was unfolding. Earlier in the month, IFP leaders had called for the staging of a rally in support of the Zulu king and the Kingdom's position in a post-apartheid South Africa. This was intended to be a showstopper and IFP supporters had come out in large numbers. The purpose of the march on Shell House was to send the message that unless the Zulus had a central seat at the dinner table, any post-apartheid dispensation would be stillborn at best.

Unbeknown to the IFP supporters, ANC security personnel were lying in wait on the upper floors of Shell House. Like deer hunters waiting for their prey to walk by, they aimed their guns at unsuspecting, chanting Zulu warriors, who were brandishing their traditional weapons, and opened fire. Eight people soon lay dead outside Shell House, while 19 people were murdered in downtown Johannesburg and many more across the Witwatersrand. Some, breathing their last breath, were still clutching their traditional weapons, reminiscent of *isosha elifele empini* (a soldier dying in the line of duty).

Whether perhaps the sight of sticks, knobkerries, spears and shields reminded the ANC security personnel that Zulu warriors had fearlessly defeated the heavily armed British forces in 1879, it is still not known why the use of guns and live ammunition was considered the appropriate way to repel a group of marchers armed with traditional weapons. The subsequent hearings that took place under the auspices of the Truth and Reconciliation Commission (TRC) came to one conclusion: that the shooting of marchers by ANC security personnel was unjustified. Eleven security personnel who had fatally shot IFP supporters were eventually granted amnesty.

The tragic incident prompted a new conversation about the carrying of sticks, knobkerries, spears and shields in public. In fact, the subject had been broached in 1992, when a ban on the carrying of so-called traditional weapons was mooted. This was not the first time that a possible ban had been discussed. In the late 19th century, particularly after the decisive and embarrassing defeat of the British in 1879 by Zulu warriors armed with traditional weapons, the Natal Native Code of the (then) British colony of Natal banned the carrying of such weapons. Later, the KwaZulu homeland authorities, under the Chiefs' and Headmen's Act No. 8 of 1974, empowered *iziInduna* and *aMakhosi* to implement the same policy, particularly in unrest areas. The extent to which these traditional leaders would have ensured that no traditional weapons were carried remained to be seen, because those with weapons were largely supporters of the IFP, as were the traditional leaders.

Today, Kwa Mai Mai's collection of traditional weapons, which are sold at most of the stalls, could fully equip the members of a Zulu regiment.

## Mama Chauke, the multi-ethnic trader

The resident mix at Kwa Mai Mai has always been dominated by the Nguni group, particularly the Zulus. When the compound moved from the old site to its current location, the Nguni constituted 83 per cent of residents, while the Sotho and other ethnic groups accounted for 5 per cent and 12 per cent respectively.

In a letter from the Office of the Town Clerk to the Native Commissioner, dated 26 October 1955, no breakdown was given of who the other 12 per cent were, but they would have been the ethnic groups from the north. In the letter, the Town Clerk clearly states: 'Although the Nguni group predominate among present tenants, it is nevertheless considered equitable that the lease of the trading rights should be available to the members of all ethnic groups.'[32] Apart from the Sotho, who occupied 5 per cent of the available trading spaces and beds, it is safe to assume that the other 12 per cent comprised Venda, Pedi, Ndebele, Swati and Tsonga individuals.

Although running a solo operation in her Kwa Mai Mai shop, Nkiyase Rose Mabasa-Chauke essentially carries the entire culture of the people from Limpopo province on her shoulders. Limpopo province accounts for the largest population of BaPedi at 52 per cent, followed by Tsonga at 24 per cent (about 15 per cent of Tsongas reside in Mpumalanga province), and then Venda at 16.7 per cent. Limpopo's diverse culture and traditions are consolidated in a single shop where Nkiyase has worked to affirm and reinforce the indigenous cultural heritage across all demographic groupings in the province.

What is particularly popular in Nkiyase's shop is Pedi traditional attire, comprising the most colourful of South Africa's traditional dresses, mainly in bright pink and turquoise, and sometimes in yellow, blue and white. These vibrant colours are said to represent happiness. Women's attire is quite different from that of men. The Pedi women's regalia consists of inner fabric (*hele*), tied at the waist, and of a cloth tied to the top of the dress (*metsheka*), which matches the head gear (*moruka*). Of course, no outfit would be complete without the famous colourful beadwork. Calf-length dresses, with pleated blouses and voluminous skirts, are common among women, sometimes with embroidery or just trimmed with colourful ribbon.

A particularly intriguing feature of Pedi traditional attire is the colourful kilts that Pedi men wear as part of their official regalia. How the kilt became part of the Pedi's traditional outfit remains a mystery, but it is rumoured that it was first brought to the country during the South African War, also known as the Anglo-Boer War, and worn by the Scottish soldiers.

Nkiyase Chauke's work has been made easier because animal skins, which used to feature in traditional Pedi attire for women, such as a front apron (*ntepa*) and a back apron (*lebole*), have been dispensed with. The previous animal–skin aprons have been replaced with aprons made of cloth.

Nkiyase, a Tsonga herself, has been making Tsonga traditional attire since she arrived in Kwa Mai Mai in 2008, to take over her grandfather's business. He had been a Kwa Mai Mai trader and resident since 1968, originally hailing from Zebediela in Limpopo province. Nkiyase's people are known for their vibrant and bright colours, often using different shades of pink, yellow, purple, blue and green. She offers a full range of women's attire, with the *xibelani* skirt a particularly striking piece. It is a wraparound, woven and beaded skirt, sometimes called *tinguvu*, and is worn mostly during the traditional *xibelani* dance. The *xibelani* dance, common in the north, involves a spectacular display, and has been popularised by artists such as Thomas Chauke and Sho Madjozi.

Nkiyase's work extends beyond her own ethnic boundaries. Her traditional attire includes that of the Zulu, Ndebele, Xhosa and Venda.

She holds culture and tradition close to her heart in an approach she claims is a sign of respect for other ethnic groups and their heritage. Her shop also has an array of Zulu traditional wear, particularly for women, which differs according to their age and stage in life. For instance, a young woman who has yet to get married, known as *intombi*, wears different traditional attire to that of a married woman or a woman about to be married, known as *inkehli*, who is expected to cover herself with *ibhayi* (a shawl), and wear *isicholo* (head gear) and *isidwaba* (a cowhide skirt). Nkiyase also stocks young Zulu women's traditional attire, including a short, beaded skirt (*isigege*), with other accessories such as beads to circle the head and waist, and twisted beads (*ucu*) for tying around the ankles and elbows.

Nkiyase's other colourful clothing collection is that of the Venda women, mainly the upper garment called *wenda*, made of multi-coloured striped cloth, and *maredo*, which are worn by young women. *Maredo* are narrow strips of cloth that hang between the legs in the front and the back.

Traditional attire at Kwa Mai Mai would not be complete without that of the Ndebele people, who are known for their intricate beadwork and lavishly decorated aprons for both young and adult women. The apron is the most elaborate clothing item. Nkiyase's versatile work ensures that different aprons are produced for different age groups. For example, small, beaded aprons are for girls and *isiphephetu* are reserved for older girls and young women. Ndebele attire also has very distinctive beaded hoops which women wear around their neck, arms, legs and waist. Included in Nkiyase's Ndebele attire collection are *isigolwani* and copper rings (*idzilla*), which married women wear around their neck, ankles and arms.

Ndebele married women also wear long aprons made of hardened skin, which are richly decorated with geometric designs. Girls and unmarried women traditionally do not cover their breasts, whereas married women cover their upper bodies with blankets in multi-coloured materials with stripes or beaded designs. The only items that Nkiyase does not stock in her shop are animal-skin aprons, which Ndebele men wear, and beaded breast plates (*iporiyana*), which men hang from their necks. *Iporiyana* is a significant item for men. It is a symbol of manhood and young men receive it from their fathers after undergoing initiation. It is worn with skin headbands and ankle bands, sometimes accompanied by a cape.

## MaNdlovu and the sacred clothing of the Nazareth Baptist Church

Legend has it that when the founder of the Shembe Nazareth Baptist Church, Prophet Isaiah Shembe, was about to depart from this earth, he called on Nela Buthelezi, Nondayiso Dlamini and Muntuwezizwe Buthelezi. Shembe painstakingly explained to the three of them how to sew various pieces of garment that would complete the Shembe sacred uniform. Thereafter he said, 'My children, the time will come, when all maidens will dress in this way, and the women will dress in this uniform; they will wear skin petticoats and they will wear topknots on their heads. A woman who does not wear a topknot is not perfect' (Buthelezi 1995:n.p.).

Shembe then prophesised to someone called Matsheketshe, saying, 'You, Matsheketshe, shall sew these dancing uniforms for the women, and they shall pay you money for them' (Buthelezi 1995:n.p.). Today all the women in the Shembe Nazareth Baptist Church dress in skin petticoats with topknots on their heads, unless they are wearing a white robe called *umnazaretha*.

On 28 September 2021, thousands of members of a particular faction in the Shembe Nazareth Baptist Church descended on the City of Durban in a march that would prove to be unprecedented. The traffic came to a standstill when the congregants marched from Dinizulu Gardens to the City Hall, a distance of about 2.2 km. What was striking was what the Shembe followers wore on the day – all-white robes, known as *umnazaretha*, in keeping with the church's denomination. Men, women and children were all in white, differentiated only by their head gear, with men wearing *umqhele* (men's head gear made of leopard skin) and women wearing topknots.

*Umnazaretha* has become synonymous with the Shembe Church and is always visible under the tree circled by stones painted white (representing the church) on the Sabbath – the day of worship, which is a Saturday. There is no evidence that early Africans, particularly

Zulu-speaking people, ever wore any clothing other than animal hide. *Umnazaretha* was first worn by Prophet Isaiah Shembe in about the 1930s. Much as he claimed at the time that the type of clothing he wore had been revealed to him in visions, it bore a striking resemblance to the clothing worn by ancient Jews and later by missionaries. Some scholars argue that Prophet Shembe may have come across such designs in biblical texts and imagery.

Shembe is said to have used a tailor in Durban to make his garments, which he later sold to his followers. Today, the same *umnazaretha* (which is made of light-weight cotton) is still worn by his followers and was on display during the march in Durban in 2021. There appears to be no difference between *umnazaretha* worn by women and that worn by men, except for the length of the gown and some other, minor details. For instance, a woman's white garment is longer and has horizontal stitching, whereas that of a man extends just to the knee. Also, married women are expected to cover their backs with a scarf and to wear a belt, which is made of black cloth, indicating their marital status, and *isicholo* (a popular Zulu headdress). A female church leader (*umkhokheli*), in turn, is distinguishable by the black fabric yoke (*isiphika*) that she wears on her shoulders, while a male church leader wears a mainly dark-green gown with buttons all the way down, similar to what the founder of the church wore.

*Shembe congregation under the tree (Photo: Siphiwe Mhlambi)*

Wearing *umnazaretha* comes with a lot of responsibility. Firstly, the garment, because it is snow white, is said to be a 'garment of the heavens', at least according to Prophet Shembe. It is said to represent purity and innocence and demands, from those who wear it, strict conformity to the rules of the church. Moreover, those who wear *umnazaretha* are expected to display a certain behaviour and demeanour, both inside and out – in other words, in thought and in action.

The *umnazaretha*, whose roots are in ecclesiastical garb, is found inside shop No. 59 at Kwa Mai Mai. This is Landiwe 'MaNdlovu' Mkhize's shop. It is the only shop that makes and supplies all the accessories for the Shembe Church, which also has its own temple, eMoyeni Temple, inside the Kwa Mai Mai compound. MaNdlovu is an impressive-looking, dark and beautiful middle-aged woman with a gaze that gives you the impression she can see right through you and even knows what you are thinking. MaNdlovu, who also doubles up as the *umkhokheli* of the church and whose brother lives next door and is the *umshumayeli* (see Chapter 7), has the monopoly in terms of making and selling all the Shembe Church garments. Whether this is due to the prophecy of Isaiah Shembe, or because MaNdlovu is the female leader of the Kwa Mai Mai temple, is not clear.

## Woodworking in Kwa Mai Mai

Some people from the villages, having been retrenched from their city jobs, sought to start their own businesses in an environment that they could relate to, and they chose Kwa Mai Mai. The compound's business environment is ideal for people who enjoy working with their hands. Whether it involves doing beadwork, tanning skins, sharpening spears, or making sticks and knobkerries, the workmanship is mostly of a manual variety. Woodworking is one of the key skills that this group of village migrants has mastered.

Judging from the calibre of the woodworkers at Kwa Mai Mai, it is clear that most of them have had some prior experience of working in factories or workshops. Before losing their jobs in the city, these woodworkers would have been involved in making products such as cabinets and home and office fittings, including panelling and shelving. Woodworking is a very delicate craft, which involves reading shop drawings, schematics and blueprints, shaping and cutting timber with power tools, joining timber, and fixing it with nails, screws, adhesives or staples. Precision in the work is achieved by following measurement specifications using rulers, plumb bobs, levels and framing squares. This suggests that those working in a woodworking business would have to have had some form of technical training in drawing and measurement, or at least acquired practical, on-the-job experience. Clearly, woodworkers need to be able to operate automated equipment and woodworking tools, such as power drills, jigsaws, circular saws, routers, sanders, biscuit joiners and milling machines, as well as other wood-shaping devices.

Woodworkers' experience in manufacturing various pieces of furniture for the home, coffins, wedding kists and personal storage boxes or wooden trunks for mineworkers have made Kwa Mai Mai an excellent source of supply. There are three competing woodworking businesses in the compound, all of which have been passed down from one generation to the next. Two of the businesses are owned by two different Sithole families. They are run by sons who inherited them from their now-deceased parents.

## Sandile Sithole – a touch of wood

Sandile Sithole, whose woodworking business seems to be thriving, is the only Kwa Mai Mai trader who seems to be running a non-stop operation. With the Sithole business following a sound division-of-labour policy, the woodworkers perform various tasks, using a range of tools, with each worker having their own speciality. Although Sithole has provided his team with power tools, his most skilled woodworkers have chosen – in the interests of time and convenience – to use hand tools only, which also helps them to add character to a piece and to ensure that they have complete control over the finished product, which can be very satisfying.

Judging from the range of products that Sithole manufactures, it is clear that different products lend themselves to different types of wood. The choice of a particular type of wood is determined by its quality, the grain and how it responds to manipulation. Given the carved features and intricate designs of wedding kists and coffins, for example, it is important that the wood must be easy to work with and soft enough to be fashioned into different shapes. Sithole says that the wrong choice of wood can lead to costly mistakes, especially if the wood is damaged during processing. Knowing how to choose the right wood and how to work with it effectively is therefore crucial. A rule of thumb is that the better the quality of the wood and the greater its malleability, the easier it will be to turn it into a fit-for-purpose and durable end product.

Sithole claims that although he learned woodworking from his late father, when he arrived in Kwa Mai Mai in 1999, he had to undergo extra woodworking training at the Johannesburg Technical College. His father had come to Johannesburg as a young man and gone straight to the original Kwa Mai Mai compound, which was still situated at Wemmer and Jubilee. He later relocated to the current site, where the young Sandile joined his father in his business. Many years later, he has never worked anywhere else.

Another native of uMsinga in KwaZulu-Natal, Sithole has all the characteristics of a hands-on businessman who is forever forging ahead with his woodworking business, which is tucked underneath an open warehouse. His clients range from those wanting wedding kists to those requiring pieces of furniture. As far as the latter is concerned, Sithole is confident that his workshop can build any piece of household furniture that may be required. Sometimes people approach him after seeing pieces of furniture that they like at shops in town and ask him to make similar items.

## The famous wedding kist

There were two things for which Mai Mai made a name for itself: the first was the beer that was brewed at Kwa Mai Mai and sold at the beer hall to the multitudes of migrant workers who frequented the compound. The other was the wedding kist. The *mai mai* wedding kist was regularly spotted loaded on the roof of the Pullman or *uLoliwe* bus, as it was popularly known in days gone by. It did not matter who the manufacturer of the bus was (Oshkosh, Leyland or International); to the village migrants, the bus was either *uLoliwe* (referring to the railways) or *iPulmende* (referring to the Pullman). With its signature red colour, *iPulmende* was usually a long trailer pulled by an ugly towing head, as if it were used to separate the driver, who was always a white government official, from the natives at the back of the bus.

It was this bus, full of returning migrants, that always carried the wedding kists as standard pieces of luggage. If it were not pulling off at the local train station, it would arrive at its designated bus stop in the village where, on a daily basis, it would be received by a group of villagers anxious to see who would descend from it. Others would be there to sell some village ware, such as *amadumbe* (sweet potatoes) or *umbila* (corn meal) to those who were making their onward journey to the next village or town but wanted a quick bite to eat.

For Sithole, whose father also came from the greater uMsinga and Ladysmith, KwaHlathi area, the railway bus from Johannesburg would have travelled through Standerton, Volksrust, Newcastle, Danhauser, Glencoe, Dundee, Wasbank and Ladysmith and then branched out to the various villages, dropping off returning migrants – many proudly displaying their wedding kists. In most cases, returning migrants would be carrying these wedding kists (known as *mai mai*) on behalf of other villagers at home, who were either about to get married or were sending their daughter off to get married to their fiancés. The wedding kist could only be sourced from Kwa Mai Mai in Johannesburg and nowhere else – hence its name *mai mai;* just as the kaffir beer also became known as *mai mai.*

*Sandile Sithole with his wooden kists (Photo: Siphiwe Mhlambi)*

Today, Sithole remains true to the tradition carried in the memories of those who came before him, that is, his grandfathers and his father who also, as young village migrants, came to Johannesburg as recruited labourers to work in the mines but then found a new purpose and carved out a different future for themselves. Sithole estimates that he manufactures between 300 and 400 kists a year.

Some people, who just love a piece of art for art's sake, buy wedding kists as ornamental pieces. The kists are also sometimes found in African speciality shops, not for sale but as décor, to lend character to the place. Wedding kists have even been spotted in stores in the upmarket Sandton City Mall in Johannesburg. One such store is run by Maria McCloy, a fashion designer and collector of rare African collectables, who also specialises in beadwork. Maria is a regular customer at Kwa Mai Mai, picking up various items that she either onward sells to customers walking into her shop at the Sandton City Mall, or uses in her signature sneaker and sandal designs.

From the data gathered for this book, it is evident that the woodworkers at Kwa Mai Mai are manufacturing and shipping between 150 and 200 kists per month at an average price of R1 500, because traditional weddings are still popular among village communities and Kwa Mai Mai is recognised as the go-to supplier of kists.

*Kwa Mai Mai wedding kist inside an upmarkert Sandton City store (Photo: Siphiwe Mhlambi)*

## *Mineworkers' wooden storage trunks*

While migrant workers would have arrived from the villages with nothing except *umphako* (food provisions for the journey) and perhaps a few items of clothing, as soon as they were encamped at the compound, the one item they urgently needed was a storage box in which to keep their personal items.

This was and still is a very important acquisition in a single men's compound, where everyone sleeps in open, camp-like rooms with no privacy and just a single bunk bed allocated to them. In the absence of any lockable cupboards, the wooden trunk has always been the answer to keeping their personal items safe and secure, such as their dishes and utensils, tea bags, sugar, Lifebuoy soap, Colgate, a *waslap* (wash cloth), Vaseline and assorted clothing. This is the same trunk in which letters from loved ones back home will be kept, and also *amakhathakhatha*, which are herbal potions used for various purposes, from neutralising evil spells to achieving professional success.

Statistics released in 2019 by StatsSA revealed that the South African mining industry employs just over 500 000 people, of whom 39 per cent work in the platinum sector and 21 per cent and 20 per cent work in the coal and the gold sectors respectively. Most of these mineworkers, if not all of them, live in mining compounds or so-called single men's hostels. Gauteng province alone has almost 100 hostels spread across the province, with the Johannesburg metro having more than 40 hostels, Ekurhuleni more than 30 hostels and the West Rand about 20 hostels.

Whether all these hostel residents work in the mines or not, they still need to keep their personal items safe. In most cases, hostels that are supposed to accommodate no more than 20 people in one open room actually accommodate two if not three times that number. Without a personal storage box, belongings are not secure. This is a key reason why Kwa Mai Mai has sustained its woodworking activities for decades. Not surprisingly, mineworkers' storage trunks are among Sithole's most lucrative products.

## *Packaging the deceased*

Whether it was because of the Covid-19 pandemic (which first swept through the world in 2020) or something else, the sight of woodworkers making coffins suddenly became very noticeable, even though this type of business is as old as time. The sound of the power drills, jigsaws and circular saws and the constant friction between the wood and the sander was no longer just a day in the life of a woodworker. It was a race against time. Johannesburg, with a population of just under 6 million people (up from less than 1 million people in 1950 when Kwa Mai Mai relocated from the old Wemmer and Jubilee compound), was now facing unprecedented Covid-19-related deaths. This meant that every coffin manufacturer had to be ready to supply the undertakers at short notice.

During the Covid-19 pandemic, no fewer than 5 000 funerals were being recorded in the city per month, and undertakers were running out of coffins. When the media reported that the City of Johannesburg was preparing 1.5 million graves for Covid-related burials, reality struck that bodies could not just be thrown into graves; the deceased still needed to be given decent burials. The race to produce as many coffins as were likely to be needed also meant that places like Kwa Mai Mai, which had been manufacturing coffins for decades, would soon be overwhelmed by the high demand.

News media reported that coffin manufacturing businesses were going strong, but that families were also opting for cheaper coffins as there were fewer people to impress at funerals owing to the restrictions on the number of mourners who could attend. At the same time, coffin manufacturers were scrambling to source chipboard to make less-expensive coffins, but this type of wood, which had to be approved by the South African Bureau of Standards, was becoming hard to come by. Woodworkers at Kwa Mai, like Sithole, faced the challenge of having to make as many coffins as possible in anticipation of walk-in customers or calls from undertakers suddenly needing coffins. They also had to deal with higher prices for chipboard from suppliers in the face of growing demand.

As if this were not enough, Sithole's woodworkers at Kwa Mai Mai, who were mostly migrants from the villages, shelved their plans to return home in December 2020. Elsewhere in the city, workers had to cut short their leave over the festive season and return to work to replenish stocks of coffins that had run short.

Sithole also mentions that, the pandemic aside, his business has always taken care of the marginal customer who cannot afford to use the services of funeral parlours, particularly those that transport the bodies of their deceased relatives (migrant labourers who pass away in the city) in private transport. Most of the bereaved are walk-in customers who, due to financial constraints, come to Kwa Mai Mai because of its relatively cheap coffins.

In normal circumstances, Sithole's woodworking business ships hundreds of coffins every year, even to Zimbabwe and Mozambique. His coffins have an average price of R700 for a low-end coffin and up to R2 800 for a high-end coffin, prices that cater to Kwa Mai Mai's regular clientele.

Sithole sits in his *bakkie*, with 'Sithole Furniture & Cupboards' printed on each side, and supervises his woodworkers as they coax each piece of wood into the desired shape, from which they then fashion a final product. He will remain at Kwa Mai Mai for as long as it is necessary and convenient to do so. However, he has never lost hope of one day owning a huge furniture factory as well as several furniture shops in the villages and towns where he used to live.

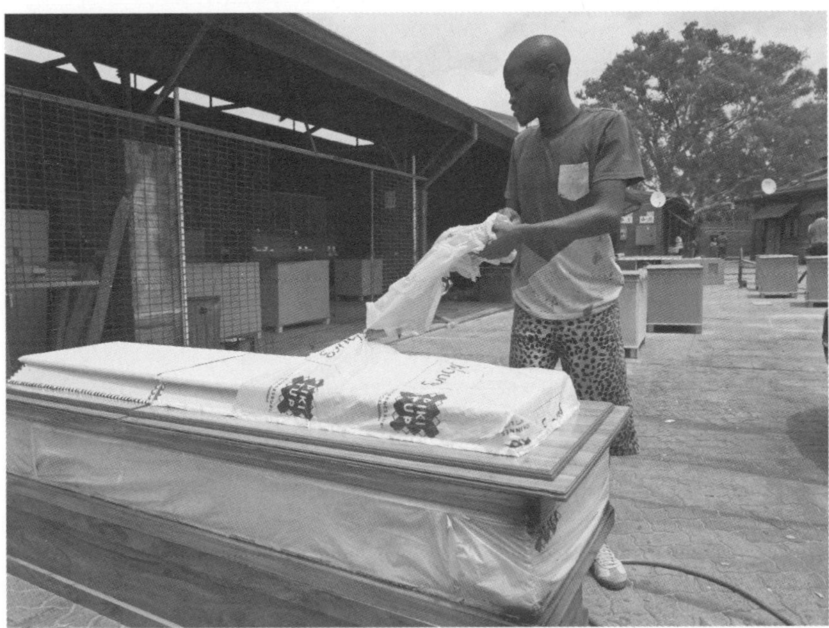

*Even the deceased are taken care of at Kwa Mai Mai (Photo: Siphiwe Mhlambi)*

## A scrap in the yard – Mshengu's panel beating business

At first glance, he would pass for a prison inmate in charge of the 26 Gang, a true *bhantinti*, a real *ngelekejane* with the gaze of *Nongoloza* himself, or a hustler who has become city-slick and knows his way around in the concrete jungle. Whether it is true or not, Mshengu, which is his clan name, confesses that he came to Kwa Mai Mai because of his hatred for the white man and thus his decision to be his own boss. Arriving in 1972 at a very young age, Mshengu initially did piece work until he found a job at Continental Panel Beaters, where he learned the trade. It was in 1978 that Mshengu suddenly experienced an overwhelming and deep hatred for the white man and decided to leave the company.

Mshengu explains: *'Ukuthi ngithathe isinqumo, kwafika nje enhliziywyeni umlungu ngavele ngamnyanya; ngamzonda. Ngathi mina ukuze singaxabani ngoba ubengikhonzile lo ebengimsebenzela kungcono ngivele ngiyekele.'* ('For me to take this decision, I had this overwhelming feeling of hatred for the white man. To avoid any further conflict, because my employer was good to me, I decided to quit.')

*Time for a facelift (Photo: Siphiwe Mhlambi)*

Because he despised the white man and felt a particular hatred towards his own boss – who, Mshengu claims, really liked him – Mshengu decided to leave to escape an untenable situation. Mshengu says he initially opened his panel beating business under the bridge at Kwa Mai Mai, starting with just two vehicles from his first two customers. This grew to three and more vehicles and the business kept on growing.

Mshengu's panel beating business focuses mainly on wrecked minibus taxis, which is not surprising considering that minibus taxis enjoy a sizeable share of the public transport market. Compared to buses and passenger rail services, minibus taxis transport more than 70 per cent of daily commuters, including those travelling long distances. Millions of daily commuters travelling to and from work, school and tertiary education institutions prefer this mode of transport, not because of its affordability but because of its extensive route network. With more than 200 000 minibus taxis (mainly Quantums) on the road daily, the taxi industry is one of the leading employers in the transport sector. It employs an estimated 300 000 drivers, supported by about 100 000 taxi marshals at over 150 000 taxi ranks.

Panel beating is one business at Kwa Mai Mai that is never short of customers. Minibus taxis arrive in droves, their damaged frames a testimony to how accident-prone they are – which is attributable to taxi drivers' often manic behaviour on the road. Notorious for their bad driving, taxi drivers have been vilified and often blamed for fatal accidents and road carnage. Said to have only one day off in a seven-day week and working up to 15 hours a day, with poor pay and no formal work benefits such as overtime or medical aid, taxi drivers often resort to clocking up as many trips as possible each day to make enough money to survive. Earning as little as R200 per week and expected to reach a daily target for the taxi owner, drivers rush to exceed the daily threshold so that they can keep the so-called 'leftover fares' for themselves. This is why taxi drivers do not observe speed limits, jump traffic lights and engage in dangerous overtaking, all of which are a recipe for accidents.

For Mshengu, minibus taxi accidents, which have caused much road carnage and ended in large numbers of fatalities, are the reason why his panel beating business is one of the most lucrative enterprises at Kwa Mai Mai. Not shy to share how well his business is doing, he eagerly shows off his workmanship and adeptness at fixing taxis that, with buckled chassis, ruined paintwork and missing body parts, appear to be almost beyond repair. Mshengu says that it can sometimes take up to a month to repair the taxis and make them look brand-new again. His yard has more than 10 vehicles in it at any one time, each having to be finished as quickly as possible because the taxi owners want them back on the road. To meet the demand, Mshengu has employed a team of mechanics with the requisite knowledge and skills in car mechanics, frame repair, bodywork, painting and spraying. Some of the damaged vehicles need to have their upholstery repaired, a service that is also available in the Kwa Mai Mai compound.

As an autobody mechanic himself, Mshengu says that when these minibus taxis are brought to his shop, the first step is to assess the extent of the damage to the vehicles' frame and bodywork. This is to determine the scope of the work that needs to be done so that he can provide the customer with an estimate of what parts may be required, when the repair work will be completed and how much it will cost. Straightening and aligning the frame, repairing scratches, dents and other damage to bodywork, replacing parts that cannot be repaired, and doing finishing and repainting are all precise, delicate operations that Mshengu and his team take pleasure in carrying out. Of course, his commitment to excellent workmanship is driven not only by a desire to give back to the customer a vehicle that looks almost brand-new, but also by the satisfaction of ensuring that the vehicle will be safe on the road again.

Mshengu stresses that panel beaters must really love their job and be capable of enormous attention to detail, especially since taxi owners' vehicles are their lifeline and so losing a vehicle on the road (particularly if they have only one) can be devastating. In his business, therefore, the ability to carry out thorough and accurate inspections of vehicles to determine the nature and extent of damage and to engage in all sorts of disassembly and reassembly activities, is not negotiable.

## Elizabeth Khumalo's automotive upholstery

Next door to Mshengu's panel beating shop is Elizabeth Khumalo's small upholstery workshop. At first glance, it does not give the impression that too much serious work is going on inside – until one sees how many of Mshengu's disfigured minibus taxis are handed over to Elizabeth for a complete fabric facelift.

Elizabeth established her vehicle upholstery business in 1994 and it is the only business in Kwa Mai Mai that faces no competition. It is also one of the few businesses that was not inherited from parents or grandparents. Elizabeth came to Kwa Mai Mai after being retrenched from an upholstery company where she had worked for seven years. Having lost all hope of finding employment, Elizabeth heard about Kwa Mai Mai, a place where aspiring, small black businesses were given space to ply their respective trades. Armed with experience of sewing car seats and couches, Elizabeth felt that this was the only business that she could do and hoped to be given a space. Today, occupying a small space measuring 2 m x 3 m, Elizabeth has built a viable business for herself, partly on the strengths of Mshengu's panel beating and autobody repair shop next door.

Elizabeth offers a specialist upholstery service for minibus taxi interiors (the roof, side panels, centre console, seats, floors and anything else requiring upholstery). Once their taxis have been repaired by Mshengu, some taxi owners take the opportunity to give the interiors of their taxis a complete makeover. This is where Elizabeth can come in and work her magic, refreshing or renewing the interiors with new fabrics and colours, and upgrading the trim. Taxi owners can either choose specific designs or allow Elizabeth to reimagine and redesign the interiors according to her own taste.

Although she has only one assistant, Elizabeth claims that no job is too big or too small for her workshop. Whether clients need carpeting, roof linings or leather seats, all the upholstery work is custom designed to meet the needs of the client. The workshop is, however, too small for the volume of work that she has, and Elizabeth hopes to get a bigger space one day. The fire that almost destroyed her workshop did not help the situation, as one of her two machines caught fire and had to undergo a number of repairs. Elizabeth is hoping that the government department responsible for small business development will one day provide financial support to her business. Funding will help her procure industrial-size upholstery sewing machines as well as various other tools to help her cope with the volume of work. For now, for as long as there is road carnage and Mshengu continues to receive damaged minibus taxis, the wheel of Elizabeth's upholstery sewing machine will continue to turn.

This chapter has examined just a few of the many cultural entrepreneurs and traders at Kwa Mai Mai who are forging ahead and making the place a thriving economic hub with a captive market who remain deeply connected to their culture and traditions.

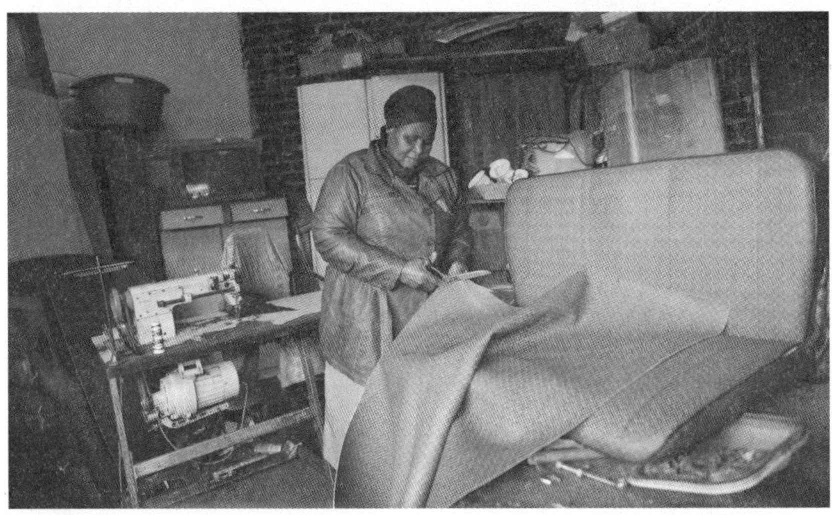

*Elizabeth Khumalo's automotive upholstery (Photo: Siphiwe Mhlambi)*

*Elizabeth Khumalo (Photo: Siphiwe Mhlambi)*

*Tholukhazi Sithole, horse-saddle maker (Photo: Siphiwe Mhlambi)*

*Nkiyase Chauke, who specialises in traditional wear of the Venda, Pedi, BaTsonga and Ndebele people (Photo: Siphiwe Mhlambi)*

*Mshengu, who runs one of only two auto repair and panel beating shops at Kwa Mai Mai (Photo: Siphiwe Mhlambi)*

*Landiwe MaNdlovu makes clothing and beadwear items for Shembe Church members (Photo: Siphiwe Mhlambi)*

*Themba Shongwe makes traditional sticks, shields and other cultural items carried by men at traditional ceremonies (Photo: Siphiwe Mhlambi)*

*Mama Zakwe produces traditonal ware for both men and women and is one of the oldest traders at Kwa Mai Mai (Photo: Siphiwe Mhlambi)*

*Mama Pikoli, one of the longest-surviving traders at Kwa Mai Mai, inherited the business from her father (Photo: Siphiwe Mhlambi)*

*Sandile Sithole is one of the manufacturers of the wooden kists and other furniture items that are synonymous with Kwa Mai Mai (Photo: Siphiwe Mhlambi)*

*Mhlongo's traditional Zulu footwear at Kwa Mai Mai (Photo: Siphiwe Mhlambi)*

*Nhlanhla Buthelezi is one of the youngest traders at Kwa Mai Mai and the owner of a hair salon, an internet cafe and a printing business (Photo: Siphiwe Mhlambi)*

*Committee chairperson Malibongwe Sithole (Photo: Siphiwe Mhlambi)*

# Correspondence related to trading applications in the 1980s

64

G.P.-S. (F-8)

REPUBLIEK VAN SUID-AFRIKA   REPUBLIC OF SOUTH AFRICA

Ref. No.   16/3/2 — 7.24
Enquiries:   MR. P.F. FOURIE
             832-2511 X 212

Mr. *N.T. Tshabalala*
*3044 Emdeni Extension*
*P.C. Kwa - Xuma*
*1868*

KANTOOR VAN DIE—OFFICE OF THE

Commissioner
Co-operation and Development
Johannesburg
Private Bag X1
FERREIRASDORP
2048

*15 . 11 .* 1984

Sir

APPLICATION FOR A GROUP AREAS PERMIT : *Thauda Bantu room 63*
*New Mai*

Applications in respect of Group Areas permits are being dealt with by the Department of Constitutional Development and Planning with effect from 1 November, 1984.

Your application has been referred to the Regional Director, Private Bag X644, Pretoria, 0001, telephone 26-9355 x 35 for consideration and a direct reply to you.

Yours faithfully

COMMISSIONER : JOHANNESBURG
/re

Die Streeksdirekteur
Privaatsak X644
PRETORIA
0001

Bogemelde onafgehandelde aansoek tesame met die volgende bylaes is vir u aandag aangeheg:-

(a)  *Aansoekvorm*        (e) *Ontwikkelingsraad se brief*
(b)  *Zary*
(c)  *S.A.P. verslag*
(d)  *Stadsklerk se brief*

KOMMISSARIS : JOHANNESBURG
/re

## City Secretariat

P.O. Box 1049
Johannesburg
2000

Civic Centre
Rissik Street
Braamfontein
2001

**City of Johannesburg**

Telephone (011) 777-1111
Ext.  2929

Our Ref.: MrDenton/DR
300/6/131

The Regional Representative
Department of Constitutional
    Development and Planning
Private Bag X718
PRETORIA
0001

2 8 -06- 1985

Dear Sir

APPLICATION FOR A GROUP AREAS PERMIT :
MR H. NGUBANE "NGUBANE HERBAL SHOP :
STAND 760 CITY AND SUBURBAN : NEW MAI
MAI BAZAAR

When this application was received from the
Department of Co-operation and Development,
Johannesburg, under their reference 16/3/2/716
it was pended due to the uncertain future of
the Mai Mai Bazaar.

As it has now been decided in principle that
the Mai Mai Bazaar will remain in existence,
there is no objection by the City Council to
the application.

Yours faithfully

TOWN CLERK

Die brief sal in Afrikaans aan u gestuur word indien u dit binne sewe dae na die briefdatum
hierbo skriftelik versoek

SS/CS

**City Secretariat**

P.O. Box 1049
Johannesburg
2000

Civic Centre
Rissik Street
Braamfontein
2001

...nesburg

Telephone (011) 777-1111

Ext. 2929

Our Ref.: Mr Denton/DR
300/6/131

The Regional Representative
Department of Constitutional
    Development and Planning
Private Bag X718
PRETORIA
0001

2 8 -06- 1983

Dear Sir

APPLICATION FOR A GROUP AREAS PERMIT :
MRS LUCY MABASA : LUCY HERBALIST : MAI MAI
BAZAAR : ROOM 113, ALBERT STREET, CITY AND
SUBURBAN

When this application was received from the
Department of Co-operation and Development,
Johannesburg under their reference 16/3/2/2-722
it was pended due to the uncertain future of
the Mai Mai Bazaar.

As it has now been decided in principle that
the Mai Mai Bazaar will remain in existence,
there is no objection to the application by
the City Council, on condition that a licence
in terms of Item 3 of the Licences Ordinance,
1974, as amended, is obtained from the Secretary,
Licensing Board, Johannesburg.

Yours faithfully

TOWN CLERK

Die brief sal in Afrikaans aan u gestuur word indien u dit binne sewe dae na die briefdatum

SS/CS

# Seven
## Converts and diviners at the crossroads

nside the Kwa Mai Mai precinct, under the bridge, there is an interesting interplay between the secular and the sacred, the shrine and the pulpit, which is symptomatic of the successes and failures of the 'civilising mission' to which African communities were subjected over many years. The convergence of the sacred and the secular makes the compound 'religiously and culturally plural' (Igwe 2014).

Today, Kwa Mai Mai does not discriminate between religious converts and atheists, or between the priest and the diviner. It is a place for healers and worshippers of all persuasions and must be understood within the context of how Africans interact and communicate with their ancestors and who they see as being closest to God as they seek His intervention.

The intersection between the two dimensions, the secular and the spiritual worlds, signals the failure of the civilising mission to introduce a single path to God, which has been conveniently packaged as Christianity, including its various sects. The civilising mission that was aimed at converting Africans to Christianity (away from ancestor worship which the Europeans regarded as barbaric), became the battleground for the heart and soul of the African. Christianity advocated the total abandonment of traditional customs, which were perceived to be primitive, and the acceptance of Jesus Christ as the Saviour. Any other practice or ritual that was deemed to fall outside the biblical discourse was seen as immoral and ungodly. Christianity dictated that a biblical text had to be cited to prove the authenticity of a particular belief or custom (Mndende 2014).

Africans believed that the ancestors were the closest beings to their living relatives, protecting them from evil and acting as a conduit to God (*uNkulunkulu*). While accepting the existence of God, the Creator of heaven and earth, African spirituality is founded on the fundamental principle that when a relative dies, their spirit plays the crucial role of mediator between the living and the Creator, *uMvelinqangi*. This stems from the belief that only the body (human flesh) is buried, but that the spirit (soul) remains among the living as their overseer and protector against all that is evil and could bring them harm.

Because the departed continue to live in the spirit as ancestors, they are worshipped by the living through rituals that are performed to honour the spiritual world and to seek guidance, prosperity and protection in the face of adversity. These rituals are underpinned by well-entrenched beliefs, behaviours and practices that are observed from the time someone is born until their death. Such rituals are performed on momentous occasions (birth, marriage, death), or to show appreciation to the ancestors for whatever the living give them credit for.

Such ancestral systems of belief or worship are either well-established traditions or are the result of active divination on the part of those seeking spiritual guidance in their quest to navigate the difficulties in life. The diviners, who have the prophetic power to interpret circumstances and events (past or present) and to predict the future, are able to translate what they see into specific interventions to be carried out by the living in order to appease the ancestors. Some diviners lack healing powers, referring those seeking divine intervention to traditional healers or herbalists.

The success of Christian missionaries and the civilising mission saw the emergence of Africanist churches towards the end of the 20th century (Kaschula 1997). These churches combined traditional African beliefs and practices with Christianity, by allowing ancestral worship to coexist with recognition and veneration of Jesus Christ as the Saviour and the Son of God. In the transition away from being either pagans or atheists, two African churches emerged: the Zionist Church and the Ethiopian Church, with the former blending African religion with Christianity.

Today, the prevalence of African traditional religion alongside conventional beliefs and customs confirms and affirms the duality of this cultural space. As a result, Africans have since found themselves caught between 'civilizing imperatives and the need to rely on indigenous norms' (McClendon 2010:21). This is evident at Kwa Mai Mai, where the secular and the sacred, the worshippers and the healers, share a common space. Because the demand for African labour and the migration to the cities overrode any discrimination between the converts and the adherents to traditional customs (*amaqaba* – meaning 'smeared ones' in reference to the ochre paste they smeared on their bodies), the city has become both a temple and a shrine.

The fact that there is no separation between the secular and the sacred appears to fly in the face of the popular view of Kwa Mai Mai as mainly a hub for traditional healers and herbal medicine. Instead, spiritual matters are handled by both the Church and diviners, and by both the herbalist and the headman. Here, traditional rulers, priests and diviners are all battling for the same souls.

This chapter examines how those who have made Kwa Mai Mai a cultural site first discovered and then came to understand their spirituality, in the context of God as the Creator and of the departed acting as intermediaries between the living and God.


## Shouting from the pulpit

Psalm 23:4 reads, 'Yea, though I walk through the valley of the shadow of death, I will fear no evil: for thou art with me; thy rod and thy staff they comfort me.' This offers a very clear biblical message: that religious converts constantly fear what life may have in store for them; yet find comfort in their belief in the Omnipotent One, who provides protection against all that is evil.

Considering the clarity of the message, one would think that human beings would converge under one religious roof to worship one God from whom they seek protection and good fortune while on earth. However, spirituality and proximity to God tend to be highly contested domains, with humans typically competing against one another, with multiple appeals to God, for the quickest route to heaven.

There are 19 churches that practise Christianity in South Africa, with over 80 per cent of the population claiming Christianity to be their religion. Among the four Christian denominations – Protestant, Pentecostal, Catholic and African-oriented churches – none claims dominance over another. The 2011 Census showed that 79.8 per cent of the 44.8 million people in South Africa, or 35.8 million people, considered themselves members of the Christian denomination. This is somewhat alarming if one considers the deliberate and well-orchestrated civilising mission that the Europeans embarked on when they first settled in this country.

It is worth mentioning that the civilising mission, which began with the arrival of the first settlers at the Cape in 1652, ground to a halt in 1744 because of a dispute between the first Protestant Christian missionary school and the Dutch Reformed Church as to whether baptised natives should be freed or remain slaves. The Dutch Reformed Church firmly resolved to keep the natives enslaved, while the Protestant Church preferred its converts to be freed after first being baptised. Unable to arrive at a solution, the European settlers eventually forced Georg Schmidt of the Moravian Brethren to leave South Africa in 1744. This brought the Christian missionary expansion to a complete halt, but it resumed again almost 50 years later (Harrison 2004; Muller 2004).

The floodgates of missionary activities opened again, and droves of missionaries arrived in South Africa from England, the Netherlands, Scotland, France and the United States. This led to the reconfiguration of African communities, as those who had converted could no longer mingle with the non–converts. The new converts settled in 'missionary-controlled communities', which Muller (2004) terms 'missionary villages'. The converts were now aligned to the missionary purpose and shared the common pursuits of evangelism and education. However, these newly converted Africans did not completely abandon their former habits; they took some of their cultural beliefs and customs along with them. Muller (2004:192) argues that the new converts were attracted to the missionaries and their work more for the hymns, where 'the singing voice poured forth its sweetness to the African ear', than for God's message.

The various Christian denominations in South Africa are also symptomatic of the racial and political character of this country. Moreover, among Africans, Christianity and religion are indicative of the extent to which certain cultural beliefs and customs have influenced religious views and practices as well as the word of God.

As a space that nurtures cultural memory and collective identity, Kwa Mai Mai offers the perfect environment in which various religious sects can find expression. There are two distinct churches at Kwa Mai Mai, all competing and even fighting for the souls of Africans who have found Christianity, in whatever shape or form: the Zulu Zionists, iBandla lamaNazaretha (the Shembe Church) and the Twelve Apostles. The presence of the Shembe Church and the Zulu Zionist Christian Church is true to the character of Kwa Mai Mai as a place of traditional healing and worship. Both these churches have blended cultural tradition and ancestor worship with Christian beliefs and practices.

## iBandla lamaNazaretha (Shembe) – Church of the Nazarites

On Saturdays, Kwa Mai Mai is abuzz with those who trade and live in the compound and those from neighbouring men's hostels, such as Denver, Wemmer and George Koch, including day visitors who come to buy cultural goods, to seek healing from herbalists and diviners, or to attend church.

Every Saturday in the compound, below the bridge and under the tree, there is a gathering of the followers of iBandla lamaNazaretha, or the Nazareth Baptist Church, one of the most traditional indigenous Christian churches in South Africa. Founded by Prophet Isaiah Shembe in 1911, it is said to be the second-biggest African-initiated church after the Zionist Christian Church, which has five million members. Notably, iBandla lamaNazaretha, popularly known as KwaShembe (Dube 1936), blends traditional and Christian religious practices.

Masondo (2004:69–79) argues that the church was founded 'with the quest to restore the Zulu to their glorious past'. Following a series of harrowing events and developments, such as the destruction of the Zulu Kingdom, land dispossession and the crushing of the Bambata Rebellion in 1906, the establishment of the Shembe Church 'provided a base for remobilizing a Zulu ethnic identity' (Chidester 1992:131), which Vilakazi et al. (1986:156) calls a 'Zulu High Church'.

Shembe sought an alternative to the way in which Zulus traditionally viewed and practised religion, based on their close affinity with the land and the use of sacred sites as points of worship and healing. The 50 acres of land that he acquired at Ekuphakameni would become a focal point and central location for his followers. The Sabbath was observed on Saturday. Shembe and his followers would gather at Ekuphakameni (in July) and at Inhlangakazi (in January) for two weeks of prayer each year. Shembe experienced revelations at an early age, including a vision in lightning (Oosthuizen 1968). During a visit to Nhlangakazi Mountain, the Holy Spirit allegedly told him to establish his own church. Later, the mountain would become the site of an annual pilgrimage (Gunner 2004.)

Kumalo and Mujinga (2017) list several factors that could have influenced Isaiah Shembe to establish the Shembe Church. Apart from visions from God, various central figures had an impact on him. For example, his brother-in-law, a preacher, is reported to have marched to Ntabazwe Mountain to pray for rain during a period of severe drought, after which heavy rains fell. Shembe was very concerned about the impact of urbanisation and colonisation on Zulu society, and how the missionaries had undermined the Zulu monarch. He felt that the fabric of Zulu society was being destroyed through forced acculturation (Shange 2013). This, together with the view that Europeans did not understand African religion and culture (Hexham 2011) spurred the creation of African-initiated churches and cleared space for African indigenous religious practices.

Defiant and determined, the Shembe Church emerged after the Natal colonial government had almost succeeded in destroying the Zulu Kingdom, two years before the death of King Dinuzulu, the son of King Cetshwayo, the last warrior king of the Zulus. Not even the notorious Natives Land Act of 1913, which allowed only 13 per cent of land to be allocated to Africans, was able to stop Shembe from securing a piece of land (Ekuphakameni) for his followers. Regarded as the 'black messiah', Shembe managed to blend the secular and the sacred in the religious practices of his church. This strategy attracted large numbers of followers who still wanted to cling to their Zulu culture and tradition, which had been shaken to the core from years of colonial conflict.

The Church has remained the home of Zulu worshippers who have fused culture and tradition with Christianity, while also displaying a penchant for Zulu nationalism. Shembe also made sure that the narrative of the Church and its interactions with God were guided by the Shembe Hymns (*Izihlabelelo zama Nazaretha*), which he wrote after 1910 and which his son, Galilee Shembe, added to in 1940. According to Muller and Mthethwa (2010), the hymns drew from the poetic African tradition of praise songs (*Izibongo*), which Gunner (1982, 1986) reports were reinterpreted in Christian worship. Shembe was an accomplished composer who, by the time of his death, had written over 200 hymns, which included elements of biblical psalms and African–American spirituals.

In his writings, Shembe reflected on the experiences of black people, their suffering and their hope. The iBandla lamaNazaretha faith was their bible, an official canon, also known as the Acts of the Nazarites that the Church commonly refers to as the Third Testament – at least as understood by Africans in their relationship with God (Cabrita 2012). This sense of cultural belonging and the fostering of Zulu identity, particularly 'traditional Zulu indigenous beliefs, values, ethnicity, religion and culture' (Kumalo and Mujinga 2017:145), are what make the Church attractive to its followers.

A church that has successfully incorporated worship, purification rituals and consultations with the prophet, iBandla lamaNazaretha defies religious norms and refuses to be confined to a bricks-and-mortar building as a place of worship. This is a church that has no physical buildings, walls or entrance to receive congregants. Each congregation worships inside a circle of white stones in an open-air location that its members refer to as 'the temple'.

*Prophet Isaiah Shembe, circa 1865–2 May 1935, the founder of iBandla lamaNazaretha, South Africa (Source: Shembe Church hymnal)*

Saturday, referred to as *iSabatha* (the Sabbath), is sacrosanct to the Shembe Church worshippers. It is the day on which *amaNazaretha* worship in their outdoor temple from the morning until the afternoon. The religion practised by the Shembe Church cannot be boxed into a specific category. It cannot be aligned to Ethiopianism just because of its Afrocentric interpretation of the bible or its music and performances; nor can it be associated with the Zionist Christian Church, which is known for its healing powers and ability to interpret prophetic dreams and visions. Muller (2004) posits that iBandla lamaNazaretha has a more eclectic character, because of the way in which it has adopted most of the African traditions and beliefs while discarding some of the remnants of the Christian civilising mission.

As Harrison (2004:11) argues, 'Instead of building shrines or temples, African belief has invested nature with powers. For example, a great tree, or a striking rock outcrop or a mountain might be considered sacred.' For Shembe followers, Saturday is the day of worship, a day of complete abstinence from everything that the heart desires. Not even drunkards, thugs or vagrants can be found loafing around the sacred ground on which the Shembe worshippers walk. The site has to be free from any evil stampede. The duality of this religion is anchored by what Du Bois (1903) sees as the worship of the Western concept of Christianity but interpreted partly within the context of African religious beliefs – what he calls the 'double consciousness' of Africans in relation to God and Christianity.

It is not the intention of this chapter to fully explain and interrogate the congregation of the Shembe Church: rather, it wishes to locate it within a context in which culture finds its expression and reconnects migrant communities to their roots in more ways than can be imagined.

In the Shembe Church, sermons from the Protestant Church are combined with African rituals expressed in dance and celebration. The Shembe Church thus fits perfectly into the Kwa Mai Mai environment, which is all about song, dance, ritual, ancestral worship and celebration. A strong tenet of the Shembe Church is celebration and dance. The sacred dance, accompanied by music, is what connects the ancestral world with the living. The supernatural and the living are then joined at the hip, so to speak. It was Isaiah Shembe who introduced the music, singing and dancing – things that Africans were already familiar with, as they formed part of daily ritual and provided a connection with the ancestors. Fusing ritualistic displays with religion, including keeping African traditions such as polygamy and ancestral worship alive, set this religion apart from the type of Christianity that the Europeans envisaged for the Africans.

The Shembe Church offers a unique proposition, which appeals to many. This is explained in the testimony of one of the leaders of the Shembe Church in Kwa Mai Mai, described below.

### *A testimony by Mshumayeli uNdlovu of eMoyeni Temple*

The eMoyeni Temple, the name given to the Kwa Mai Mai congregation of the Shembe Church, is led by Mphatheni Ndlovu, who is a preacher, a trader and an iron smith who makes *iklwa* (spears). It seems to be a contradiction that a man of God should be manufacturing traditional weapons that could be used in clashes between clans or in faction fights between chieftaincies. As he is also an iron smith, the preacher is a go-to person for those looking for *iklwa*, a shorter version of the *assegai*, which was invented by King Shaka as a mid-range weapon. This is the type of spear that was used by the king's warriors in the many wars that they waged to conquer other tribes.

It is difficult to imagine that such a weapon, which was responsible for the demise of so many of Shaka's enemies, could be in the hands of a man of God. What the people who come to buy an *iklwa* from Ndlovu in his shop at Kwa Mai Mai intend to use it for, is not known. For now, the focus will be not on Mphatheni Ndlovu, the spear maker, but rather on uMshumayeli Mphatheni Ndlovu, the preacher of Shembe's gospel.

***

Shembe's followers had gathered under the bridge, as they did every Saturday. We caught up with uMshumayeli Ndlovu during the recess after the morning's sermon, which stretched from 9 am to 11 am. We took the opportunity to interview him before the start of the second sermon (after lunch).

uMshumayeli Ndlovu took his place in front of the cameras. Initially a chair had been arranged for him but, realising that he could be breaking some of the Shembe rules, he asked to kneel down. It transpired that only the leader of the Shembe Church, uNyazi lwe Zulu – loosely translated as the 'Lightning of the Heavens' – can sit on a chair. To show respect towards the head of the church, even in absentia, Mshumayeli Ndlovu put down a towel and then knelt, with his back straight, in preparation for the interview. There was clear order, discipline and humility in the way he conducted himself. With an inexplicable aura around him, Ndlovu folded his hands in front of him as a sign of submission – not to us, the interviewers, but to uNyazi, the leader of the Church, to whom he must show respect at all times, whether present or not.

Ndlovu explained that the church at Kwa Mai Mai had arisen out of a need to shorten the distance that worshippers had to travel to the nearest Shembe Church. Initially, Shembe followers travelled to Soweto every Saturday, but this practice stopped when the leader of the Church authorised the building of a temple at Kwa Mai Mai, which would be called eMoyeni. Mrs Mbatha, a trader who manufactured wedding kists in the Kwa Mai Mai compound, used to be spotted praying alone in her room. Later she was joined by five more people and the church continued to grow. Today, more than 100 worshippers gather beneath the trees under the bridge that crosses over the Kwa Mai Mai compound. The site of worship, the temple, is clearly visible from its signature circles of white stones.

*Shembe women worshippers (Photo: Siphiwe Mhlambi)*

Inside the temple – in other words, inside the circles – there is a particular seating arrangement, with specific areas reserved for designated groups. Married women or those engaged to be married sit in one spot, while young girls (virgins or 'princesses') sit in another spot. Married men and young men, in turn, have their own spots some distance from the women and young girls. Furthermore, no one is allowed to enter the circle wearing footwear of any kind, not even sandals. In the absence of a door, a specific area has been designated as the entrance to the temple, with sections of grass planted on either side. Every worshipper is required to enter the sacred temple through the imaginary door and then take their allocated seat according to their age and status in the church.

Men wear their distinctive leopard-print headband and *ibheshu* (a cowhide that covers a man's buttocks), as well as *isinene* (twisted strips of civet skin that cover his genitals). A white robe is worn over *ibheshu* and *isinene* during worship. Only during Shembe dances and celebrations would men wear their traditional garb without the white robe. Similarly, women are identifiable by their *isicholo* (head gear). Betrothed and married women wear a traditional pleated skirt or kilt made of cowhide or goatskin, wraparound cloths and other, colourful, accessories.

To uMshumayeli Ndlovu and other followers, Isaiah Shembe is God and can therefore solve all problems. His followers believe that once they plead their case with uShembe, through their current leader, uNyazi lwe Zulu, nothing is impossible. Isaiah Shembe is the *isiqalo* (the beginning) and *isigcino* (the end). To most of Shembe's followers, he is *uMvelinqangi* (God) (Magwaza 2011) or *ubabamkhulu* (the grandfather) (Oosthuizen 1968) or even the Lord of amaNazaretha.

When asked how the Shembe Church differs from other religious denominations, Ndlovu replied that the founder of the Church emphasised that his followers should not abandon their tradition but to come as they are, as long as they believe in God. Unlike conventional Christianity, which demands that converts dispense with their former culture and tradition, the Shembe Church accommodates followers' traditional beliefs and practices. A Shembe follower, therefore, exists both in the ancestral realm and in a religious environment. The worshippers can pray to God and later visit a traditional healer, herbalist or *isangoma* to seek ancestral interventions. A Shembe worshipper, therefore, has 'double cover'. If God takes time to respond (as He always does), worshippers quickly summon the ancestors by slaughtering a goat or by burning *imphepho* (incense). They then address the ancestors using various totems and epithets, to honour their deeds while they still walked on earth. The ancestors are called by name, from many generations ago to the most recently departed.

In contrast to Christianity, where only three names are called – the Father, the Son and the Holy Spirit – a Shembe follower can call any or all of the departed leaders of the Church. To encourage an immediate ancestral intervention and positive response, a Shembe follower may launch into poetic verse in which they heap praise on the succession of leaders in the Shembe Church. For example, in the passage below, iNkosi Shembe and those who came after him are praised and acknowledged for their achievements and the impact they had on the living.

*Shembe wama Nazaretha*
*Shembe ka Mzazela*
*Ka Sokhabuzela*
*Ka Nhliziyo*
*Ndlamhlathi ka Mayekiso*
*Sibiza wena langa phuma sikothe*
*Nabalothayo liyabahangula*
*Sibiza wena Nyanga yeZulu*
*Sithi qhibu khobe*
*Thingo lenkosazana*
*Igwalagwala elimajubane amabili*
*Elinye elokuya, elinye elokubuya*
*Gembu mbana phansi*
*Kwelase Mzumbe*
*Utikoloshe owavuma wathi*
*Ukube ngangiwumuntu*
*Ngabe ngiyayikhetha*
*iNkosi yase Kuphakameni*

The English translation is:

Shembe of the Nazarites
Shembe the Son of Mzazela
Son of Sokhabuzela
of Nhliziyo
Ndlamhlathi of Mayekiso
We call upon you Sun in which we bask
Those who bask in it suffer sunburn
We call upon you healer of Heaven
We say bulge like a mushroom
Rainbow of the Princess
The turaco bird with two speeds
One for flying away and one for flying back
We say roar all the way down in Mzumbe
A Tikoloshe that wished if it was a person
It would choose you, Lord of Ekuphakameni


## Tithing at the altar (*umnikelo*) – the offering

In Kwa Mai Mai, no activity takes place that does not generate revenue, and generating revenue creates obligations. In the Shembe temple, worshippers are required to observe 2 Corinthians 9:7, which states: 'Each of you should give what you have decided in your heart to give, not reluctantly or under compulsion, for God loves a cheerful giver.' Giving back to the Church, which often takes the form of tithing, means that followers are obedient to God and give freely, without expecting anything specific in return.

Towards the end of a service, worshippers (men on one side and women on the other) are invited to offer whatever they can afford. They join a single line, kneel in front of *umshumayeli* (the preacher) and request the latter to plead their case (whatever their wishes are) to Prophet Shembe, while placing money in the collection bowl positioned on a grass mat. No one else hears what issues are troubling the worshippers, as the conversation between the preacher and the followers are closely guarded secrets (and would even defy eavesdropping attempts).

When everyone has given their tithe, the preacher announces how much money has been collected and what it will be used for, while also expressing the hope that everyone's wishes will come true. Ultimately, the collected offerings will be channelled to the leader of the Shembe Church. Shembe temples throughout South Africa compete with one another (though this is not discussed openly) to supply weekly collections of the highest possible value. Now and again, one hears of trips being arranged to the Shembe Church's headquarters outside Durban to deliver the collected money to the leader.

## Ibandla laseZayoni (Church of Zion)

The word of God and the practice of Christianity have been fiercely contested terrain when it comes to evangelism in South Africa. Africans have always known God as the Creator of heaven and earth. Therefore, the existence of God was not a foreign concept to Africans when missionaries arrived on the continent. However, the ways in which Africans communicated and engaged with God were not congruent with Christian teachings. Changing Africans' spiritual beliefs and habits was the battle that missionaries were keen to engage in and win at all costs.

In the early 1900s, the Zionist missionaries arrived in the country to establish congregations. Among their distinctive characteristics, apart from wearing white robes, were performing divine healing and barring people from eating pork. Pewa (1997) observes that some converts were inspired by the Christian teachings delivered by the missionaries and appeared prepared to completely abandon their traditional African beliefs in favour of this new Christian faith. However, there were other converts who accepted the fundamental principles of the Christian faith but preferred to retain and practise their traditional beliefs and customs. The Zionist Church falls into the latter category. It is one of the many African indigenous Christian churches that have found an affinity with the more traditional African communities. Known as Isonto lamaZayoni (the Church of Zion), the Church has its roots in the Christian Apostolic Church founded in Chicago in 1896. With the formation of that church and the start of a campaign to spread the Christian gospel to the rest of the world, South Africa was a target.

The duality of Afro-Christian religious practices and the ability to remain African, in the true sense of the word, was a bone of contention among Christian missionaries. It was also a trying time for the Zulus, particularly during the attack on the Zulu Kingdom and the creation of a new class in society which necessitated a difficult choice being made between becoming converts (*amakholwa*) or remaining heathens (*amaqaba* or *umhedeni*), the name given to those who did not convert. Those who fully embraced Christianity and were assimilated into mission reserves were expected to abandon their traditional practices, including notable Zulu practices such as polygamy and the payment of *ilobolo* (the dowry).

To illustrate how converting to Christianity meant losing part of one's 'Zuluness', a magistrate in Weenen pointed out in 1897 that 'when a Native becomes an *ikolwa* he or she actually loses caste in the eyes of their (*sic*) heathen fellow-creatures' (Lambert 1995:50). Converting to Christianity involved breaking with some cherished beliefs and practices, such as the head of the family (*umnumzane*) being entitled to a huge homestead with many wives. Becoming a Christian and practising Christianity meant that wives in polygamous arrangements had to divorce their husbands when they converted. In the same way, men were expected to have just one wife. Breaking with their sacred traditional values in order to become members of a new, Eurocentric society proved difficult for some people to stomach. In the annual survey of missions conducted by the American Board of Commissioners for Foreign Missions, a Mr Grout reported on his encounter with a 'company of men, young and old, where one of them addressed him saying, "Teacher, white man! We black people do not like the news you bring us. We are black, and we like to live in darkness and sin. You induce our children to abandon our practices; you break up our kraals and eat up our cattle; you will be the ruin of our tribe"' (*The Missionary Herald* 1853:38).

After the split in the Zionist movement, which saw some missionaries migrating to other countries in Africa, the Church had to adapt and accept some of the traditional beliefs and practices observed by its newer members. In wooing would-be converts and leaders, the Church had to accept that African tradition and ancestral worship were central to their social system and were never going to be discarded outright. As a result, the Zionist groups began to mix traditional African beliefs with Christian principles and practices. Central to this were the veneration of the departed, *ukubholofida* (prophecy), *ukuboniswa* (revelations) and *izithunywa* (spirits), which is the ability to divine through the voices that descend upon those possessed of such powers.

This is a church that prides itself on (i) having been established on the basis of a mandate received by a prophet in a dream, vision or death–resurrection experience; (ii) practising healing through confessions, repeated baptisms, purification rites and exorcisms; (iii) its followers' receiving of revelations and power from the Holy Spirit through prophetic utterances and Pentecostal phenomena; (iv) engaging in ritualistic and Africanised worship at innovative festivals characterised by the wearing of special garments, singing, dancing, clapping and drumming; (v) enforcing bans against certain foods (such as pork), alcohol and tobacco (although it tolerates polygamy); and (vi) resorting to traditional practices such as divination and ancestral worship, to find meaning in certain events.

## *A colourful Sunday*

Every Sunday in African communities, in rural, urban or semi-urban settings, worshippers from different denominations are seen heading towards their places of worship – on foot, on the back of *bakkies* and in kombis. It is the day of worship but it is also the day on which churchgoers are seen, and their distinctive uniforms and sacred fashion styles are on display. Donning their vibrant white, green, blue or multi-coloured robes, they criss-cross their neighbourhoods as they make their way to their respective churches. Their distinctive robes are adorned with other pieces of cloth, which function as a belt or a cross belt and are associated with the Zionist Church. Another common accessory is the medieval-type double cross belt across the chest, where a rope functions as a belt, its ends hanging freely and stylishly at the side of the body. The design was inspired by the crossed skin cords that a traditional diviner wears across their chest.

Those whose robes testify to some form of divination stand out from the other members of the congregation, as their designs were communicated in a prophecy. Anyone familiar with the African Zionist Church will have come across a worshipper who, having been diagnosed with some sort of illness or received a bad omen, is instructed to make a very specific garment – sometimes with crosses on different parts of the robe. They are instructed to bring the robe to the church, where it will be blessed, sprinkled with purified and divine water, and placed in a candle-lit corner representing the shrine (*umsamo*). This is believed to be a virtual manifestation of heaven, where God and the ancestors converge.

Each colour in people's robes, whether mixed or pure, has a particular meaning in the African Zionist Church. The colour black is never seen among these churchgoers, because it is considered bad luck and an *isinyama* (a bad omen); so is the colour red, which is associated with various taboos. In most Zionist churches, white dominates as it is considered to be pure. Green reflects the power of the spirit and blue symbolises faithfulness (Oosthuizen 1979).

Completing the outfit is the accompanying *isikhali* (a stick), which comes in all shapes and sizes, depending on congregants' tastes. With reference to these sticks, Tsedu (2017) writes: 'Some walk with sticks with intricate circles, while others, mostly men, carry sticks, some with woollen ropes either tied to the sticks or wound around their bodies.' He adds: 'It is not unusual to find a gardener in suburbia transformed on Sunday into a raging preacher and leader, teaching his few flock under a tree and praying for the sick.'

Worshippers' songs are interwoven with beautiful harmonies, with tenors, sopranos, altos and baritones contributing to the melody in their own special ways while following the lead of the principal vocalist (the preacher). Unlike the hymns of the Shembe Church, the songs of the Zionist Church have been passed down from generation to generation. They are sung from memory, without a hymn book, because they have never been written down. As a result, they have undergone some changes over the years. In typical griot style, the master congregant, the preacher, leads the singing, with occasional pauses as if to check that the worshippers are listening and properly engaged.

## *A song, a sacred drum and a dance*

Dancing and singing are key elements of worship and praise in the Zionist Church, unleashing spiritual powers and transforming congregants into floating spirits who enter spaces reserved only for those with godly powers. The Zionist Church's syncretic religion, a fusion of Christianity and traditional African beliefs (Oosthuizen et al. 1989; Pewa 1997) is rooted in African religion and anchored by music, dance and rituals. Pewa (1997:2) asserts, 'In trying to search for African identity and culture, the Zionists as well as other African Christian churches have begun to explore the resources of indigenous music and dance.'

The drum, a sacred instrument in African communities, could not be abandoned with the conversion of Africans to Christianity. It was one instrument that missionaries had to come to terms with and accept as a necessary pre-condition of Africans agreeing to convert. Even though drumming, according to Hastings (1976), was prohibited by the missionaries who associated it with ancestral worship, it tied together the song, dance and worship that formed important pillars in African indigenous churches. The drummer, who has no formal training in counting or time signature, creates a rhythm to suit the congregants. They start to dance in a trance-like state, occasionally clapping and hitting their sticks on the ground as if to wake the ancestors.

Each song has a different drum pattern and rhythm, which reflects the message behind it. The drummer cannot simply decide to adopt a particular approach according to how they feel that day, or without taking the mood of the worshippers into consideration. Each drum pattern and accompanying rhythm has been passed down from one generation to the next. It is therefore not unusual to see a master drummer angrily snatching the drum from a young drummer if the latter is failing to capture the right mood through the music, in keeping with the occasion.

Feelings of suffering and despair are temporarily suspended during the drumming, the singing, the dancing and the clapping, which build up to the right mood for *inkonzo* (the sermon). It is at this point that the sacred voices reach their zenith, united in harmony and melodically invoking the spirit of the departed while inviting God to be present.

The choreographed dancing and occasional spinning by those imbued with the spirit are signs that the participants in this sacred performance are now connected to the Omnipotent One, oblivious of their earthly surroundings. If, by now, the preacher has not started speaking in tongues, you are in the wrong church.

## Prayer and hope

Because the preacher or evangelist is believed to possess supernatural powers, including an ability to commune with *umoya* (spirits), to interpret dreams and to determine the cause of a troubled soul, the preacher's recommended intervention must be accepted. The preacher is also believed to be able to connect the congregation with God. As a result, the congregants 'believe that the church is able to give them spiritual power and confidence to face the ups and downs of daily life' (Pewa 1997:82).

It is common for people to come to the church for divination when they are troubled or have some sort of burden, such as intolerable pain or inexplicable dreams. Dreams are believed to be 'modes of communication' (Makhathini 2020) through which the living and the departed are able to connect. Those who have had the privilege of attending this type of church will have witnessed diviners praying for people with troubled souls or physical problems, such as inexplicable, excruciating pain in a certain part of their body. All is revealed through divination, when the person with the power to do so speaks in tongues.

Kiernan (1978) explains that the processes of divination and healing never involve the use of *umuthi* (traditional herbs); instead, the healing powers of blessed water are invoked. According to Kiernan (1978), this water is prescribed as medication to repel evil spirits or cure pain. Blessed water is sometimes sprinkled around the house to provide protection against sorcerers. It can even be imbibed or used to cleanse oneself of suspected bad omens. Called *isiwasho*, which literally means something that is used to make something clean, the water must be ingested in large gulps and then spat out, symbolising the cleaning out of the dirt from inside.

Part of the healing process for the person who is troubled or in pain involves spinning them around, shaking them and hitting them repeatedly on their shoulders and back, in what resembles a violent, physical attack. During this time, the person appears to be consumed by the spirit (*umoya*), oblivious of the pain being inflicted on their body through the physical assault.

At the end of it all, the preacher leads the group in prayer. While not specifically choreographed, the call to prayer follows a certain format, with members of the congregation all praying simultaneously. They do not start reciting 'Our father who art in heaven', or anything like that. Each congregant launches into an individual and very passionate and spirited prayer. There are no rules, there is no leader, there is no time limit, and there is no volume control on congregants' voices. Congregants can pray about anything and everything, such as praying for someone they care about or praying for their own good fortune or prosperity.

The prayer session reaches a climax when everyone has been transported spiritually, with some squeaking and others shouting at the top of their voices in a deafening cacophony, as if God only hears those who shout the loudest. At this point, some people are crying and their voices are trembling as if they are engulfed by pain or emotion. Others are breathless, as if they have just completed a 400 m relay race. When the frenetic mood subsides, one of the congregants suddenly breaks into a song, which prompts the others to follow. Some of the more spirited worshippers continue praying for a while, but eventually there is silence.

The congregants feel assured that their prayers have been received by God and are comforted by the words of Psalm 17:6: 'I have called upon You, for You will answer me, O God; Incline Your ear to me, hear my speech.' Now the worshippers will wait for God to respond, but no one knows when this will happen. As Jeremiah 33:3 reminds us: 'Call to Me and I will answer you, and I will tell you great and mighty things, which you do not know.'

## The divination

At the end of the prayer session, the preacher focuses on the person whom each congregant has prayed for. The preacher assures the congregants that their problems or challenges are now in God's hands.

Whatever may have been revealed to the preacher is now shared with the one whose soul is troubled. Most of the time, the prophecy is linked in some way to the ancestors who are clearly upset about the living not having met an obligation that the departed wanted met. The feelings of adoration and fear that people have for the dead are driven by the belief that ancestors require the living to perform certain rituals if they are to be protected from life's iniquities.

As the ancestors are believed to have the ability to positively or negatively influence people's lives, the prophet is able to determine what needs to be done to appease the ancestors. The ancestors are also believed to demand appreciation. Every now and again, they expect *ukuhlatshelwa* (a slaughtered animal as an offering). This is an example of the sacred converging with the secular.

The blending of Christianity and African indigenous beliefs is what has attracted many Africans to the Zionist Apostolic churches and to the church at Kwa Mai Mai, led by one Mavuso. The church at Kwa Mai Mai has both a Christian and an indigenous character, including the belief in possession by *umoya* (spirits) and the power of divination. A key tenet of this church is the conviction that the ancestors can mediate on behalf of the living because, once people have passed, their close proximity to God allows them to appeal to Him to hear the prayers of the living. Ancestors are believed to have a very clear understanding of the plight of the living, as they once walked among their relatives on earth and are well versed in the family's circumstances.

This church at Kwa Mai Mai is the product of what Dube (cited in Masikane 2017:24) calls a rebellion against 'the white man's missionary churches, particularly because they rejected and demonised African traditional religion, which had well-entrenched communication modalities, such as referring to God as *uNkhulunkhulu, uMveliqangi* or *"uHlanga"*, among other principles'. Furthermore, Masikane (2017) sees the Zionist Church as distinctive in that, unlike conventional Christian churches of various denominations, it has continued to refuse to change and be modernised based on a culture it does not embrace. The refusal to discard traditional customs while accepting Christianity as a parallel passage to God is what attracts most of this religion's followers. This serves Mavuso, a traditional healer and herbalist, very well.

## The intriguing figure of Mavuso, the resident priest at iBandla laseZayoni

As with most black Zionist churches, the congregation at Kwa Mai Mai displays all the traits of the Zionist tradition. It is inside the Kwa Mai Mai compound that the Zionist Church, an alternative to the traditional Christian mission in Africa, has found a place. It is a church that highlights sections of the Gospel that are believed to be part of the biblical message but do not feature overtly in the teachings of mainstream churches. As Kwa Mai Mai is a cultural hub, its church has a foundation of African tradition and heritage that is sprinkled with ancestral veneration.

The church at Kwa Mai Mai is led by an *mfundisi* (priest) by the name of Mavuso. Mavuso has an interesting character and demeanour. At first glance, he looks as if he is completely 'out of it', resembling a vagrant who is out of place in a community of productive traders. Mavuso is not what one would expect from a priest of the Zionist Church – in fact, he is the exact opposite. *Inyanga* (traditional healer) would be a more fitting description for him, or *umngqayi* or *umantshingelani* (as one would describe a night guard) because of the signature heavy coat he wears, come rain or shine. A man with a short temper, Mavuso does not hesitate to tell anyone who cares to listen that he carries a gun, which he can draw at any time if circumstances dictate.

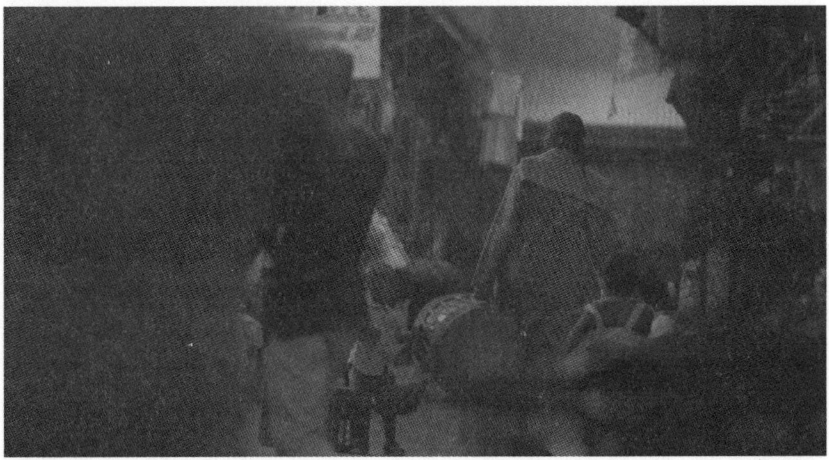

*Mavuso's son carrying the church drum (Source: Kwa Mai Mai documentary produced by the author)*

Mavuso reportedly once worked in a steel factory somewhere in Johannesburg but retired from that job. He came to Kwa Mai Mai in the late 1980s and ran a thriving church until the late 1990s, when the members of his congregation started leaving one by one. Like many adult men living at Kwa Mai Mai, Mavuso is also a traditional healer, and acts in this capacity in between being the leader of his church inside the compound.

Mavuso certainly has a strong presence in the compound, and it is impossible to miss him. Other than a couple of regulars, including a parking attendant, visitors to the trade zone have to walk past Mavuso as they enter the gate from Albert Street. Wearing his usual 'uniform' – his trademark coat, a jersey and two or three under shirts – Mavuso has become a permanent feature inside the Kwa Mai Mai precinct. He is always seen leaning against the wall, from morning until sunset, with no apparent purpose or agenda, ready to engage in a trivial conversation with anyone who happens to be around and is willing to listen to him.

Rumour has it that Mavuso came from Mpumalanga province, except that nobody remembers when he last returned home. He once had a wife (now deceased) who managed to hold the church together until her demise. Regardless of what Mavuso claims to be at Kwa Mai Mai, he is very different from the other residents, who are traders, herbalists, carpenters, healers and diviners. Except for having ordained himself a priest in the Zionist Church, with a questionable number of followers, Mavuso has no business being at Kwa Mai Mai. Legend has it that his church once had a sizeable following in the late 1990s. Today it is as a good as non-existent.

Although I had scheduled a visit to his church, it did not take place because, for three Sundays in a row, nobody came to worship. However, Mavuso persists in preparing a sermon every Sunday. He puts on his church regalia – white pants, shirt and white overcoat, with colourful *isembatho* (a piece of clothing thrown over the shoulder) – and strolls confidently down the long walkway leading to the hall at the end of the compound.

As he walks past the traders' stalls, he seems unconcerned about whether or not anyone will emerge and accompany him to the church. Mavuso has to pass Ngxongo's herbal medicine consulting room, which normally has over 100 people queuing to buy his *amakhathakhatha* (herbal concoctions). These are people whom Mavuso would love to have as his congregants. However, they are not into praise and worship; they are more interested in receiving herbal remedies that will hopefully solve their earthly problems. Even more embarrassing is the fact that Mavuso has to walk past uMshumayeli Ndlovu (the Shembe priest) who, every Saturday, has a congregation that would fill the hall twice over if they did not worship out in the open, under the trees beneath the bridge.

In less than 10 minutes, Mavuso is making the return journey back to his stall. He tries to avoid making eye contact with the people he passes, such as uMshumayeli Ndlovu, who refrains from asking his colleague how the service went. It is obvious that nobody showed up for church today: hence Mavuso's hasty return. He then loudly volunteers, for all to hear: '*Eish … abantu abakabuyi ku Gudi emakhaya*', which means that people have not returned home since they went away for Good Friday (one of the Easter holidays). Now, this is very interesting because a priest in the Zionist Church would also have gone to some or other venue to officiate at a service during the holy weekend. The sad truth of the matter is that since the passing of *umkhokheli* (the female head and assistant to the preacher, who also happened to be his wife), his church has not had any congregants for quite some time.

As the religious leader of a church, Mavuso has authority over his congregants, and is able to perform sacred rituals and act as an intermediary between those still living and the departed who, in turn, are believed to facilitate contact between God and humans. Mavuso also has the authority to perform religious rites, especially rites of sacrifice and the propitiation of deities. However, Mavuso's followers also need to believe in his spiritual powers and capabilities. The very small number of followers and the size of his church say a great deal about the power and influence he has (or does not have). With the remaining congregants supposedly numbering about five people (his daughter, son and grandchildren), his church has become a venue for family meetings rather than legitimate religious gatherings.

Some say that Mavuso's loss of followers is attributable to his poor interpersonal skills. He is said to be *ibhimbi lokukhuluma* (one with a sharp tongue) and leaves a bitter taste in people's mouths every time he speaks. When *umkhokheli* (the wife) was still alive, she had a way of sanitising her husband's preaching style, effectively cleaning up after his regular diatribes. At the time, those who still attended the church services did so out of respect and loyalty to *umkhokheli*. As soon as she passed away, they abandoned the church and never returned.

One Sunday, when Mavuso's daughter, son and grandchildren had quietly retreated from the hall and he saw that nobody else was coming to worship, he sat there momentarily, cutting a lonely figure and reading his bible, as if to say, 'I am still here, God. Don't mind them as I am your faithful and loyal servant.' When he left the church and took off his garb, he headed over to see his friend and *induna,* uNdwandwe (the hostel headman), who is also a herbalist and traditional healer.

Mavuso has been holding onto the idea of a church, with a reference to Matthew (18:19) being particularly meaningful to him: 'Again, truly I tell you that if two of you on earth agree about anything they ask for, it will be done for them by my Father in heaven.' To Mavuso, it really does not matter how many congregants assemble to pray to God and ask for His intervention because, as stated in Matthew (18:20): 'For where two or three gather in my name, there am I with them.'

## This is a place of healers too

Duma Ndlovu, a highly celebrated arts practitioner and producer of the television series *Muvhango*, said in a Facebook post on 8 May 2020: 'When I humble myself to my ancestors and ask for something, they give me. They are my intercessors with the most high, *Umvelinqangi*.' Kwa Mai Mai, also known as 'the place of healers', has become a drawcard for those seeking help from their ancestors and who believe that their problems can only be addressed through traditional healing and the use of indigenous medicine.

Writing in *The Lancet*, Kubukeli (1999:24) argues, 'To understand the African traditional healer and the whole traditional process, one needs to understand African religion. The whole African belief system is so fundamental that any form of healing process that ignores these beliefs is psychologically unsatisfactory and in some cases unaccountable.' Kubukeli (1999) contends, further, that the practice of African traditional healing is the only form of healing that Africans understand. It is the only combined sacred and secular practice to have brought order and sanity to Africans' social systems, assisted by the fact that it is passed down from generation to generation.

Benatar (2001) argues that no amount of Western influence has succeeded in rendering traditional medicine and healing practices extinct. According to this author, traditional healers outnumber Western medical practitioners in South Africa. For example, in 2001, there were only 25 000 trained medical practitioners in the country, compared to over 200 000 practising traditional healers.

Traditional healing will never be devoid of culture or out of touch with people's day-to-day encounters with and impressions of life as it unfolds. Whenever those who subscribe to traditional healing start to suspect that something is amiss in their lives and they cannot make meaning of what is going on around them, they seek guidance and healing from traditional healers. Quite often, when people fall ill, they associate their illness with some cultural or cosmic phenomenon and not necessarily a biological condition that calls for scientific intervention. Similarly, some sort of mishap or misfortunate, such as losing a job or being unable to find employment, is at times attributed to a bad omen of a supernatural origin, which only a traditional healer or diviner can explain and help to resolve.

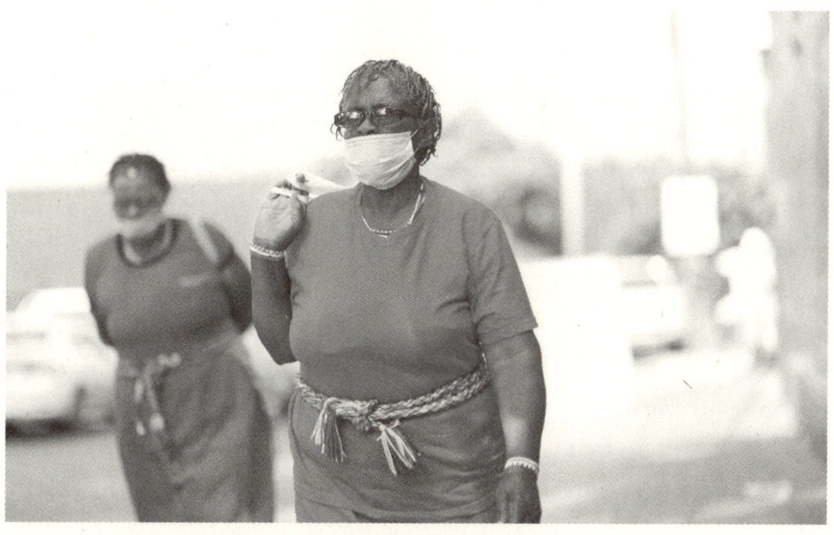

*Traditional healers at Kwa Mai Mai (Photo: Siphiwe Mhlambi)*

The ingenuity behind African medicinal practices and prescriptions for illness, whether of a spiritual or physical nature, often makes a mockery of science by defying lab-tested, chemically formulated medicines. The fact that traditional healers can diagnose a health condition, whether psychological or physical, has been a source of amazement or, alternatively, scepticism among health scientists, physicians, psychologists and even psychiatrists. This is because Western medicine is the result of lab-tested, chemically derived medications. According to Mothibe and Sibanda (2019:12), 'Traditional medicine is an object or substance used in traditional health practice for the diagnosis, treatment or prevention of physical or mental illness; or well-being in human beings.' Mothibe and Sibanba (2019:1) add that 'African traditional medicine (ATM) has been used by African populations for the treatment of diseases long before the advent of orthodox medicine and continues to carry a part of the burden of health for the majority of the population.' Therefore, there is no reason for it to fail now.

One of the fundamental mistakes that Westerners and those who practise Christianity make is to assume that traditional healing does not accommodate a belief in the existence of God. Chidester (1992:xii) warns against this careless assumption, arguing that the 'complex distinctive character of South African religious life has taken shape within a particular economic, social and political context, and pays special attention to the creativity of people who have suffered under conquest, colonialism and apartheid'. Strijdom and Charnick-Udemans (2018) support Chidester's views that, by embedding religion within the cultural, economic and political context that has shaped religious formations, anything can be made sacred through intensive interpretation and ritualisation.

If there is any truth in Chidester's argument, then this condescending attitude towards anything African, and the suggestion that African religion and spirituality are not inspired by God, must be rejected. Van Dyk (2001) argues that because the ancestors are the 'living dead', their relatives on earth believe that they are compassionate and will always show an interest in their daily lives, acting as concerned mediators in their communication with God. However, the power to decipher the instructions relayed from the departed to the living has been conferred on the traditional healers and diviners. They are the ones who understand the intricacies of ancestral veneration and reverence, and are able to instruct the living on how to appease the ancestors, who in turn will shower them with ancestral blessings.

Mokgobi (2014:3) asserts:

Because African religion reveres and holds God in the highest regard, worshippers do not speak directly to Him. Their prayers and wishes are communicated to Him through the medium of the ancestors. This is often aided by enlisting the services of a traditional healer who advises on how to communicate with the ancestors, depending on the purposes of the communication and the type of ritual that needs to be performed.

## Scattered bones and flaming incense

The concepts of *ubungoma* (divination or the power to divine) and *ukuthwasa* (training to be a diviner) remain deeply entrenched in the African spiritual realm. Studies have been conducted on the ontology and epistemology of *ubungoma*. Until 1978, when the World Health Organization (WHO) officially recognised African traditional medicine, the practice of *ubungoma* was seen as witchcraft. The WHO advocated that a holistic approach be adopted to the practice of traditional medicine – from environmental, social and spiritual perspectives – something that even Western health practitioners had never done (Ogana and Ojong 2015).

For a time, popular Western scholarship associated *ukuthwasa* and *ubungoma* with pagan practices that were particularly prevalent among rural women. Scholars such as Lee (1969) viewed *ukuthwasa* and *ubungoma* as forms of escape for women who suffered the stress of social exclusion and therefore opted for *ubungoma* as a way to attain a higher social status. Lee (1969:141) argued: '… to become diviners is for pagan Zulu women the only socially recognized way of escape from an impossible situation in family life; it is also the only way outstanding women can win general social prestige.'

*Herb-grinding is a full-time job at Kwa Mai Mai (Photo: Sipho Mhlambi)*

This type of approach testifies to the dangers of those strands of Western scholarship in which authors write about African social life from an outsider's perspective, without the necessary lived cultural experiences. Such scholars' lack of insight is especially evident from their suggestion that women who become diviners are merely seeking attention because they feel neglected. Ogana and Ojong (2015) dismiss the above view, saying that it is condescending and based on shallow, Eurocentric theoretical constructs. They reason that if it were true that women become sangomas to escape their social circumstances, then large numbers of women would be flocking to become *sangomas*. However, this profession is confined to relatively few individuals.

It was not only individual Europeans who intervened in the local 'authoritative' narrative; even colonial governments and their related authorities in Africa battled with the cultural and spiritual dimensions of African communities. In 1891, the colonial government of Natal passed legislation prohibiting the practice of *ubungoma*. The Natal Native Code of 1891 outlawed this practice, classifying it as witchcraft. This was not surprising because the *izangoma* (diviners) and *izinyanga* (herbalists) could well have been instrumental in strengthening *amabutho* (regiments) when they went to war against the British in 1879. Even under Afrikaner rule, new pieces of legislation were enacted to further suppress *ubungoma*. The Witchcraft Suppression Act No.3 was passed in 1957 and the Witchcraft Suppression Amendment Act No.50 was passed in 1970, with both pieces of legislation designed to ensure that *ubungoma* was completely prohibited. In fact, practising *ubungoma* remains prohibited to this day, as per the 1996 Ralushai Commission Findings.[33]

*Izangoma* live inside and outside society simultaneously. They are cherished and admired by those who consult and engage with them but are frowned upon and feared by those who do not understand their world. They live behind an invisible wall, and you will sense an 'approach with care' warning should you try to enter their world. Courtships between a female *sangoma* and a male suitor are seldom seen in public. In villages it is common, especially at traditional ceremonies, to see young men making advances towards some of the women folk in a practice of *ukushela* (courtship), where a young man declares his interest or love to a woman. However, a female *sangoma* enjoys a certain level of authority, which is sometimes confused for a form of matriarchal control over men.

Phiri (2016) argues that *izangoma* are not part of patriarchal culture, which lumps together women and children as 'powerless subordinates'. Even referring to a female *isangoma* as *makhosi* (king), a title reserved for chiefs (who are mainly men), confirms that *ubungoma* defies the gender norms that typically favour men in traditional societies. The world of *izangoma* is the underworld of ancestors – those whom they consult for the purpose of divination and who in turn give them the power to solve life's puzzles for the living. Acquiring the power to divine is not a chosen journey in life; it is a calling that cannot be refused, lest it invokes the anger of the ancestors.

Accepting the calling to be a diviner does not allow you to choose who your *gobela* (trainer) will be as you undergo *ukuthwasa* (the journey of becoming an *isangoma*). Your *gobela* is revealed to you in one form or another, and you may even have to travel far to find the *gobela* whom the ancestors have identified. Becoming a sangoma is inborn – something gifted to you by *amadlozi* (ancestors). The calling can manifest in many ways, such as in an ill-defined illness. Trying to ignore a calling can be disastrous and lead to mishaps in life; hence it is regarded as unavoidable. Ellis and Berglund, respectively (cited in Ogana and Ojong, 2015:60), observe that the call to become a *sangoma* is accompanied by a wide range of somatic, psychological and social symptoms, such as 'sneezing, belching, hiccupping, yawning, restlessness, sleeplessness, anxiety, mental confusion … *izibhobo* (pain in shoulders and between shoulder blades), and withdrawal from social life'.

Broster (1981) indicates that, if left unattended, an ancestral calling can cause emotional or mental difficulties, manifesting in the person (as if possessed) weeping uncontrollably, hurling themselves on the ground, tearing off their clothes and occasionally lapsing into unconsciousness. The longer the calling remains unanswered, the greater the number of physical ailments that the *ithwasa* (initiate) has to contend with, the author argues.

There seems to be a rising number of initiates, particularly young women and even teenagers, who are heeding the call of *ukuthwasa*.

Recently, a new phenomenon has emerged in South Africa – celebrities who are responding to the call to become a sangoma. An online magazine article on the subject read: 'Some of Mzansi's biggest stars have heeded their ancestral calling.'[34] The article identified more than 10 celebrities who had responded to the call. Leading the list were female musicians and actresses, and some male singers.

The magazine article revealed that South Africa has no shortage of celebrities who are *sangomas,* reporting that over the previous decade many famous children of the soil have accepted their ancestral gift of *ubungoma* (traditional healing). Even *Sowetan Live,* one of the country's largest daily newspapers, reported a rise in local celebrities embracing their ancestral calling and undergoing 'their *ukuthwasa* (spiritual emergence) training'.[35] This trend is not addressed in this book, but needs further research.

The phenomenon of being called to be a *sangoma* has popularised *umsamo*, a sacred place or a place of spiritual reconnection, where ancestors or the gods interact, albeit in the spiritual realm. This sacred space, which is sometimes in a special section of someone's house, is a kind of shrine where offerings are made and incense is burnt to interest the ancestors in responding positively to appeals for help from the living. For those who use the space for prayer, this same *umsamo* becomes a place of solitary worship of their specific god. For *ubungoma*, the space is arranged in a specific way. As a place of spiritual and ancestral worship, *umsamo* has certain items that cannot be touched or removed by any person other than the owner of the place. Items usually found in *umsamo* are a prayer mat, *udengezi* (a fragment of a clay pot) on which to burn incense and sometimes a white cloth, representing purity.

As *ukuthwasa* gains momentum, large numbers of young initiates are coming to Kwa Mai Mai. Some are seeking spiritual guidance and others wish to start the *ukuthwasa* journey. Still others are simply advised by the diviner that they need to have *umsamo* if they want *izindlela zabo zikhanye*: that is, if their path in life is to be free of obstacles and open to opportunities, and if any illnesses they or their family members may be experiencing are to be cured.

Whereas *umsamo* has always been a sacred place inside the main ancestral house, usually a *rondavel* (a circular house with a thatched roof) called *kwaGogo, umsamo* is a place where the father figure in the home is allowed to address the ancestors. A married woman, who has acquired a new surname, cannot enter *umsamo* or address ancestors, which can be a problem if the same woman's ancestors demand *umsamo* of their own.

Compounding the problem with young female celebrities, in particular, who now have their own *umsamo*, is the fact that *umsamo* has always been understood to be a place where only a father figure can burn incense and talk to the ancestors. Where a female matriarch is the head of the household, she, too, is allowed to engage with the ancestors at this sacred shrine. This new phenomenon of young women suddenly having their own *umsamo* is foreign to some cultural communities, unless they have fully undergone the process of *ukuthwasa* and become *isangoma* (a diviner) themselves.

A *sangoma* does not just have the power to divine. A *sangoma* must also have the ability to prescribe the right type of treatment in the event of illness and treat such an ailment. Some *sangomas* combine this gift with religion (particularly African traditional religion) and become preachers.

Kwa Mai Mai is not short of *izangoma* (diviners) and *izinyanga* (herbalists). In fact, it is the norm for diviners to act as herbalists, and vice versa. One such person is MaNsimbi.


## *MaNsimbi – A woman of steel*

People are sitting in a long line on benches that stretch along the wall, up to the entrance to the shop of uMama Zilondile Nsimbi. Inside the shop, MaNsimbi, as she is popularly known, is in consultation with troubled souls who have come to seek elusive answers to questions about their various infirmities. Some of them have come to ask for concoctions of herbs that will hopefully solve their problems. Some are here in search of fortune and need *umuthi wenhlanhla* (a good luck potion or lucky charms) to enable them to win a lotto ticket or find a job after an extended period of unemployment.

Zilondile Nsimbi is a self-proclaimed herbalist, diviner and traditional healer who responded to the calling at a young age. As a traditional healer, MaNsimbi has over the years received people with a range of problems: some have shown signs of mental illness and dementia, while others have been dumped by their girlfriend or a fiancé who has abandoned the relationship and gone back home. MaNsimbi claims to have the power and practical skills to heal all types of problems, including troubled relationships. Where someone has walked out of a relationship, MaNsimbi claims she can bring the person back by supplying the customer, who has lost their love, with various traditional herbs. Among her herbal concoctions are *udelunina*, *abangqongqozi*, *umabuya*, *umthunyelelwa* and many others, which she gives to those in need of help. Different circumstances demand different concoctions, in keeping with the intended results. For instance, *udelunina*, simply translated, means one who would abandon her family and choose to run to her man, regardless of the consequences, while *umabuya* means that someone will return, even if they slammed the door behind them.

MaNsimbi also claims to be able to heal those who, having been brought in by their families, suffer from some form of insanity. Insanity is not always regarded as having been triggered by a chemical imbalance; it can be associated with witchcraft. If she suspects the latter, she says, putting the afflicted person in water and hypnotising them results in their being able to reveal the person responsible for bewitching them. Once the source of the problem has been identified, MaNsimbi is able to heal the person.

MaNsimbi shared a story of a woman who was brought in by her family for a consultation a week before our interview. The woman had multiple personalities, spoke in tongues and appeared completely insane. Upon her arrival at MaNsimbi's place, she was calmed down, given traditional herbs and made to inhale burnt incense. By the time she had regained her senses, the woman was asking her family what had happened to her and how she had got there; she left completely healed. A diviner since 1981, MaNsimbi claimed that she has never caused a rift between family members by revealing any person's name (normally that of a family member) as the cause of strife. This means, she says, that nobody has died or been killed by a family member because of her divination. Moreover, she has never supplied a customer with poison to kill someone.

The discussion delved into some of the most embarrassing problems that people have brought to MaNsimbi, such as couples who are failing to satisfy each other in bed or individuals who wake up in the throes of an orgasm after dreaming about sleeping with an animal. MaNsimbi pointed to a dried iguana hanging from the roof of her shop, which she said she used to treat women who dream about sleeping with an animal. The same iguana is used to help women fall pregnant, or to help men develop an erection.

Her traditional shop, which she calls a pharmacy, is a veritable library of medicine and herbs. They are stored in big and small bottles and wrapped in plastic or paper. There are herbs in powder form as well as roots, leaves and plants, which together offer a spectacular sight for those intrigued by traditional medicine.

MaNsimbi is well-travelled, having been to most southern African countries (including Mozambique, eSwatini, Zimbabwe, Botswana and Lesotho) to collect herbs. A successful business woman, MaNsimbi claims to have amassed her wealth as a traditional healer and *isangoma* just by working at Kwa Mai Mai. She sees hundreds of people every year, who come to consult her either at her main business premises in the compound or in her consulting room at her place of residence. She also owns a passenger transport company – with a string of taxis operating in and around Johannesburg and Soweto – and has built several properties for herself and her children.

To her, Kwa Mai Mai is a symbol of black entrepreneurship and pride, a place where tradition has unlocked an economy that operates separately from the mainstream businesses in Johannesburg.

## Meet Mkhulu Mamba, the diviner

*'Ngokufika abantu, awubabizi, bayazifikela. Ubabona bengene nje. Omunye ephakanyelwe lidlozi. Ubese uyalibuza lifunani.'*

Mkhulu Mamba explained that diviners do not solicit clients; they come of their own accord, seeking help for their various problems. Because *'mkhulu'* means grandfather, her practice or craft name could pass for that of a male sangoma, but Mkhulu Mamba is a female diviner who carries the ancestral power of a man from her family. Mkhulu Mamba has the confident gaze of a man and also conveys a type of male authority in her speech, mannerisms and actions.

As a sangoma, Mkhulu Mamba carries the spirit of her own descendant group from her paternal and maternal side, not that of the family into which she was married. Because of this, and even though Mkhulu Mamba is already married, when coming out of *ukuthwasa* she had to return to her paternal home because she carried the *idlozi* (ancestral spirit) of her family and not that of her husband. So that she could return to her marriage with this gift, her husband had to buy *idlozi* (the power of the ancestor she now possesses) from his in-laws; otherwise, the *idlozi* would have remained at Mkhulu Mamba's parents' home.

This practice is confirmed by Ngubane (1977:142), who asserts: 'The spirits in their complete state as ancestors return to this world through their daughters, not through their wives, mothers or daughters-in-law.' Ngubane (1977) further emphasises that a sangoma is principally possessed by the spirits of her own descendant group, not that of her husband. A female sangoma clearly enjoys gender supremacy in her role as a mediator between the living and their ancestors, with Ngubane (1977:88) arguing that 'it is through a woman that the transition of spiritual beings is made'.

Mkhulu Mamba underwent her *ukuthwasa* training in 1995 in Daveyton on the East Rand, near Johannesburg, but first had to go home to Piet Retief before returning to Kwa Mai Mai to start up her combined trade of *isangoma* (diviner), *inyanga* (traditional healer) and *umthandazi* (preacher). Mkhulu Mamba would not have been able to practise her craft if her husband had not gone to her home to buy the ancestral power she now possesses; and to fetch her, together with her new gift of divining.

As a resident of Kwa Mai Mai, Mkhulu Mamba is also a *gobela* (trainer) with her own *amathwasa* (diviner trainees). Three of Mkhulu Mamba's *amathwasa*, all women, look young enough to be at school or college and still under the care of their parents. They avoid eye contact, as if they have been told that under no circumstances must they connect with the outside world. Their feet, arms and legs have been smeared with white ash and they have *ibovu* (red ash) on their faces. Beads and strips of goat skin criss-cross their chests. Their wrists are adorned with bangles made of goat skin, a sign that blood has been spilt so that they may connect with the ancestors.

*Mkhulu Mamba's initiates (Photo: Siphiwe Mhlambi)*

These young sangoma initiates are not here by choice or by chance. They have been guided by the spirit of their ancestors, who led them straight to Mkhulu Mamba's shrine and training facility. Some of them, not knowing where they were meant to go, would have been led by their ancestors to Mkhulu Mamba's place, arriving in the early hours of the morning. Upon their arrival, they would have immediately burst into a song – a song they never knew before – and gone into a trance-like state and started dancing like they had never danced before. Even their families would not, at that stage, have known where they had gone. None of these initiates would have known Mkhulu Mamba or where she lived or practised. But, possessed by the ancestral spirit, they embarked on a journey that they had no prior knowledge of. Irrespective of the distance, they would have arrived at the place that the ancestors directed them to.

As Mkhulu Mamba explained in Zulu:

*Ngokufika abantu, awubabizi, bayazifikela. Ubabona bengena nje. Omunye ephakanyelwe lidlozi. Ubese uyalibuza lifunani. Bese liyakhuluma, liyabajagela ngokwesiZulu. Kudala ukufika komuntu wayevuka ebusuku enqunu angene kwakho. Akhulela , amemeze, abhodle ngokwedlozi. Ubone ukuthi hhayibo lomuntu uzothwasa, kodwa okwamanje akusafani nasekuqaleni. Idlozi likubiza ngokuthi mhlambe lingangidlulisa lapha phambi kwakho. Bafike bagoqane izinyawo la phambi kwakho wena Gobela, engabe esakwazi ukusukuma. Kufanele wena umsize, umelule, bese uyabuza ukuthi bafunani. Uze afike kuwe nje, kusuke kwenzenjani.*

Loosely translated, Mkhulu Mamba explained that nobody comes to her place by invitation; they are led to her by the ancestral spirits. Some are already possessed by the spirit of the ancestors who have entered their body and are oblivious of their whereabouts or who they are. When someone is possessed by *idlozi* (the ancestral spirit), it is *idlozi* that is speaking through them. As a diviner, she is able to enter that spiritual realm and engage *idlozi* directly. Speaking through the one possessed, *idlozi* is then able to explain who the person is and where they came from. 'Some arrive and break into a trance, sing a song they never sang before and dance a dance they never learned before,' confirmed Mkhulu Mamba. She also explained that *ukuthwasa* is two-fold: there are those who *thwasa* as *'makhosi'* and those who *thwasa* as *'thokoza'*. These are different paths to becoming a *sangoma*, with some being trained through *amandiki* and others being trained through *amandawe*.

The three *amathwasa* who are under Mkhulu Mamba's care came to embark on a spiritual journey that would see them becoming *izangoma*, eventually graduating to trainers (*gobela*) with their own *amathwasa*. Mkhulu Mamba explained that there is no set time frame for *ithwasa* to come out of *idlozi* (to complete training). Some have a clear path, and their ancestors are quick to show them the way, and they are soon released to their families as fully trained *izangoma*.Others have a more difficult path and remain in training (*edlozini*) for several years, until their ancestors eventually convey the message that they have completed their training.

Mkhulu Mamba revealed that some trainees find it difficult to pay for the training, especially if their training period is lengthy. However, as a compassionate *gobela* who understands each *thwasa*'s (initiate's) individual circumstances, Mkhulu Mamba allows her trainees who have completed *ukuthwasa* to leave and seek work. This allows them to start earning money to cover the cost of *ukuthwasa*.

Mkhulu Mamba also revealed that people who come to consult her have many reasons and problems that prompt their visit, from family or marriage-related strife to assorted illnesses. She claimed that she is able to fix all these problems with herbal remedies: *'Ngiyawuhlanganisa umshado, kuningi nje, nogulayo ngiyamelapha. Onezinto ngaphakathi esiswini ezihambayo ngizelapha.'* ('I fix broken marriages, and other things, even the sick I heal them. Some have gremlins inside their stomach and I am able to heal them.')

Those who come for divination do not necessarily reveal their exact circumstances to Mkhulu Mamba. She divines with bones, scattering them on the floor and analysing their shape and direction. She is then able to interpret what the bones are saying. Guided by and talking to her ancestors, she is able to determine the reason for the person's visit. Those who come for a consultation never return home if the divination suggests a process of *ukuthwasa*; instead, they will remain for an uncertain period of time until they have completed the process.

Mkhulu Mamba and her three female *amathwasa* are just a handful of the many men and women who have responded to the call and gone on to become traditional healers with the power and ability to divine and heal broken and lost souls. In Kwa Mai Mai, there are at least three *izangoma* with between three and six initiates undergoing *ukuthwasa* at any one time. Until their training is over, initiates continue to perform tasks and chores that are necessary to prepare them for their calling. Chores include sweeping the entrance to the diviner's premises and walking to the nearby shop. Irrespective of the task at hand, initiates always work in pairs.

There appear to be unwritten rules that initiates must observe at all times, such as: Don't look at strangers, don't talk to them, don't respond, always maintain an aloof attitude, and look really mean and angry. These are in evidence at Kwa Mai Mai, where the initiates do not talk to anyone except their *gobela*. The rituals they are expected to perform, often at odd hours, could be the reason why they display such an unfriendly demeanour. Whatever the reason for their apparent grumpiness, the process each initiate has to undergo before being released to serve in the capacity for which they were chosen appears to be gruelling.

*MaNsimbi (Photo: Siphiwe Mhlambi)*

*Mkhulu Mamba (Photo: Siphiwe Mhlambi)*

*Unkab'ewrong (Photo: Siphiwe Mhlambi)*

*uMshumayeli Ndlovu of the Shembe Church at Kwa Mai Mai
(Photo: Siphiwe Mhlambi)*

*Priest Mavuso of the Zionist Church, resident of Kwa Mai Mai
(Photo: The author)*

# Eight
# At loggerheads

Since the advent of democracy in South Africa, the government has faced the sad reality of history having conspired to create the unsavoury conditions under which rural migrants have been forced to live. The hostels have become a symbol of a colonial quest and part of a deliberate project to forcibly extract Africans from the villages and put them in cramped labour camps not fit for human habitation.

Thurman (1997:43) attributes the conditions in migrant labour hostels in the country to 'the archetypal physical manifestation of three centuries of systematic racial discrimination and economic exploitation of South Africa's African population'. These hostels, anonymous-looking buildings that the government would prefer did not exist, have become the epitome of dejection and indignation and are regarded as hotspots for violence and crime. Beyond this dubious reputation, there is no acknowledgment that the hostels have also suffered years of neglect.

At the same time, as Bank et al. (2020) observe, migrants living in hostels after apartheid, particularly those from KwaZulu-Natal (whom they refer to as 'Zulu migrants'), have not sought to integrate with their surrounding communities. Owing to their lack of participation in the struggle for democracy, these authors state, they 'were not regarded as a priority for investment after 1994' (Bank et al. 2020:7). Hence, no effort was made by City Council officials to improve the quality of these hostels. Whether these statements are true or not, particularly those around the apolitical stance of Zulu migrants, these hostels are in the same condition as they were in when the democratic government inherited them from the previous dispensation – and perhaps in an even worse state.

One reason why hostels populated by Zulu migrants have been left in a state of disrepair may well be that the ruling party views them as not having been on the side of the mass democratic movement during the struggle for democracy. However, other powerful forces are at play. The fact that residents of the hostels have been forced to live in squalid and often overcrowded conditions is complicated by the fact that, since 1994, what had originally been built as single men's hostels have seen the arrival of residents' wives and children, which has turned these places into family establishments. Moreover, the socio-political dynamics between hostel residents and their township counterparts have not contributed to cordial interpersonal relationships. Perceived by the city slick and township residents as urban outcasts who are backward, rural, traditional and unsophisticated, the hostel residents have insulated themselves against outside pressures, resorting to living isolated lives.

The steady influx of people from the rural areas in search of employment opportunities is a nightmare as far as urban settlement planning is concerned. Since there are no more apartheid restrictions, such as influx control, on the movement of who comes in and out of the city, informal human settlements have mushroomed across the metropolitan area. The hostels have not been spared the overcrowding. Whereas there used to be 2 000 hostels with about 600 000 beds across the country, hostel dwellers now number more than 1 million. Some hostels have even erected informal settlements within their compounds.

The Community Residential Unit (CRU) Programme, a successor to the National Hostel Redevelopment Programme, was established by the government to facilitate the provision of secure, stable rental accommodation for low-income individuals working and living in the city who lacked proper dwellings. Among the housing challenges that the CRU has to address are public hostels that are owned by provincial housing departments and municipalities and the so-called 'grey' hostels that combine both private and public ownership.

While the CRU Programme has noble intentions, including a desire to restore the dignity of hostel dwellers who were previously prohibited from having their wives and children live with them in the city, its main shortcoming is that most hostel residents do not fall into the low-income category which the programme targets. Most hostel residents lack secure employment – if indeed they are employed at all. Those still living in the existing hostels have not paid (nor been expected to pay) rent for their 'single bed' for over two decades (this used to be less than R20 a month). Therefore, the idea of building affordable rental housing units for the families of hostel dwellers earning between R800 and R3 500 a month, with the aim of collecting monthly rental income from them, appears not to have been carefully considered, nor is it widely accepted by hostel residents. Some, for example, view the hostels as merely a place to rent a bed, sleep, wake up and go to work, for as long as they are in the city, while returning to their homes in the villages at least twice a year.

The literature on hostels, from the early 1990s until today, paints a consistent picture of the squalid conditions that hostel residents have to endure. Writing in 1993, Ramphele (cited in Fenyane 2016) laments the unpleasant odours and overflowing garbage cans, the inadequate ablution facilities and the constant overcrowding as some of the degrading conditions that characterise the hostels. These problems are probably even more serious now than in years gone by, particularly if they have not been attended to for more than two decades. Kwa Mai Mai has not been spared this scourge.

Meanwhile, the National Hostel Redevelopment Programme has not yet achieved its stated aims, namely: (i) to promote humane living conditions for hostel residents; (ii) to include hostel residents, neighbouring communities and other stakeholders affected by the redevelopment in decision-making processes; (iii) to promote social integration within hostel communities and also between hostel and neighbouring communities; (iv) to include plans for accommodating those who will be displaced by the redevelopment project; (v) to initiate the inclusion of local institutions and administrative procedures in the system in order to sustain improvements and promote socio-economic development; and (vi) to boost development that is orientated towards empowerment, participation and the promotion of economic opportunities.

It comes as no surprise, therefore, that even Kwa Mai Mai hostel residents and traders are taking matters into their own hands and demanding better treatment and improved service delivery.

## Battle for control of Kwa Mai Mai

In 2014, the City Council, working through the Johannesburg Property Company (JPC), appointed Stim Logistic-FGZ Consultants to enter into a joint venture for the alleged revamp of Kwa Mai Mai at a cost of more than R3.2 million. This investment was part of a planned rejuvenation of the market that would attract more tourists to the compound. The massive project included major maintenance work and renovations, such as painting, paving, tiling, upgrading of security, electrification, plumbing, glazing, cleaning of gutters, welding and repairing of toilet facilities.

At the time, the Member of the Mayoral Committee (MMC) who was responsible for the city's economic development plan, Councillor Ruby Mathang, described Kwa Mai Mai as 'a special space' whose facelift was aimed at attracting more tourists and ultimately stimulating the tourism sector by showcasing the compound's traditional heritage. According to Councillor Mathang, the place consisted of 'several stalls run by authentic traditional healers in traditional regalia who use real traditional herbs and ointments to cure the sick'.[36] This half-hearted description of the place, which also boasts a lively trade in cultural goods and services (including woodwork, upholstery and traditional wear), showed that Councillor Mathang had either never been to the place or thought the various offerings were inferior. Whatever the reason, this description of Kwa Mai Mai was a sign that the City Council itself lacked a clear understanding of this creative and culturally rich market.

The planned revamp of Kwa Mai Mai was an acknowledgement by the City Council that the precinct, having been neglected for a long time, needed to become a safer environment for residents and traders. It also had to be cleaned up and made more attractive to visitors. With this investment, the precinct would be given a new lease on life. Striking all the right chords, the City Council even went so far as to say that the tourists were now returning to the area, which was abuzz with trading activity, and that business was booming. This, however, was a far cry from what the market was experiencing on the ground.

Three years later, Kwa Mai Mai had clearly not received the boost it had been hoping for when the investment was made in 2014, or perhaps no visible improvements had been made of the kind that would attract large numbers of tourists to the market. In 2017, a further R10.9 million was allegedly allocated to the market for infrastructure maintenance and upgrades. This multimillion-rand maintenance and upgrade project was at the centre of tensions that developed between Kwa Mai Mai traders, through its committee, and the JPC, which had been overseeing the project.

Besides bringing their main complaint about alleged mismanagement and maladministration of the R10.9 million project, traders were complaining about the poor upkeep of the compound, particularly in respect of waste collection and the overall management of the area. At the centre of the brewing storm was Pikitup, a waste-collection entity run by the City of Johannesburg. Whereas the municipality views Pikitup as being responsible for ensuring that streets are swept, litter is picked up and illegally dumped goods are cleared away to reduce environmental pollution, it would appear that these services did not apply to the Kwa Mai Mai hostel and bazaar. The piles of waste that remained uncollected and the rising stench were a serious indictment of Pikitup and its supposed commitment to the daily collection and disposal of waste. Kwa Mai Mai seemed not to be on Pikitup's radar or considered a priority area for waste collection and disposal. Instead, the fumes of uncollected waste continued to greet visitors at the gate and became a permanent feature of the compound, repelling many regular patrons and potential customers.

The infrastructure and services improvement project, valued at more than R14 million but with no visible impact, stretched the tolerance levels of the Kwa Mai Mai community towards the City Council and the JPC. To understand the scale of the tension between the City Council and the Kwa Mai Mai community, it is important to examine the hierarchical structure, leadership and social system that existed within the Kwa Mai Mai trade zone and hostel.

## Traditional authority at the single men's hostels

To appreciate the nature of the confluence between the outside world and the residents of hostels, it is useful to examine how hostels are managed.

Approximately 100 hostels are spread across Gauteng province, with the City of Johannesburg accounting for the bulk of these hostels, including those in Soweto and Alexandra townships. These are followed by Ekurhuleni and the West Rand, with 21 and 11 hostels respectively. In City and Suburban in Johannesburg is a cluster of so-called men's hostels, all within walking distance of each other, comprising the Wemmer, Denver, George Koch, MBA, Murray & Roberts, and Kwa Mai Mai hostels. Because the majority of hostel dwellers in Johannesburg are from the Nguni group, mainly Zulus, they represent an extension or even a replica of the rural social system. Here in the city, traditional leadership has entrenched itself in a fashion similar to how chieftaincies are organised in rural KwaZulu-Natal.

Today, hostels in the city are still run along the same lines as when they were first established all those years ago. Just as rural homesteads and tribal wards (*izigodi*) are overseen by an *induna* (headman) on behalf of a chief, hostel residents continue to acknowledge the authority of chiefs, even in places as far away as Johannesburg or Durban. Each hostel has appointed an *induna* assisted by an *isigungu* (*induna*'s council), comprising *abanumzane* or elderly men of character. Even though there is no chief physically present among them with authority and oversight over the hostels, it is assumed that hostel dwellers remain directly connected to the chief's authority back home. For that connection to manifest itself, an *induna* has to be appointed as an overseer on behalf of the chief.

As the most important leader of a clan and within a particular ward (*izigodi*), the *induna* administers localised issues, including rituals and ceremonies, on behalf of the chief, and handles conflicts and scuffles. The *induna* is also responsible for receiving and presenting to the villagers those families seeking to *khonza*, which means to fall within the clan, settle their families in the ward and become subjects of the chief.

Similarly, in the city, the *induna* has the difficult and ultimate responsibility of maintaining a complex structure within the hostel, which accommodates men from diverse rural settings and different tribal authorities or chieftaincies. For instance, KwaZulu-Natal has approximately 300 *aMakhosi* (chiefs) spread across the province. Each *iNkosi* is a tribal authority overseeing different wards (*izigodi*), which can number more than 30, depending on the size of the *iNkosi*'s territory. With each ward having an *induna*, when the wards are amalgamated under one tribal authority they acquire a chief *induna* – known as *uNdunankulu* – above the various *iziNduna*. The head *induna* reports directly to the *iNkosi* of that clan. Just as in the pre-colonial era, this type of traditional leadership plays a prominent role, particularly among the Zulu people. The traditional, day-to-day social system of the Zulu people is administered by *iziNduna*, acting on behalf of *aMakhosi* (the chiefs).

In each ward there is *ubhekeni wezinsizwa* (a man tasked with overseeing and ensuring discipline among adult men in the ward). This is the person responsible for ensuring good behaviour and instilling certain character traits in the young men of the village, including motivating them to attend ceremonies and other rituals. In the past, during the fight against colonialism or between warring tribes, *ubhekeni* assumed command of the regiments as they prepared to go to war. This high level of discipline and supervision over young men in the village has been central to the maintenance of an efficient communication engine, and to the relaying of messages to the entire village, the clan or the tribe across the various wards. When the *induna* needed his own council of 'men of character' in *isigodi* to assist him in overseeing the ward and maintaining discipline, it was these men (*oBhekeni*) who constituted the council, otherwise known as *isigungu* or, for lack of a better word, committee.

This rural template of traditional leadership, which is applied in a granular form across a ward, has been used in urban hostels. The *induna* plays a primary role in managing the hostel eco system, particularly by maintaining peace and good relations in the hostel. Hostel residents have accepted and adopted this system, with each hostel becoming a ward similar to the one found in chieftaincies, and with the *induna* overseeing the hostel on behalf of the *iNkosi* (the chief). It is this socio–political unit that has come to define the character and organisation of the hostel. This extension of the chief's tribal authority to the cities suggests the emergence, far from home, of a type of shadow tribal identity and social unit.

Once new migrant workers arrive in the city and take up residence in a hostel, they are not separated according to their tribal authority or clan back home. No distinction is made between various *aMakhosi* to whom they *khonza* or pledge allegiance. The fact that they come from Zululand means that it is the Zulu Kingdom that becomes the conduit between the home and the city. These migrant workers are thus conjoined through their 'Zulu-ness' or Zulu national identity.

For *iziNduna* to function effectively and carry out the duties expected of them, they are assisted by a council (*isigungu*). The purpose of the *isigungu* is to advise the *induna* on matters affecting the people under the latter's care. In the villages and in traditional tribal communities, the *isigungu* administers the affairs of the village in a specific location. Its responsibilities range from dealing with petty crimes and stock theft, through defusing tensions over grazing and the ploughing of fields, to preventing faction fights and other crimes that do not warrant the involvement of a chief or a criminal or civil court.

In the city, the *induna* and his *isigungu* are always on the lookout for any tension that might result in a full-scale faction fight between clans or even ethnic groups residing at the hostels, as this could spill over into faction fights back home in the villages. The *induna* and his *isigungu* are also responsible for ensuring that hostels do not become hideouts for people committing various types of crime in the urban areas. More importantly, the committee is there to ensure that culture and tradition permeate the hostel, by, among other things, being the conduit between what is happening back home and those living in the city's hostels. The preservation of the rural arrangement, albeit in an urban setting, underpins the rural–urban political and administrative life of a migrant worker.

With the head *induna*, who is appointed as the chairperson of *isigungu*, rules of engagement in the compound (hostels) are established, including who enters and who leaves, who is visiting, and who is coming to stay and from where. The flow of information between *iziNduna* and their councils, both within and between the hostels, including on activities taking place within the hostels, has to be channelled through each *induna* and his council.

Of particular importance is the maintenance of peace, social cohesion and harmony between the various clans, whose members suddenly find themselves thrust together into cramped men's compounds. Given the long history of ethnic violence and tribal wars dating back to the days of Shaka, tribal conflicts and faction fights are not relegated to the past: they could be sparked by anything at any time. Even when such faction fights erupt back home in the villages, the possibility of their spilling over into the city is not far-fetched. They could, for example, quickly manifest in the hostels. This is when the *iziNduna* in the hostels straddling the city need to quell possible bloody encounters. (This assumes that they will not be inciting them on occasions where it might suit their purpose to do so.)

## Nkab'eWrong – Induna uNdwandwe and his council

Like any other hostel in the city, Kwa Mai Mai has its *induna*, with their own *isigungu* (council). *Induna* uNdwandwe is *induna* but doubles up as the *inyanga* (a traditional healer) too. Ndwandwe also has a nickname, Nkab'ewrong, which is a worrying name for someone who is supposed to be ensuring peace and stability at the hostel. The name *inkabi* is associated with hitmen – feared and faceless gunmen who are available for hire to carry out any type of hit, whether political, tribal or commercial. However, the nickname simply means 'the wrong person to mess with' who, if crossed, could orchestrate their opponent's demise.

*Induna* uNdwandwe does not at all resemble someone with violent tendencies. On the contrary, he has a very calm demeanour, and is a good listener who pays attention to the conversation before he responds. In his capacity as both an *induna* and a herbalist, he always has company in his consulting room–cum–living quarters in the evening (consisting of other male residents of Kwa Mai Mai). His visitors are either just hanging out with him or discussing traditional matters – whatever they may be. Nobody knows who actually makes up *induna* uNdwandwe's *isigungu*, except that a group with familiar faces are always in his company. They comprise young adult men who live in the hostel and some fairly old men who appear not to have returned home since they came to Johannesburg decades ago.

Everyone wants some sort of status, as if that gives you permission to live in the hostel. If you are not a trader, you are a herbalist, a *sangoma* or a leader of some church. Leading the group of old men who are always gathered inside *induna* uNdwandwe's quarters is one Mavuso, the leader of the Zionist Christian Church at Kwa Mai Mai. None of the men who gather inside Ndwandwe's quarters are part of Mavuso's congregation, but they do form part of the *induna*'s council. When Mavuso is with the council (*isigungu*), his character changes. He is no longer the man of God, but becomes a feared, gun-toting individual who is quick to threaten men and women with violence whenever a member of the Kwa Mai Mai community expresses a view that is contrary to his own.

Therefore, there is no clarity on the composition of the council of the *induna*, but whoever they are, they have formed a strong bond with him and support his leadership. Of particular concern is that any other structures formed at Kwa Mai Mai are perceived to be inimical to the *induna* and the *isigungu*.

### *Role confusion between the* induna *and his* isigungu *and the traders' committee*

Because of the complex nature of Kwa Mai Mai, both as a hostel and as a trade zone, the role of the *induna* and his council is not as clear as it should be. This could be a case of deliberate role confusion on the part of the *induna* and his *isigungu*; or simply a widely accepted view that, to deal with anything requiring attention at the hostel, one has to go through the *induna*. In any event, some sectors in the hostel contend that the *induna* and his council are involving themselves in matters that exceed their mandate.

The service delivery problems discussed in this chapter are having an adverse effect on the community of Kwa Mai Mai – both the traders and the residents. Whether the *induna* understands that these issues warrant attention and action by a special committee appointed to address such matters, or whether he believes he is ultimately responsible for providing a solution, it has created serious tensions between the traders' committee (see below) and the *induna* and his *isigungu*.

Ndwandwe and his council have been accused by the traders' committee and by some individual traders of running a clandestine council or committee that remains faceless. They have accused him of arranging meetings with Kwa Mai Mai stakeholders, including entities under the control of the City of Johannesburg – which his council lacks the mandate to do. They have also accused *isigungu* of being in cahoots with the JPC, which has allegedly failed to address the problems affecting them at Kwa Mai Mai and whose failings they detailed in a petition submitted to the Office of the Mayor on 11 November 2020.

Complicating matters is the fact that, instead of meeting with the traders through their elected traders' committee, the JPC has co-opted the *induna*'s council and prefers to meet with the *isigungu* instead. The traders have even alleged that the *isigungu* has gone out to secure funding or sponsorships for Kwa Mai Mai but has never disclosed the details of these visits or arrangements to the trading community.

The allegations against the *induna* and his council came to a head at a meeting held at the Kwa Mai Mai hall on 27 October 2020, when the traders attributed the breakdown of the relationship between the traders' committee and the JPC to the *isigungu*. One trader at the meeting volunteered, '*Kunjenjenje Kwa Mai Mai, Induna nebandla layo*' ('Things are like this because of the *induna* and his council'). Even more concerning was a warning issued by one of the traders that people would hear gun shots at Kwa Mai Mai very soon: '*Kwa Mai Mai kusazodutshulwana*' ('Bullets are going to fly here at Kwa Mai Mai').

The meeting resolved that the JPC must be asked to liaise with just one committee, the one elected by the hostel community, failing which the JPC official (a Mr Zakwe) must be requested to vacate his office. The meeting also resolved that the *induna* must step down, together with his council. This meant that the traders did not recognise the *induna* as the traditional leader at Kwa Mai Mai, which was quite surprising considering the traditional leadership pattern at hostels. Needless to say, the *induna* and his council were not present at the meeting and all the allegations were later vehemently denied by the *isigungu*. Evidently these tensions caused the rift between the traders and their elected committee, and the *induna* and his *isigungu*.

### The chairperson and his committee

As a trade zone and market, Kwa Mai Mai established a committee of traders whose role is to liaise with the facilities management company, the JPC, which falls under the control of the City of Johannesburg. Governed by specific terms of reference, the committee acts as a multi-party representative of business enterprises and the City Council-owned informal trading market. Regarding the latter, the committee is expected to provide guidance, oversight and advice to the facility and act as a legitimate institutional and coordinating structure with which the Council liaises, while also providing support to ensure the effective management of the facility. To ensure effective communication with the JPC, an official from the latter is deployed to and maintains an office in the Kwa Mai Mai trade zone. This allows daily interaction and communication between the traders, through their committee, and the property company.

In the beginning, the establishment of the committee and the physical presence of an official from the property company in the Kwa Mai Mai precinct seemed like a sensible idea. With the committee (acting for the traders) liaising directly with the JPC, the stage was set for the property company to disseminate information intended for the traders in a timeous manner and for the market operation to run smoothly. More importantly, this structure was intended to find amicable solutions to problems (including infrastructure and service delivery shortcomings) that traders might encounter from time to time, of the type preventing them from running their businesses effectively. The committee is elected for an effective period of three years and comprises six people who are registered traders at Kwa Mai Mai.

On paper, the committee's governance requirements look fairly straightforward. However, this has not been the experience of the Kwa Mai Mai traders and their committee, who complain that the JPC has adopted a divide-and-rule strategy in respect of the *induna* and his *isigungu*, and the committee of traders. The fraught relationship between the committee and the JPC is at the centre of the tensions between the committee and *isigungu*. The terms of reference clearly state that the committee, elected by the traders, is 'to become a legitimate institutional and coordination instrument through which the city, government and other development institutions would be able to engage with business formations in the City of Johannesburg'.[37]

Clearly, there is no mention of the *isigungu* or the *induna*, either as an extension of or an alternative to the committee, or the role they should play in meeting the committee's objectives. However, the committee has accused the JPC of favouring the *induna* and his *isigungu* when dealing with matters that affect Kwa Mai Mai traders. The committee alleges that the property company has over the years been having clandestine meetings with the *isigungu*, knowing full well that it lacks the mandate to oversee maintenance and other service delivery issues at Kwa Mai Mai. The committee believes that the JPC prefers interacting with the *isigungu* and the *induna* because of their high level of sophistication and literacy, even though in doing so it is breaching governance protocols at Kwa Mai Mai. The committee has even started accusing the JPC of bribing the *isigungu*, including by allocating some of the required maintenance work to it.

## When enough is enough

Tired of the lack of service delivery and maintenance at the market, and what they perceive as the mismanagement of funds allocated to Kwa Mai Mai by the City Council, the traders decided to take matters into their own hands. They were advised by the committee to suspend their rent payments to the City Council until their list of demands had been met. The tense atmosphere reached boiling point when the official from the property company was ordered to exit the office he occupied inside the compound and leave the premises. The traders resolved that the committee should demand the keys from the JPC official and take over his office.

The committee had tabled a list of demands, which the JPC had failed to address. The demands appeared in a memorandum that was delivered to the Office of the Mayor on 11 November 2020. The latter promised to respond within seven days and to ensure that a dedicated official was assigned to the matter.

### Arrest of the traders' committee chairperson

Tensions boiled over when the JPC opened a case against the chairperson of the traders' committee for alleged trespassing and malicious damage to property. The JPC charged that the committee chairperson, Malibongwe Sithole, had forcefully opened the office occupied by the deployed JPC official (Mr Zakwe) after he had been ordered to leave the premises, at which point Sithole assumed responsibility for addressing the traders' complaints. The property company perceived this to be a criminal act on the part of the committee and opened a case against it with the police.

On 2 March 2021, the Johannesburg metro police arrived at Kwa Mai Mai and found the chairperson of the committee occupying the office of the JPC. After a brief discussion, the police suggested that it would mediate at a meeting between the JPC and the committee. The police agreed to come back later with an official from the JPC so that the proposed meeting could take place. The metro police returned on 23 March for the said meeting, but the official from the JPC failed to arrive and/or had decided not to be part of the mediation. The following day, on 24 March, a huge police contingent from the Jeppe police station arrived at Kwa Mai Mai to issue a warrant for the arrest of the chairperson of the committee for illegally occupying the JPC office. The committee chairperson was locked up in a cell at the police station. He appeared in court the following day, having spent the night in his cell, and was released on bail.

Notwithstanding the suggestion from the metro police that the matter should be resolved through mediation, the JPC clearly preferred to go the legal route, which would explain their no-show at the mediation session. At this stage, it was clear that the JPC had declared an all-out war on the traders' committee, which the committee later called an 'abuse of state power'. The traders at Kwa Mai Mai claimed that, ever since the appointment of the committee, they had been voicing their concerns about the JPC, particularly its alleged mismanagement of the precinct and failure to maintain its infrastructure. The decision to forcefully remove the official of the property company and have the chairperson of the committee occupy his office had been taken at the traders' meeting. In deciding to open a criminal case against the committee chairperson, the JPC had opted to ignore the legitimate concerns raised by the traders.

The dilapidated state of Kwa Mai Mai was becoming increasingly evident – even to first-time visitors who were drawn to the place by the word on the street that it had stayed true to its cultural roots. The tweet

above, posted on 28 March 2021 by one @Rorisang, could not have been too far from the truth, with the traders at Kwa Mai Mai obviously watching helplessly as their trading environment deteriorated in front of their eyes amidst growing piles of filth.

The post speaks to the general conditions at Kwa Mai Mai. With all the economic and tourism opportunities that Kwa Mai Mai presents, the lack of upkeep of the compound has been a huge obstacle to the realisation of the market's potential. What is extremely disconcerting is the poor sanitation in the compound and the unsightly environment that is evident from the entrance. Pikitup boldly states that waste collection and disposal are its core mandate, which should include this part of town. On its website, the company's pledge to keep 'the City clean, and preserving an attractive and hygienic environment for all residents, and visitors alike'[38] does not apply to Kwa Mai Mai, as evidenced in the pile of uncollected garbage inside the entrance to the compound. It is clear from the Twitter post that the traders at Kwa Mai Mai were justified in seeking an alternative to the management of their market, including taking over the JPC's office.

Shocked by the Twitter message, but not surprised, I (not for the first time) sent a scathing message to the Mayor, threatening to take the City Council to the Human Rights Commission and the Constitutional Court over the manner in which it was treating the residents of Kwa Mai Mai and allowing their environment to rot. Councillor Geoff Makhubo kindly responded and referred me to the Acting CEO of the JPC, Mr Ruby Mathang, who the Mayor said had been alerted to the conditions at Kwa Mai Mai.

## *Appeal to the Mayor of Johannesburg*

During the course of my research for this book, I was shocked by the clear abuse of power by the property company. These traders had come from the margins of society, arriving in Johannesburg as reluctant migrant workers and finding themselves relegated to the men's hostels. Reacting to this situation, I sent the following message to the Mayor of Johannesburg, the late Councillor Geoff Makhubo, on 24 March 2021:

Cde Geoff –

This is Cde Sipho Sithole. I am reaching out to you, as a last resort, to seek your intervention in an escalating crisis. For the past three years I have been doing research on Kwa Mai Mai for a book I will be publishing, called *Below the Radar: The Invincible Economy of Kwa Mai Mai* [the original proposed title of this book] as well as a documentary.

What the Joburg Property Company is doing there is both a gross injustice and inhuman. This will end up as the proverbial egg on the City Council's face.

I know that the residents of Kwa Mai Mai delivered a petition to you and you instructed Cde Justice to look into the matter. A follow-up meeting was promised with your office but this has not happened. The place is seriously neglected; sometimes garbage is not collected for a week or more. There are sections of Kwa Mai Mai that have not had electricity for more than a year. This is supposed to be a tourist attraction but has turned into something that even the residents who have been there for more than 40 years cannot recognise.

The residents ended up chasing the JPC official out of his office in the compound, took the key and gave it to the traders' committee so it could handle their affairs. The committee has been accused of committing a crime and has been harassed by the Johannesburg Metro Police Department for the past three weeks.

The JPC has waged war against the chair of the traders' committee at Kwa Mai Mai and has even opened a case of malicious damage to property. He was locked up today at Jeppe Police Station for an offence that we all know is a smokescreen.

I have done a great deal of research on how the Joburg City Council bought the original Kwa Mai Mai compound, when the Jubilee and Salisbury mining companies went under before the First World War, and how the compound was later moved to the new site.

I have reached out to Cde Mpho Moerane and Cde Justice Ngalonkulu, but to no avail. As the ruling party, we need to be more caring and concerned, especially about how hostel dwellers have suffered indignation at the hands of the previous regime. I don't want my book and documentary to end up as an exposé on how the City has ignored this place. I am appealing to you, as the Mayor and my comrade, to intervene. We need to fix this before it reaches a point of no return. We can regain control of the situation. Please call me back.

## *Meeting with the Office of the Mayor*

At long last, Mayor Makhubo instructed officials from his office to attend to the matter. On 30 March 2021, I attended a meeting with officials from the Office of the Mayor and the JPC. The meeting was attended by Sizeka Tshabalala (Acting Executive Manager at the JPC), Councillor Zondo (Ward 61, Inner City, Johannesburg), Simphiwe Ngejane (Executive Manager, Informal Trading at the JPC), Lipson Malate (Service Delivery Unit in the Office of the Mayor), Lwando Sibeko (Executive Secretary, Service Delivery Unit in the Office of the Mayor), Mbulelo Ruda (Chief of Staff in the Office of the Mayor), Justice Ngalonkulu (Director, Service Delivery Unit in the Office of the Mayor) and Ruby Mathang (Acting CEO of the JPC and Advisor to the Mayor on economic issues).

It was chaired by Mbulelo Ruda, who confirmed that the meeting was the result of an instruction from the Executive Mayor following my complaint regarding the quality of management at Kwa Mai Mai, particularly in connection with service delivery issues and how the City Councilwas hampering the Kwa Mai Mai operation. What was notable was that Ruda made specific reference to what was preventing the City Council from doing what it was supposed to be doing at Kwa Mai Mai. I was interested in where this would take the meeting.

As expected, Sizeka Tshabalala, the Acting Executive at the JPC, kickstarted the meeting. Tshabalala first pointed out that the facility at Kwa Mai Mai is occupied by traders who have no signed leases, which has affected the management and service delivery at Kwa Mai Mai. She added that the allocation of trader shops is done by the Department of Economic Development in the City Council; the JPC only comes in to verify whether the traders have the necessary permission to be in the facility and whether the right person with the right permit is occupying a particular shop. Tshabalala specifically raised the issue that for a number of years traders have operated without the necessary permit and have also lived in the facility with their families, in contravention of the city's by-laws.

Compounding the problem, according to Tshabalala, were the vehicles parked in the facility whose owners could not be traced. In addition, a certain section of the facility, which used to be a beer hall in Kwa Mai Mai's heyday, had been converted into an early childhood education centre without the necessary permit. Tshabalala also called attention to the lack of electricity in various parts of the facility, which required urgent attention by the JPC and which Councilor Zondo had also raised with the property company, regarding the unsatisfactory state of the facility.

Tshabalala went on to discuss some of the infrastructural challenges, such as the absence of a storm water drainage system and insufficient public ablution facilities, which required attention from the Housing Department. Tshabalala then focused on the crux of the matter: the tension between the JPC and the traders' committee at Kwa Mai Mai. She said that Councillor Zondo had alerted the JPC that one Kwa Mai Mai resident had, without permission, occupied an office in the compound and that the matter required the attention of the metro police in terms of its law-enforcement duties. The fact that it had become a legal matter was the result of the action taken by the metro police, which had led to the arrest of Malibongwe Sithole. As previously mentioned, the community and the traders at Kwa Mai Mai had resolved to chase away the JPC official, Mr Zakwe, with Sithole promptly occupying his office and taking over the job of dealing with the day-to-day matters affecting the traders.

The JPC contended that one of the challenges of ensuring the proper upkeep of the facility and efficient service delivery was that there was now an informal settlement at Kwa Mai Mai. The informal settlement had created a power overload because of illegal electricity connections. Simphiwe Ngejane also highlighted the strained internal dynamics between the traders, with opposing structures wanting to manage and lead the facility.

Councillor Zondo acknowledged the JPC officials' input, but stressed in the meeting that the Kwa Mai Mai community had put in a request for the separation of the trading and residential areas. He explained that the Kwa Mai Mai community did not want to live in the place in which they traded and would prefer to be moved to an alternative residential area, while keeping Kwa Mai Mai strictly as a trade zone. Councillor Zondo also admitted that the place had been poorly maintained and that some areas were falling apart. This had prompted the JPC to appoint a service provider to fix up the precinct, except that the community liaison officer did not come from within the Kwa Mai Mai community, which the traders had not taken to kindly. This had then precipitated the appointment of Malibongwe Sithole, the interim chair of the traders' committee, to oversee the execution of the maintenance project. Councillor Zondo then alleged that the involvement of the interim committee had created many problems for the management and administration of Kwa Mai Mai, such as Sithole having instructed the traders not to pay rent for the shops they occupied and having told those trading in the *shisanyama* area to pay the traders' committee directly. The creation of new rules by the interim chairperson was a source of major frustration for Councillor Zondo.

It was clear from this meeting that the problems at Kwa Mai Mai were multifaceted: a facility that needed serious maintenance; illegal electricity connections; illegally parked vehicles; an informal settlement with all its attendant challenges; a committee that did not see eye to eye with the *induna* and his *isigungu;* a fractious relationship between the traders' committee, the City Council and the JPC; traders not paying rent; and so on. Councillor Zondo then dropped a bombshell, boldly stating that the JPC was not the problem at Kwa Mai Mai: the biggest stumbling block to the facility's development was the committee led by Malibongwe Sithole, who did not even own a shop at Kwa Mai Mai and yet was dictating the facility's agenda. Zondo said that the traders wanted the City Council to find them alternative accommodation, but that they were no longer paying rent under their shop leases, as per Sithole's instruction. According to Zondo, moreover, the JPC was failing to maintain the facility because the traders' committee interfered every time the property company came to fix a particular problem.

Clearly, as far as the City Council and the JPC were concerned, the traders' committee was the problem. Councillor Zondo went so far as to say that the committee should be dissolved, which would enable the JPC to proceed to fix the problems at Kwa Mai Mai. What the JPC and Councillor Zondo failed to address, though, were the reasons why the Kwa Mai Mai traders were refusing to pay rent. The JPC had proposed a 12-month renewal of traders' leases. However, the traders had rejected this proposal outright and resolved to stop paying rent until their grievances had been addressed. The Kwa Mai Mai traders also demanded that the JPC transfer ownership of the stalls to them in the form of sectional title deeds, arguing that their businesses had been in their families for seven decades, passed down from generation to generation.

The traders did not believe that they should be compelled to pay rent to the JPC in the light of the poor infrastructure and maintenance standards at the property, particularly the shared communal toilets, the poor drainage system, the unbearable working conditions in the stalls and poor lighting throughout the facility. The fact that a large part of the market had not had electricity for almost a year was yet another reason why the community at Kwa Mai Mai did not want to continue under the management of the JPC; instead, they preferred to revert to being managed by the City of Johannesburg.

However, both the Acting Executive Manager, Sizeka Tshabalala, and Councillor Zondo had legitimate frustrations, such as the cluttering up of the facility with ownerless vehicles, illegal electricity connections, informal residents occupying a building that had been earmarked for the Kwa Mai Mai trading community, and the fact that a trade market should not double up as a place of residence. The meeting ended well, though, with a clear programme of action that would see all stakeholders getting involved in removing obstacles to service delivery and committing to restoring the dignity of the hostel dwellers who had faced various forms of marginalisation over many years.

True to the commitments expressed at the meeting, officials from the Office of the Mayor, together with representatives from various entities under the control of the city, including the JPC, City Power, Pikitup, the Department of Social Development and the Johannesburg Metropolitan Police Department (JMPD), conducted a site inspection on 8 April 2021, which I attended. Justice Ngalongkulu and Mbulelo Ruda from the Office of the Mayor and the Acting CEO of the JPC and some colleagues were also there.

It was obvious to the Office of the Mayor that Kwa Mai Mai needed urgent attention, with priorities including the regularisation of trading activities, which had not been the focus when Kwa Mai Mai started up many years before. Among the well-established operations were the panel beating business, which had been around for decades, and the informal early childhood education facility, which now occupied the former beer hall. It was clear that the Office of the Mayor, which had political oversight, saw issues differently from the administrative officials from the various entities. The latter appeared to be taking a hard line over what they perceived to be contraventions of city by-laws. The attitude of the Office of the Mayor was more along the lines of: 'Well, these are our people; they are here now, and we might as well regularise their presence and operations.'

Unfortunately, Mayor Geoff Makhubo died of Covid-19 complications on 9 July 2021. The officials from the various entities now had to deal with another mayor, Councillor Jolidee Matongo, who may well have had other priorities before his tragic death in a car accident on 18 September 2021.

## *My earlier attempts*

Before Councillor Mpho Moerane became a caretaker mayor (after the death of Councillor Jolidee Matongo) in the period leading up to November 2021, I had made contact with him from as early as 20 March 2020. In his role as MMC responsible for infrastructure development, I alerted Councillor Moerane to the unfolding events at Kwa Mai Mai and warned him that the place was not being taken care of and had become dilapidated. On 29 September 2020, I followed up with another message to Councillor Moerane, and sent two further messages on 13 October 2020 and 26 October 2020.

On 27 October 2020, the traders convened a meeting about the situation at Kwa Mai Mai and the indignity that they were suffering at the hands of the JPC. The following issues were highlighted:

- The JPC does not respect the community of Kwa Mai Mai.
- Issues must now be taken straight to the Mayor.
- *Kunjenje Kwa Mai Mai, induna nebandla layo* (the situation at Kwa Mai Mai has been caused by the *induna* and his council).
- Kwa Mai Mai *kusazodutushulwana* (soon there is going to be a blood bath at Kwa Mai Mai).
- The toilets are dirty, and people have to queue to use them.
- There are traffic jams inside the premises, which would be a serious impediment if someone experienced a medical problem and needed emergency rescue.
- Taxis are becoming a problem at the entrance.
- The place is not suitable for human habitation.

One trader complained that one of the trading blocks had not had electricity for eight months, and that this was affecting eight shops.

Then, on 28 October 2020, I sent the following message to Councillor Moerane:

> Comrade Mpho —
>
> Call me when you get a chance. Big shit is about to hit Kwa Mai Mai. The outcome of the meeting I attended today is going to land right in the Office of the Mayor. It is not going to be good. You need

to give me an ear before it gets out of hand. There is a lot going on there between the Johannesburg Property Company, the traders and *abahlali* Kwa Mai Mai, the committee elected by the community of Kwa Mai Mai, *isigungu seNduna neqembu lakhe*.

Having researched what's going on there, I feel I owe it to you as comrades [*sic*] to manage that situation before it gets worse. I am now prepared to meet you even in the evening to really give you a heads up. Your department is responsible for Kwa Mai Mai in as far as the environment and infrastructure are concerned; so is Economic Development. Konakele and I think you must press that lid down before it explodes. I also don't want to expose what I am discovering there without getting to know what the City is planning in terms of developing and preserving that place. Give me an ear please.

Councillor Moerane eventually responded on 30 October 2020, with the message: 'Morning, Cde Sipho, I will give you a call. But it looks like JPC is responsible for Kwa Mai Mai, EISD [Environment and Infrastructure Services Department] is not responsible, but I will still call you.' I responded: 'Yes, JPC is responsible but it's a big mess.'

On the same day, 30 October 2020 (30 days after the new Mayor assumed office), I sent a final alert to Councillor Moerane:

There is a planned march to the Mayor's Office in November, as per the resolution of the meeting I was observing. Kwa Mai Mai was bought by the Johannesburg City Council around 1918 from the Jubilee Gold Mining Company after it went under, following the Second World War. The City wanted to accommodate two day-time job seekers who needed a place to stay after completing a piece job. The place was different from the other hostels, as we know them, because it also had a bazaar (market), which it still has today. The City later moved Kwa Mai Mai to its current site in the 1940s and it has been economically vibrant since then. But there is a huge disconnect between the traders and the City; the biggest culprit is the JPC.

I really would like to brief you, Cde Geoff, so that we are seen to be caring for the semi-formal economy in which the marginalised communities in the City operate. If the Chinese and the Indians can

have such big and successful businesses in the city, we cannot fail
our people. Kwa Mai Mai is an African market, and we must help it
to be just that.

My interventions, which I sent to the Office of the Mayor and to every
official who could help to defuse the growing tensions, were designed
to persuade the City Council to put its energies into revitalising the
only black-owned – but fast-deteriorating – trade market in the heart of
Johannesburg. Moreover, I sent them because it was becoming very clear
that the City Council did not regard the Kwa Mai Mai trade market and
hostel as a strategic pillar for the preservation and promotion of African
culture or a cultural drawcard for local and international visitors. To the
City Council, Kwa Mai Mai was just another hostel – a Zulu hostel full
of illiterates who were nothing but a headache to the officials responsible
for its upkeep and marketing.

By early October 2021, Councillor Mpho Moerane had been
installed as the caretaker mayor of the City of Johannesburg. He was in
office from 1 October 2021 to 22 November 2021, his continued tenure
dependent on the outcome of the local government elections. The ANC
did not garner enough votes to retain the City Council, which it lost
to the Democratic Alliance (DA). Sadly, Councillor Moerane died in a
tragic car accident in May 2022.

## *The Human Rights Commission intervenes*

Unfortunately, with a legal case still hanging over the head of
Malibongwe Sithole, the chair of the Kwa Mai Mai traders' committee,
the committee decided to approach the Human Rights Commission to
alert them to what it believed had been a violation of human rights and
abuse of power by the City Council – and by the JPC in particular. The
Human Rights Commission scheduled a meeting with the committee for
2 June 2021 in the hall at Kwa Mai Mai, which I also attended. The issues
raised were no different from those detailed in the petition dispatched
to the mayor on 23 November 2020. Again, the committee highlighted
the inhumane conditions in which the residents–cum–traders at
Kwa Mai Mai were forced to live and the indignation they had suffered
at the hands of the JPC.

Because a meeting invitation had not been extended to the *induna* and his *isigungu* – who nevertheless decided to join the meeting halfway through – the Human Rights Commission scheduled a follow-up meeting on 14 June 2021 in the Kwa Mai Mai market. That meeting was also attended by the JPC, who eventually had to be asked to leave the meeting as the Commission felt that it was proper that a separate meeting be held with the JPC before all the parties gathered for one consolidated meeting. Echoing the sentiments of the traders' committee, the *induna* and his *isigungu* were also of the view that the JPC was failing in its duty to address the problems at Kwa Mai Mai (including a lack of visible security, no control over who entered and exited the precinct, and general filth and degradation) and to improve the conditions under which the traders conducted their business.

The meeting also raised concerns about perceived mismanagement of maintenance contracts for the refurbishment of the Kwa Mai Mai hostel and bazaar in 2017, with some work having been abandoned in the middle of a project. In this regard, the meeting looked to the Human Rights Commission to demand that the JPC submit a more detailed report on the 2017 project, which had apparently not been completed. The meeting ended with the Commission promising follow-up discussions after they had heard the JPC's side of the story.

During my interactions with the officials from the Office of the Mayor and the Acting CEO of the JPC, Ruby Mathang, I pointed out that the ongoing so-called criminal case against the chairperson of the traders' committee was not helping to reduce the tensions between the Kwa Mai Mai community, the City Council and the JPC. On several occasions, I asked them to drop the charges and resolve the impasse politically and not through the courts. My requests fell on deaf ears as Sithole continued to appear in court on several occasions, with his last appearance postponed to 24 August 2021.

At the time of writing this book, there had been no visible intervention by the City Council, the JPC or even the Human Rights Commission, save for their attending meetings. What has become clear is that City Council officials have an urban outlook and do not appreciate or understand what life is like for those living in hostels or, indeed, what motivates them. Because they remain 'double-rooted' (Bank et al. 2020) by retaining their connection to their rural homes, village migrants are still regarded by City Council officials as 'birds of passage' (Wacquant 2008), who are in the city just to generate sufficient resources for their families and dependants back home. Therefore, where they stay in the city does not warrant finding a permanent solution.

# Nine
# Betrayed, but not defeated

Visitors and tourists come to a country because they want to interact, discover and learn. Some are keen to see what products and services the country and its cities and towns have to offer, or even to experience some of its intangible cultural attractions. Smart countries understand that for cities and towns to thrive, they should have a vibrant culture and a creative environment, which in turn gives rise to a sustainable and inclusive economy.

All countries have their own, distinctive cultural heritage, and those that have provided outlets for cultural beliefs, traditions and customs to find commercial expression are likely to flourish economically and socially. A culture–led economy is one in which the preservation of culture is at the heart of urban planning and design. Culture is homegrown and authentic; it is not borrowed. If it is not preserved and nurtured, people's history and identity are slowly erased. Yet putting culture on display is not simply about showbiz and entertainment; it is about reaching into the near and distant past and retrieving memories, insights, experiences, attitudes and values – which together give a country (or a city) its rich, colourful and unique identity. It is also about keeping culture alive by ensuring that artists and other creative people have the opportunity to grow in their profession, so that they can (with a few modern twists and turns) take well-entrenched and cherished beliefs and traditions into the future.

There is no shortage of beautiful cities in the world where history and culture are visible on every street and building and are evident in how people dress, speak and behave. The French Quarter in New Orleans, the Latin Quarter in Paris, Covent Garden in London and Soho in New York are artistically and culturally sublime and are home to a fascinating cross-section of people. Some cities, such as Melbourne and Edinburgh, have boldly declared themselves to be cultural capitals. These and many other cities have successfully integrated residential areas with commercial districts, encouraging a rich interplay of economic and leisure activities, which is the perfect spawning ground for innovation and limitless creative expression.

When someone asks: 'What makes a great city?', the answer should invariably be: one that mobilises and harnesses the creative spirit of the city's planners, administrators, architects, businesses and residents, while also recognising and celebrating arts, culture and tradition as a steady source of tourism-related revenue. Great cities are those in which creative industries are an integral part of the total economy, providing an important foundation for a wide range of economic sectors, not just tourism. A culturally rich economy (evidenced in well-run and well-maintained museums, galleries, theatres, monuments, libraries, performing arts centres and cultural markets) is a happy, connected and forward-looking economy.

Culture-led cities do not happen by accident. They are the result of clearly defined and well-implemented strategies that weave together living, working and entertainment spaces into a vibrant, integrated whole. Johannesburg has the potential to become that kind of city, where culture and heritage converge in new and interesting ways, where people are free to celebrate the city's historical high points and remember its low points, which will always remain an important part of the story. African arts and culture are known and valued in different parts of the world, but much more needs to be done to put them on the world stage. This starts with creating a local environment in which those whose work involves creative entrepreneurship are able to fully utilise their talents and skills, and develop thriving, sustainable businesses.

The various City Council entities that, with their differentiated resources and responsibilities, are entrusted with the task of making

Johannesburg work have the collective capacity to create a cultural hub where residents can enjoy a good quality of life and productive livelihoods. However, for this to happen, the City Council must first acknowledge that there are certain non-negotiables that must be in place, which other cities around the world have worked hard to implement and sustain. At the top of the list of these non-negotiables are the provision of viable and appropriate infrastructure and services, and a safe and secure environment that enables entrepreneurs to reach and confidently trade with clients who are less interested in chain stores and more interested in unique product and service offerings whose workmanship and quality speak for themselves.

Kwa Mai Mai has the ingredients and the drive to become an admired cultural hub for the City of Johannesburg and South Africa as a whole. The city already has vibrant cultural precincts, such as Newtown, Braamfontein, Constitution Hill, Maboneng and Melville; and other, more distant, attractions such as Vilakazi Street in Soweto. Including Kwa Mai Mai in this line-up should be a no-brainer.

Kwa Mai Mai is located in City and Suburban, a suburb established in 1896 and named after the original City and Suburban mine. The suburb, which is both a residential and business area, has a population of almost 3 000 people. It is sandwiched between Marshalltown on the west and Jeppestown on the east, on what was once farmland before the discovery of gold on the Witwatersrand. Residents and small businesses and retailers rely on the municipality to provide the necessary infrastructure and services to enable them to live and work in the area.

However, despite the municipality's grand growth and development plans and strategies, which promise an inclusive and productive city, the City and Suburban area (and therefore Kwa Mai Mai) does not appear to be on the city's radar. There seems to be a glaring lack of political will on the part of City Council officials not only to provide basic services to the suburb's residents and businesses but also to earmark Kwa Mai Mai for special attention and support, given its potential to become an important economic driver for the city. Far from ensuring that Kwa Mai Mai becomes a sought-after, inner-city gem, the authorities appear to see it as being low down on the priority list – despite their claims to the contrary.

## Strategy … what strategy?

The City of Johannesburg's Strategy 2040 has five strategic deliverables: (1) a well-governed city; (2) a clean and safe city; (3) a sustainable city; (4) a productive city; and (5) an inclusive city. Moreover, its Integrated Development Plan 2020/21 (an area-based management framework and partnership initiative) states that the City Council's vision is:

> A well-governed, transformed, safe, clean and sustainable inner city of Johannesburg, which offers high-quality, sustainable services; supports vibrant economic activity; and provides a welcoming place for all residents, migrants, commuters, workers, traders, investors and tourists. [39]

In a constitutional democracy, there is no discrimination (where economic opportunity and service delivery are concerned) between the 'haves' (the rich) and the 'have-nots' (the poor) or between groups of people on the basis of colour, ethnicity or religion. The South African Constitution places the responsibility for ensuring that all citizens have access to basic services that meet their daily needs with cities or municipalities. Whether people are sophisticated or otherwise, literate or illiterate, hostel dwellers or residents of up-market estates, business tycoons or emerging entrepreneurs, South Africans have the right to expect the government to provide basic services in the form of water, electricity, refuse removal, sewerage management, street lighting, storm water drainage, road maintenance, parks and recreation facilities, health services and housing support.

Citizens also have a civic duty to engage municipalities on service delivery issues. They should be able to do this through various structures and forums that have been established either through a systematic, democratic process or more organically, thus ensuring that decision-making takes place following proper consultation and information-sharing. At the local government level, for example, there are ward committees and planning forums where citizens should be able to express their views about issues that affect their neighbourhoods.

Ensuring that the objectives of the City Council's Strategy 2040 are met requires action (and actionable plans), facilitated by well-functioning, supportive infrastructure and funding support, especially for small and/or marginalised businesses such as those in Kwa Mai Mai. This will go a long way towards alleviating widespread poverty and unemployment. Often, all that is needed is to build on what is already there – helping existing enterprises to grow and become sources of employment, decent lives and livelihoods, in keeping with people's right to dignity and social mobility.

The trouble with visions and strategic plans and initiatives is that they often look good on paper but are difficult to implement because of capacity and financial constraints, among other reasons. The failure to bring these plans and initiatives to fruition is felt most acutely by those who, living on the margins, are most in need of government support. The government's expressed commitment to create a vibrant, well-resourced and inclusive city appears to fly in the face of what many of Johannesburg's residents experience on the ground. Indeed, the sharp economic and social divide (the result of the uneven allocation of resources) is glaringly apparent in this 'City of Gold'.

Service delivery (or the lack of it) is at the heart of the problem. The situation was aptly captured in a 2002 blog titled 'South Africa: What does "service delivery" really mean?' Its message was that government could not be relied upon to deliver and maintain services, thus greatly inconveniencing, and even endangering, whole communities.[40] Unhappiness over the state of service delivery in many of South Africa's cities (though people's experiences differ, depending on the area) has become a new national anthem and has been expressed in all sorts of ways – from organised marches to the offices of local authorities and petitions aimed at those who walk the corridors of power, to violent protests and widespread destruction of infrastructure and other property. Many choose to be less demonstrative, but the common refrain in communities across the country is that basic service delivery leaves much to be desired; and has to be fixed in a non-discriminatory manner.

The Kwa Mai Mai community has been on the receiving end of service delivery problems for some time, and things are getting worse. The City Council acknowledges that the precinct needs regular maintenance of its infrastructure, efficient service delivery and periodic upgrades to facilities if it is to present an attractive value proposition to traders and visitors alike. However, the City Council's ongoing neglect and failure to create a clean and attractive environment is a serious indictment of the Johannesburg municipality and its ability to follow through on its plans and commitments.

The City Council claims that the Kwa Mai Mai market forms part of Johannesburg's rehabilitation programme, which is directed at attracting more tourists to the area. However, City Council officials appear to be largely oblivious of, or unconcerned about, the real potential of Kwa Mai Mai as a cultural hub and tourist magnet which, ironically, could help to solve some of the pressing socio-economic challenges in that part of the city. Moreover, some of the existing, loyal visitors are deterred by the precinct's deteriorating aesthetics and security standards. What complicates the situation is that Kwa Mai Mai is both a trade zone and a human settlement, which means that its residents cannot, at the end of their working day, go home to a better-serviced suburb elsewhere in the city.

There are several entities that are responsible for municipal service delivery, including Pikitup, City Power, the Department of Economic Development, the Department of Tourism, the Gauteng Tourism Authority, the Johannesburg Metropolitan Police Department (JMPD), the Johannesburg Property Company (JPC) and the Johannesburg Roads Agency (JRA). Each has a special role to play, and together they should be providing a seamless, enjoyable experience to the city's residents. However, traders and residents of Kwa Mai Mai report ongoing lapses in the performance of several of these entities. There is no evidence that the City Council is using all the resources at its disposal or working with its stakeholders to provide an environment that would put Kwa Mai Mai, and the surrounding City and Suburban district, on the tourism and investment maps.

In addition to its commitment to providing shelter for the indigent, the municipality has identified housing as one of its strategic priorities and anchors in its drive to create sustainable human settlements. In this regard, the City of Johannesburg has identified 'corridors' aimed at reversing apartheid spatial planning, which will see the creation of mixed-income, rental and quality (higher-density) developments with improved access to economic and social amenities as well as the rejuvenation of hostels. This will help to address the serious gaps in the market for these types of accommodation. Likewise, the provision of basic services and infrastructure to these new developments, it is claimed, will not discriminate according to type of settlement, whether formal or less formal.

## On the defensive

Hostel redevelopment has been identified as a key priority area in terms of the City Council's human settlements mandate. Council officials acknowledge that the redevelopment of hostels has faced significant obstacles, but they attribute the lack of progress to criminal activity in the hostels themselves. Another problem, they say, is that hostels are occupied by large numbers of people who stay there illegally or informally (under the radar). The combination of crime, illegal occupation and overcrowding, the Council officials argue, has made it difficult for them to access hostels and conduct proper assessments of service delivery needs and gaps. The City Council has proposed the establishment of an inter-ministerial security task team, which will report to the Office of the Mayor, whose function will be to address problems of criminality at the hostels as an important precursor to the formulation of appropriate solutions.

Attempting to blame crime for the City Council's failure to deliver basic services to the hostels under its administration is unfortunate, to say the least. It is also fraught with administrative injustice, as it is tantamount to saying that all hostels are the same, which is clearly not true. Kwa Mai Mai is a case in point.

First, it should be stressed that the Kwa Mai Mai hostel and bazaar does not pose any risk from criminals or act as a deterrent to Council officials who may wish to access the premises, provide basic services or manage the various facilities. In fact, the JPC, which is responsible for the administration of the precinct, has a permanent office on the premises. The only impediment to attracting more visitors to Kwa Mai Mai is the deteriorating upkeep and aesthetics of the common areas in the compound. In contrast, the traders have gone out of their way to ensure that their own stalls are as clean and inviting as possible, although – because of their small size – they can sometimes look cluttered.

Second, Kwa Mai Mai is a combined trade zone-cum-hostel, with a long history of producing and selling goods and services to a culturally inclined market. It also gives visitors the opportunity to enjoy social engagement, musical entertainment, and spiritual enlightenment and healing. In other words, it has an unusually diverse range of offerings. However, the combined trade zone–residential character of the compound is not desirable, according to the Kwa Mai Mai community.

When traders were moved to the new site in the 1940s, they were forced to combine their living space with their trading space – a situation they perceive to be inhumane, particularly as the City Council has neglected to provide adequate facilities and services to make the place habitable. Residents, who now number about 500, have complained to the City Council and the JPC on numerous occasions about the undignified conditions under which they are forced to live. Besides leaking roofs (which can damage or destroy their merchandise), the absence of private ablution facilities is a huge problem. There are no individual toilets or bathing facilities in the various stalls/living quarters, which means that men, women and children have to use communal facilities in the compound. These ablution blocks (and indeed the stalls/living quarters) were not originally built for women or children, but women and children have been forced to accept these facilities, with associated concerns for their comfort and security. Whether a trade zone and a hostel should, in fact, coexist is a contentious issue.

## Sending the right message

The City of Johannesburg's Economic Growth Strategy (EGS) claims to be aligned with the municipality's mission of creating an enabling economic environment and facilitating economic growth, with job creation as its core objective. Central to this mission and objective is a thriving trading environment. While I was conducting research at Kwa Mai Mai for this book, however, I found no evidence that City Council officials understood why the hostel and market exist or knew Kwa Mai Mai's early and later history. Even in the its Integrated Development Plan, there is no mention of Kwa Mai Mai having been earmarked, long ago, as a trade zone, let alone one that thrives on culture and tradition and is an important tourist destination.

The responsibility for promoting the trade zone – which one would think would fall within the purview of the Department of Economic Development (DED) as one of its sectoral, community-based projects – appears to have fallen to the traders themselves. This is an indictment of a City Council that prides itself on being caring. The DED, for example, should have taken steps to provide additional training to Kwa Mai Mai traders to enable them to expand their markets or access new ones, an aspect that should underpin any serious growth and development strategy. Although the DED regards tourism promotion as part of its contribution to developing and supporting micro, small and medium enterprises, it has neither identified Kwa Mai Mai as a focal point for any of its promotional strategies nor ensured that the compound features on online trade and consumer portals.

Similarly, the Gauteng Tourism Authority appears to have overlooked the historical and cultural significance of the compound, dating back to the early 20th century, while also ignoring its potential to become a sought-after cultural corridor for tourists and other visitors. This entity is responsible for the promotion of entrepreneurship, innovation, enterprise growth and competitiveness, regarded as critical for growing the economy and creating jobs in the city. Yet it makes little reference to Kwa Mai Mai, other than to say that it is a place of traditional medicine and healing. The following appears on the tourism authority's website:

> Kwa Mai Mai Market is a traditional South African medicine market located in Johannesburg's central business district. One of the oldest traditional markets in the city, here you'll find dozens of stalls run by African traditional healers who have dedicated themselves to healing the sick. It's one of the best places to visit in Johannesburg, if you're looking for that genuine, traditional African tourist experience.

This limited and misleading description is accompanied by a photo of the entrance to the compound, with the name 'Kwa Mai Mai' appearing on the red brick wall above the steel gates. Noticeable by its absence is an informative photo collection, showcasing the various cultural goods and services that the market has to offer.

Why would a tourist from Italy, Japan or Sweden bother to visit a place where, according to the Gauteng Tourism Authority, '…you'll meet Sangomas who use real animal parts to cure ailments and read your fortune…'? Similarly, how tempted would an Irish visitor be to visit MaNsimbi or Mkhulu Mamba for a love potion to lure back a fiancé who has run off with another lover?

This is a clear sign of a City Council, with its various departments and agencies, being far removed from what communities on the margins of society are doing to reimagine economic opportunities and survive in the urban jungle. Do informal traders not matter? Do they not perhaps have treasures that would appeal to those looking for 'that genuine, traditional African tourist experience'?

Despite the lack of – or at best half-hearted – support from the City of Johannesburg, members of the Kwa Mai Mai community have nevertheless displayed plenty of resilience and a resolve to grow their businesses and customer bases. They owe it to themselves, to their forebears and to future generations to keep their customs and tradition alive.

Kwa Mai Mai may have been betrayed but it has by no means been defeated.

# Ten
# Formalising the informal?

Johannesburg is the second-largest city in Africa, with more than 6 million people calling this large and bustling metropolis home. 'Joburg' or 'Jozi', as some people affectionately call it, offers visitors experiences as unique and as diverse as is the city itself. Whether you are on business, in search of a cultural treat or an adrenaline rush, or you simply want to relax and unwind for a few days, Johannesburg has everything a visitor could wish for, and more. Johannesburg is a transit city, a destination city, a place to live and a place to work. It is also an immigrant city, with many of its residents hailing from other provinces in South Africa or elsewhere in the continent and the world.

With its diverse cultures and creative offerings, the city has the potential to become a real magnet for business people and tourists, but in pursuing this vision a difficult road lies ahead. The city is full of hope, disappointments, dreams and despair. It is rich in opportunity, but only if enough people dare to dream and keep the possibilities alive. It buzzes with an eclectic mix of people with talent and good ideas, but it is vulnerable to short-sightedness, bureaucracy and greed. There is so much latent talent in the city – particularly in the creative industries (cultural performers, designers, craftspeople, artists, musicians, event planners and wellness practitioners) – but government's attention is often elsewhere. So much energy, both in government and in society at large, goes into trying to get a bigger slice of the pie. But if everyone focused instead on creating a bigger pie, the individual pieces would take care of themselves.

Johannesburg is home to Kwa Mai Mai – a hostel, a small business hub, a market, a training ground, a source of spiritual guidance and a place of worship, all rolled into one. Its long history and the colourful personalities who have written its story make Kwa Mai Mai a truly unique entity, one that leaves an indelible mark on the minds of those who visit the place and take the time to absorb its many sights and sounds. At times shocking, at times inspiring, Kwa Mai Mai shows that effort and imagination can be lethal weapons in the face of displacement, uncertainty and loss.

The inner city of Johannesburg is not for the faint-hearted, given its tough exterior and proliferation of opportunists and thugs. It lacks the order and decorum of the suburbs, and is unfailingly unpredictable. Danger and uncertainty are always in the air, and courage is essential. But it is alive. And where there is life, there are opportunities for growth and renewal. Kwa Mai Mai, situated in downtown Johannesburg, is a community of survivors – not just because they have learned to navigate the dangers on the streets and in the alleyways but also because they are still holding their own and looking confidently to the future after years of personal and professional hardship.

A residential, business and semi-industrial district, the inner city throbs with activity, thanks to its commercial disposition, vibrancy and sense of urgency. At the centre of it all are its cultural agency and the entrepreneurial spirit of its many inhabitants. The never-say-die attitude, the will and determination to make it – come what may – put pressure on City Council officials to create a space that facilitates working, living and playing. The inner city is also an important transportation hub that fans out in different directions to innumerable destinations, both near and far. Though much of the infrastructure is old and worn, there are some wonderful historical buildings that City Council officials have recognised as being worth preserving, notwithstanding the fact that there seems to be no clear plan on how this should be done. Finally, the inner city remains an important location for many informal business operators to ply their trade, with many of them living a hand-to-mouth existence.

## Small businesses in a big city

The question must be posed: What does the City Council do about those who are operating on the fringes of society and economic opportunity – those who are desperately calling out for economic inclusion and an environment in which they are free to hustle in pursuit of the dreams that brought them here in the first place? What does the City Council do about the people of Kwa Mai Mai?

The answer lies in whether or not City and Suburban, which is Kwa Mai Mai's locale, forms part of the City Council's oversight function. If it does, one would expect various stakeholders from government, the private sector and civil society to be actively involved in delivering what is best for businesses and residents in the area. However, it does not appear that the City Council has any particular interest in this part of town, much less a transformation roadmap.

Chapter 8 highlighted that Kwa Mai Mai residents and traders are crying out for proper operational and financial oversight from the City Council, for responsible and committed spatial planning, for a roadmap for the rejuvenation of their compound, and for swift action – all the things that are promised in the Integrated Development Plan. The basis of their cries is the desire to improve the image of the area so that they can ply their respective trades in comfort and confidence. This will snowball into more sustainable and lucrative business opportunities, and lift the tone of the neighbourhood. In such a scenario, everyone wins.

As things currently stand, the Kwa Mai Mai community are being deprived of that yearned-for sense of pride in their city. Yet they have not allowed their hopes to die. Though Kwa Mai Mai as a cultural centre is hamstrung, it still has great potential. Examples from around the world should teach us (and City Council officials) that culture can be a bright beacon leading an economy's growth and development efforts. What Kwa Mai Mai has going for it (apart from its appealing diversity of product and service offerings) is that it is a *self-driven* cultural community, hell-bent on making ends meet with the limited resources it has at its disposal. Kwa Mai Mai's competitive edge is that it has taken its collective cultural heritage (generational knowledge, beliefs, customs and skills) and commercialised it in different ways, but without yielding to mass production.

The fusion of people and activities in a relatively confined space can pose significant challenges to city managers and planners. Charman et al. (2020) posit that spatial ordering is particularly complex in areas faced with a 'multiplicity of logics'. For example, it may be desirable to encourage economic activity but not to the extent that it leads to unfettered competition, which can have many adverse consequences. What makes Kwa Mai Mai a spatial development challenge is that its community of micro enterprises would normally occupy about a kilometre radius, either in separate stalls or clusters of stalls. However, Kwa Mai Mai's traders are housed under one roof in an area measuring less than $200\,m^2$. In addition, the diversity of product and service offerings (such as fruit and vegetables, wood products, upholstery services, panel beating, childcare, hair care, herbal medicine and traditional healing) calls for specific infrastructure and facilities for the different shops. Street-side markets also have a broader reach than it does.

Just as the township economy is built on the social relations of the community it serves, Kwa Mai Mai is anchored on its long-established 'social connections' (Watson 2009), which can be traced back many years, often to previous generations. Kwa Mai Mai has become a space for social interaction and intercultural engagement, particularly among Zulu migrants (acting as traders) and urban Zulus (as consumers). Watson (2009:120) refers to this interaction between the two Zulu groups as 'rubbing along', a setting where urban Zulus, in particular, like to be seen with their rural counterparts. This is often an attempt by the urban Zulu to achieve 'cultural affirmation', to assuage the fear of missing out for not having grown up in a rural setting.

The concept of the city (or a section of the city) being a place where people can work, live and play emphasises the importance of a culture-led urban regeneration and development strategy. In this regard, Kwa Mai Mai is a neighbour of an established area where the privileged work, live and play in a lively juxtaposition: the Maboneng precinct. The apparently thriving economy of Maboneng is founded on four pillars: (i) a space to live, (ii) a space to work, (iii) a space to make and (iv) a space to sell. Maboneng boasts a mixture of restaurants, small venues for entertainment gigs, coffee shops, clothing boutiques, art galleries, and retail and studio space. Attracting those living downtown as well as the chic, art-loving crowd from the suburbs, the precinct is helping to bring life back to what was once a very dubious part of the city.

What is interesting about Kwa Mai Mai is that it offers almost everything that Maboneng offers, except that it lacks the aesthetics and the well-heeled clientele that Maboneng enjoys. In other words, Kwa Mai Mai is a space to live, a space to work, a space to make and a space to sell. Unlike Maboneng, however, Kwa Mai Mai is not a place where friends hang out (except for the braai area at the entrance to the market), or a place to have drinks and snacks or even dinner while enjoying some musical entertainment. Those who visit Kwa Mai Mai have a specific purpose and destination in mind; they do not come to linger or fraternise.

Research conducted at Kwa Mai Mai involving more than 50 of the traders revealed high levels of frustration among these cultural entrepreneurs, who complained that the City Council still fails to recognise their businesses as being part of its mainstream economy. Although they are self-employed and mainly run businesses that have been passed down through the generations, their goods and services meet the needs of their clients, just as clothing, pharmaceuticals and other products from retail outlets in suburban shopping malls meet the needs of shoppers who frequent such establishments. Williams (2005) concurs, saying that the informal sector should be recognised and supported as a launching pad for many entrepreneurial business ventures. As a result, national and local government need to play a more active role in legitimising and/or formalising these businesses.

There is widespread agreement and acceptance that the informal economy is here to stay. Therefore, it cannot be wished away or ignored. Even trying to formalise informal businesses may not be a good idea, apart from it being difficult to do in many cases. Studies show that the informal economy accounts for a large share of the economies of many developing and transitional countries, although less so in South Africa. Some of the comparative figures are surprising. Globally, there are hundreds of millions of poor people who operate in the informal economy, with many beyond the reach of government in terms of regulatory requirements, oversight and protection (Lewis 2016). Sometimes governments do not acknowledge their existence – perhaps as a way of absolving themselves of the obligation to provide the necessary infrastructure and support to help informal workers create sustainable livelihoods.

According to the Organisation for Economic Cooperation and Development and the International Labour Organization (OECD/ILO 2019:12), 'Informality is the norm in developing and emerging countries. Informality represents 70% of all employment in developing and emerging countries, compared with about 18% in developed countries. There is also substantial variation across regions, from 86% in Africa to around 68% in the Arab States and Asia and the Pacific, 40% in the Americas and 25% in Europe and Central Asia. Globally, 81% of all enterprises is informal.' The OECD (2007:76) adds that the informal sector accounts 'for 42% of value-added in Africa, 41% in Latin America and 35% in the transition economies of Europe and the former Soviet Union' and 'for only 13.5% of value-added in the OECD countries'.

The ILO notes that 'The informal economy absorbs workers who would otherwise be without work or income, especially in developing countries that have a large and rapidly growing labour force'.[41] The OECD (2007:76) further attests that the informal economy provides employment and income for many who have lost their jobs or cannot find work in the formal economy, adding that it includes a 'disproportionate number of women, young people and others from disadvantaged groups'. In 'The transition from the informal to the formal economy in Africa', Kiaga and Leung (2020) state that a higher propotion of women (89.7%) than men (82.7%) are found in the informal employment sector on the continent. This is a cause for concern, even for South Africa, which has a relatively small informal sector relative to other countries.


## The case for an informal economy

South Africa is one of many countries facing the challenges associated with a sizeable informal sector. Informal traders play a crucial role in producing a range of goods and services, often for their immediate communities, but they remain on the periphery of society, often unknown to the authorities and out of reach. However, it would be wrong to assume that all small businesses operating informally would want to be part of a very structured, formal economy that imposes registration, licensing and taxation requirements. In fact, such a prospect could be a serious deterrent to informal business owners, prompting them to retreat further into the shadows, far from the scrutiny of various regulating authorities. Although some informal sector workers might be swayed by the prospect of receiving pension and other benefits if they formalised their businesses, others are more interested in obtaining government support in the form of facilitated business opportunities and the opening up of distribution pipelines, without succumbing to red tape such as licensing and tax regulations, financial reporting requirements, and so on.

A trader at Kwa Mai Mai, for example, who sells traditional clothing and beads and relies on walk-ins, may not generate enough revenue to hire a bookkeeper to keep formal financial records. Yet that trader knows exactly what she earns in a month, and it is probably just enough to buy food and other necessities. Informal workers rely heavily on social networks and traditional forms of communication. Formalising their businesses and following different operating norms may disrupt the daily rhythm of the business and compromise established business relationships.

At Kwa Mai Mai, Mama uMaNsimbi is a well-established and experienced traditional healer and diviner. Her business is reliant on customers whose cultural belief system encourages them to seek solutions to their problems through divine intervention. MaNsimbi has no business with, or interest in, the government, other than that she expects her consulting room to have electricity and running water. She has no desire to formalise her business or change her work routine. She is a one-woman show, for whom the formalisation option makes little sense. If she is not in her consulting room divining and prescribing traditional medicine, she is out in the veld looking for healing plants, roots and weeds to create herbal concoctions.

Even the OECD has argued that there is no evidence to suggest that the benefits enjoyed by the formal sector will attract informal sector players. While having access to, for example, credit, the title deeds to property, procurement opportunities, technical assistance and management support – which are available to formal businesses – may look appealing, there is little evidence to suggest that this access represents formidable inducements to informal business owners to switch to a more formal business model. Nevertheless, according to the OECD (2007), a worrying reality is that local authorities often lack a proper understanding of how the informal sector works and/or lack the capacity to provide the type of support that would make a difference in informal workers' lives.

It is possible for informal businesses to operate within a formal business environment without actually being formal themselves. However, if government is keen to encourage more informal businesses to become formal, it can do so by:

- Removing regulatory barriers that make it difficult, costly or impossible for small, informal businesses to operate;
- Removing unnecessary administration and paperwork that are designed for the formal sector and big business;
- Simplifying tax administration and compliance requirements to suit small businesses, e.g. by introducing a fixed tax regime with easy payment arrangements; and
- Simplifying business registration and licensing procedures.

In *The South African Informal Sector: Creating Jobs, Reducing Poverty*, Fourie (2018) suggests new ways of encouraging the formalisation of the informal sector. Typically, government authorities assume that when informal business owners ask for support from government, it means that they are asking to go the formalisation route, which will involve (at a minimum) registration, a business permit and tax compliance. Taking such a step could make them vulnerable to punitive measures in the event of non-compliance. This scenario is usually very different from what informal business owners are looking for. Fourie (2018) indicates that, for many informal business owners, formalisation – in whatever form – must translate into improved livelihoods and more self-sufficient, sustainable operations. What informal enterprises need from government, above all, is the type of support that enables them to survive, become stronger and, if possible, create more employment – even if this employment remains informal in the initial stages.

It is no longer a valid argument that taking people out of informal, often precarious self-employment and putting them into formal, wage-paying jobs constitutes the formalisation of the informal sector. The argument is even more difficult to defend when even the formal economy cannot ensure job security. In such a case, it may be wise for self-employed, informal business owners to rely on their own creativity and talents to survive.

What is becoming increasingly obvious, according to the ILO, particularly in terms of its Recommendation 204, is that attempts to formalise small, informal businesses must be accompanied by appropriate incentives and other inducements that relate to these businesses' operating environments.[42] These, according to the ILO, should include improved access to business services, finance, infrastructure, markets, technology, promotional assistance, and marketing and distribution networks (such as cooperatives). The informal (and largely hidden) economy can and should form part of government's support programme, which is designed to ensure that the production of goods and services occurs in a conducive environment that will help to drive the sustainability of the business. The informal sector should, in fact, have access to the same market opportunities as those enjoyed by the formal sector. This could help to increase demand, enhance production efficiency and produce more competitive outputs.

The above suggests a more gradual, developmental approach to business formalisation, one focusing on support and sustainability rather than on regulation for regulation's sake. One recommended condition for informal businesses to secure government support in this way is some form of registration or licensing. This would enable government to track these small businesses and local authorities to provide basic services such as water and electricity. It would also facilitate access to additional (optional) services, such as basic bookkeeping training; management training; banking services; credit and loan facilities; business insurance; government subsidies; contract advice; and public procurement systems.[43]

This slow and measured approach to formalisation would unfold differently for different businesses, with different owners opting for a bouquet of services that errs on the side of informality or formality, as the case may be. They may prefer to keep their options relatively open and not be bound to something that would be difficult to extract themselves from if their circumstances changed. Fourie (2018) suggests that formalisation might usefully comprise a bouquet of support elements with matching elements of formalisation, allowing a business owner to select elements of formalisation as needed, at various intervals. He adds that, as the uptake of these support and formalisation elements bring progressive benefits and induce better business outcomes, business owners will be incentivised – voluntarily – to continue along the developmental formalisation trajectory.

Fourie (2018) contends that the extent of formalisation should depend on where the business is on the development scale, its specific needs, its current circumstances and opportunities and its aspirations. In other words, there is no 'one size fits all'. Of course, efforts to formalise the informal will not eliminate micro, small and medium enterprises, many of which will continue to operate outside the mainstream economy even though they contribute to it. While government efforts to create a more enabling environment will help all small businesses, those that opt to remain in the informal economy will require their own strategies and support mechanisms.

Formalising the informal will only work if local government recognises, firstly, that a wide range of goods and services is necessary to keep the economy going and, secondly, that the value thereof has an important social impact on surrounding communities, including through the creation of employment opportunities (even of an informal nature). The informal sector remains crucial as it contributes not only to the broader economy but also to the labour market by creating employment and boosting income (Rais 2016).

Of course, there is no single way for the government to intervene and assist the informal sector to become part of the mainstream economy. It will also take far more than merely drawing up plans and strategies. It is what is done at a practical level that will be felt by informal businesses at the coalface, that will signal whether or not government is committed to an effective process of formalisation. In particular, interventions are needed that stimulate entrepreneurship and mobilise financial and other resources through a well-integrated approach.

The mistake that most proponents of business formalisation make is to assume that the process centres on the regulations and incentives necessary to enable informal sector operators to make the transition into the formal sector, thereby ignoring specific circumstances that may call for other types of assistance.

At the Public Dialogue on 'Forging a Path towards Recognition and Inclusion of Informal Workers in South Africa' held in November 2018, Sally Roever, of Women in Informal Employment: Globalizing and Organizing (WIEGO), opened the event by saying, 'We're here to discuss one of the most profound challenges of our time – how to create jobs, how to increase incomes, and how to improve working conditions in today's globalized economy.' Her opening statement, noble as it was, missed an important point regarding the ability of entrepreneurs to create jobs, even of an informal nature.

For example, one of the small informal businesses at Kwa Mai Mai is Sithole Furniture. At first glance, it seems to be a decent outfit which manufactures coffins, wedding kists and wooden storage boxes and employs a few carpenters to do the work. However, looks can be deceiving. What is often overlooked are the lengths to which a business owner – of what appears to be a viable business – has to go to operate under very difficult circumstances. Sithole Furniture's workshop is nothing more than a shaded area covered by a corrugated roof, with no protection from the elements or, indeed, theft.

Sithole, a saddle maker who repairs and rebuilds horse saddles, is a one-man show who does not need to contend with regularising his operation, including introducing structured employment conditions for his workers. He has a different problem. He has no workshop in which to operate. His room in the Kwa Mai Mai compound doubles up as his sleeping quarters and his work premises. He also has no saddle-stitching machine. During our interview, and in response to a question about the types of business development support and resources that he needed, Sithole listed, among other needs, more efficient trade tools and a bigger space in which to work.

Informal businesses do not necessarily require a financial injection; instead, they may need business development support that serves to link them to local and even international markets, thereby helping their businesses to grow and become sustainable. For businesses relying heavily on physical resources, such as the woodworking business at Kwa Mai Mai that makes coffins, wedding kists and wooden storage boxes for miners, the best type of support from government may be the provision of machinery and a proper workshop. Informal businesses also need marketing and advertising support to drive foot traffic to the compound. For example, a website could be created showcasing the goods and services offered by the various businesses, together with their contact details.

What the informal sector needs more than anything are self-reliant enterprises that receive support in the form of efficiency-enhancing infrastructure and the tools of trade, as well as access to markets and a distribution pipeline. Formalising the informal – in the broadest sense – may not be a viable policy objective. Instead, a 'mini' formalisation option, such as the registration of informal businesses so that the government can contact them and determine the types of support they need, could be the way to go. In other words, government should be focused on growing and capacitating the informal sector rather than on shrinking it or eliminating it completely. A formal–informal hybrid is necessary for the sector to survive.

A policy framework that sets out to bridge the gap between the informal and the formal must take into account the different stages of development and the maturity of the businesses in question, and even their appetite for growth. Fourie (2018) notes that any intervention to formalise micro, small and medium enterprises must consider their stage of maturity, sophistication, size and whether they are a one-person show or feature multiple actors. He cautions against introducing a policy framework that is not holistic and ignores pertinent issues such as businesses' start-up and developmental phases, profitability, capital strength, growth potential and aspirations, and entrepreneurial aptitude.

Fourie (2018) further advises that formalisation should not be the only solution for informal enterprises. An effective policy framework for the informal sector should not only have formalisation objectives; it should also incorporate at least three types of measures:

- Cross-cutting, generic support measures, including an appropriate regulatory framework; property and infrastructure; foundational business and accounting training; and access to finance, among other aspects;

- Tailored support measures for designated groups (employing firms, one-person enterprises or own-account workers, and new entrants), or to achieve certain goals; and
- Industry-specific measures designed to give 'teeth' and substance to the process of integrating the informal and the formal components of an industry or supply chain, which would require industry-specific analyses.

The gap between the potential and actual performance of the Kwa Mai Mai market and bazaar is symptomatic of the socio-political distance between the government and the informal economy and its actors, who are producing much-needed goods and services. This gap can be attributed to the perpetuation of colonial policies which turned those coming from villages into a constant source of labour in the cities, with no prospects of controlling the means of production. Migrant workers, particularly those living in so-called single men's hostels, are merely expected to offer their labour in return for meagre wages, and head back to their rural homes at least twice a year.

To those who are suddenly, and because of their official positions in government, expected to accept and treat these migrant workers as new business owners who demand equal treatment to that given to 'white monopoly capital', it is a difficult mind shift. De Soto (cited in Skinner 2018) claims that the growth of the informal sector was a natural, counter response to the introduction of government regulations that made it impossible for small entrepreneurs to participate in the formal economy.

Kwa Mai Mai presents an interesting contradiction because of the visibility of its marginal informal businesses. The traders all operate in a specific location in clearly demarcated stalls, with each stall numbered and having a trader registered to it. Kwa Mai Mai is operating in a boundary-less environment without a physical location capable of being traced by government officials. Having said that, Kwa Mai Mai has a deployed government official occupying an office from 9 am to

5 pm on weekdays. What is astonishing is that although this official has supposedly been deployed to see to the upkeep of the compound, there are serious problems: broken and leaking toilets, one section of the compound without electricity for almost two years, leaking roofs on the traders' stalls – the list goes on. The reason for the government's failure to deliver much-needed services and create a business-friendly environment is what this book has tried to determine.

Unlike the township economy, where informal businesses serve a captive market in the neighbourhood, Kwa Mai Mai has no captive market. It occupies no neighbourhood niche as it does not provide the day-to-day neighbourhood essentials. It therefore requires special and innovative strategies as a trade market operating in the informal economy. Much as it may be based on a 'survivalist' strategy, in line with what Charman et al. (2020) refer to as the 'pursuit of day-to-day economic survival' in the township economy, Kwa Mai Mai does not trade in items needed for survival. The survivalist nature of Kwa Mai Mai as a collection of micro enterprises stems from traders' need to shield themselves from harsh economic conditions and to accumulate sufficient money to sustain their homesteads back home.

The informal economy comprises both the powerful and the weak, with some social groupings exercising dominance over others. This may call for what Charman et al. (2020:120) describe as a 'repertoire of intercultural skills, which ... enhances economic opportunities for diverse participants'. The dominance of one ethnic group at Kwa Mai Mai, for example, might pose a threat to 'outsiders' wanting to enter the same social space. The use of common space by disparate social groupings or by 'insiders' and 'outsiders' must be underpinned by a networked and relational economy (Charman and Govender 2016:312).

Although the reason for the government's failure to address the needs of Kwa Mai Mai traders remains elusive, the different paradigms advanced by various scholars are instructive. Skinner (2018) points to different schools of thought or perspectives regarding the treatment of informal traders. One is the *dualist* approach, which calls for support measures to be given to informal traders, such as credit facilities, training and skills development, and basic infrastructure. Another is the *legalist* approach, which considers the nature and impact of state regulations that exclude small, informal businesses from the mainstream economy. Skinner (2018) also cites the *voluntarist* approach, which recognises the right to reject a business formalisation process, and the *structuralist* approach, which acknowledges the need to understand the linkages between informal and formal businesses and the unequal power relations between the two.

Irrespective of the different views about the conditions under which informal traders operate (and why), it is ultimately the government, from its ideological vantage point, that should determine the conditions under which these businesses conduct their operations. The historical circumstances from which South Africa's new democracy emerged – including how Africans were treated in the cities – cannot be ignored. The Group Areas Act No. 41 of 1950, for example, prevented certain blacks or Africans from being in the city or restricted their movements once they arrived. It is not surprising, therefore, that the country has not been able to completely overturn the harsh realities that informal traders find themselves facing. In fact, there is still a covert perpetuation of the rules of exclusion according to class and status in the city.

Despite the formulation of various policy frameworks and pieces of legislation since 1995, there appears to have been no measurable progress in transforming informal sector workers into real players in the mainstream economy. Government initiatives include introducing white papers (such as the 1995 White Paper on the Development and Promotion of Small Business) and gazetting new laws (such as the National Small Business Act No. 102 of 1996), as well as establishing specialised agencies to help small businesses. Most of these efforts have been geared towards the provision of financial assistance to small businesses, completely ignoring their need for market access and distribution pipelines for their goods and services.

Today, it seems that City Council officials are unable to differentiate, from a policy perspective, between informal traders operating in public spaces and those running their businesses in designated spaces in a specific location and, importantly, inside a building. The specific case of Kwa Mai Mai needs to take into account, from a policy perspective, the socio-cultural influences that steer the various businesses. Because the Kwa Mai Mai hostel and bazaar produces both cultural goods and services, with the cultural and creative economy being at the core of the market, it cannot simply be regarded as a factory where goods are produced according to a standard design. The creative people behind the businesses and the market are the essence of the goods and services on offer.

Therefore, the cultural nuances found at Kwa Mai Mai call for a multifaceted range of government support measures, taking into account the fact that:

- culture and heritage have long informed the production of goods and services at Kwa Mai Mai;
- various historical periods and milestones led to the establishment of the hostel and market;
- businesses have been passed down from generation to generation, something current traders are committed to preserving;
- Kwa Mai Mai also acts as a site of cultural reaffirmation for those looking to reconnect with their roots; and
- Kwa Mai is a unique tourist attraction for those looking for homegrown, culturally authentic goods.

Any policy interventions must be informed by the need to build on existing expertise and integrate Kwa Mai Mai into the City Council's economic development strategy, as a cultural corridor and tourist destination as well as a creative hub for entrepreneurs who wish to keep long-held customs and traditions alive.

# Eleven
# Conclusion

**M**uch has changed at Kwa Mai Mai since the early 20th century. What once was a men's-only compound, subject to the intense scrutiny of compound police, is now a vibrant community whose members wake up every day and open their doors, without fail, to welcome their first customers.

In this unique part of Johannesburg, men and women, young and old, all work, live and play in the same space. Four generations in a family are often found in one room, which has been modified to conceal its kitchen-cum-bedroom from the front store downstairs. A makeshift mezzanine area has been created to make space for an extra bedroom. A wooden panel acts as a dividing wall between the front store and the sleeping and cooking area, but what lies behind the wall is left to one's imagination. How a family of four, and sometimes eight, share such a small space while making sure that the store front remains attractive to customers, is nothing short of amazing and is a testimony of their steely determination to survive. Behind the makeshift wall is the family's humble abode, measuring less than 2 m x 2 m, where they keep their sparse belongings.

What is not in dispute is that the Kwa Mai Mai market and bazaar is similar to other cultural markets: it is what Chinatown is to New Yorkers, and it is what the Oriental Plaza is to Joburgers. Just as Chinatown offers many of the things that Chinese people (outside China) are looking for, other than factory-made goods, Kwa Mai Mai offers many of the things that Africans (away from their rural villages) are looking for. It is also the only place in the city where village migrants converge with urbanites who visit the place just for an acculturation experience. It is a convenient place for anyone wishing to visit the hinterland of Zululand and kwa Xhosa, or the lands of the Tsonga, baPedi or VhaVenda, without leaving the city.

Much as the place has enjoyed reasonable success, its still-untapped potential is far greater than what it has delivered so far. Kwa Mai Mai is yet to come truly into its own. Its inability to reach its full potential is not an indication of the traders' failure to imagine the impossible: they have done that in abundance. Rather, it can be attributed to disinterest by the City Council and its assorted entities to help Kwa Mai Mai realise its substantial possibilities.

As I have argued in this book, none of the City Council's entities tasked with providing the site with essential services and infrastructure, including City Power, Pikitup, the JRA, the JPC or even the Department of Economic Development, appear to have the necessary political will to bring dignity to a place that is supposed to be a major cultural attraction for visitors to the city and a celebration of creative entrepreneurship. Instead, what is evident is the perpetuation of colonial and apartheid attitudes, which dismissed these compounds as mere labour reserves supplying businesses in the city. What these City Council officials have failed to realise is that these village migrants-turned-cultural entrepreneurs have refused to be a source of cheap labour for other people. Instead, they have become the creators of their own destiny, self-employed and productive in a city that, to all intents and purposes, does not care about them.

No matter what challenges they face, including the City Council's complete disregard for their existence and well-being, the people of Kwa Mai Mai take pride in the businesses they inherited from their forebears. Bolstered by their pride in their heritage, they defied the repressive colonial and apartheid regimes which sought to erase their identity and crush their spirit. In this compound lives a resilient community who, while repeatedly ignored, refuses to be forgotten.

It is this community, spanning multiple generations, that has refused to be relegated to the margins of society or to a footnote in history. Instead, it has opted to fight for its survival in a city that pretends it does not exist. Moreover, with their resilience and passion for culture and tradition, Kwa Mai Mai's people have translated their heritage into a range of businesses through which they have faced – head on – the spectres of poverty and unemployment.

The fact that no other book has ever been written about Kwa Mai Mai, its place in the history of Johannesburg or its contribution to South Africa's creative economy and legacy, is indicative of how the place has been positioned as just another hostel where migrant labourers live, except that it also happens to trade in traditional medicine.

What this book has uncovered is a community of men who, in the early 20th century, could have ended up as mineworkers or general labourers; and of women, who could have travelled to the city from time to time to visit their husbands, armed with the all-important temporary visitor's permit from the Commissioner of Native Affairs.

However, these men and women escaped that fate. Today, Kwa Mai Mai is home to a lively cohort of entrepreneurial migrants from the villages who occupy a space in the city that would have been unthinkable under apartheid. Moreover, for all its trials and tribulations, there is a new vibrancy in this neglected part of the city. A new generation of young cultural entrepreneurs who were born in Kwa Mai Mai are now taking over the reins from their parents and the cycle continues.

One of the challenges associated with ethnography is that researchers may find it difficult to separate themselves from the subject matter and the characters they are studying. Unfortunately, when I was doing the research for this book, it was extremely difficult to ignore the despair and hopelessness welling up in the eyes of young people who have only known life in the compound. Encouragingly, though, they have an innate desire to interact with a world that is bigger than their current one. Some of these young people are still at school but hope to pursue tertiary studies that will bring them into contact with that bigger world, which now they can only imagine.

As I was winding up my research, I identified nine matric learners (see photograph at the end of this chapter) who expressed a desire to attend college upon completing high school and passing matric. In response to their plight, I established a varsity legacy project that would ensure that every one of the nine learners who successfully completed their matric and was admitted to a university (of their choice), would be able to proceed with their studies. The Kwa Mai Mai Varsity Legacy Project was registered as a non-profit company, with two directors drawn from the Kwa Mai Mai community and me as the third director (see photographs at the end of this chapter). Having made the initial investment, I was delighted when a few more people raised their hands and also contributed to the fund.

Younger people who were not fortunate enough to be given such an opportunity, for instance Nhlanhla Buthelezi, who completed matric a few years ago, nevertheless started their own businesses in the compound. In this digital age and true to his youthfulness, Nhlanhla established a hair salon and an internet café that offers faxing, photocopying and scanning facilities. Nhlanhla says that his salon is popular because, in addition to older residents, more and more young people are living in the compound, having been born there. They want to look young and trendy, hence the need for fashionable hairstyles. Some young people find the internet facilities useful for sending their curriculum vitae and applications to universities or potential employers. Others, who have opted not to continue in their parents' line of work and have no desire to pursue further studies, have taken the showbiz route and entered the music industry as either music producers or musicians, sometimes building makeshift recording studios in the spaces originally built for horses.

But for many of the older members of the Kwa Mai Mai community, little has changed and they go about their familiar daily routine. Mama uPikoli, with her heavy limp, still wakes up every morning, pulls down the roller doors of her shop and waits for customers, something she has done since she took over her late father's business. uBaba uKhumalo no Mhlongo and uMavuso are familiar sights, leaning against the wall and coaxing a greeting from passers-by who are on their way to uMama Zakwe's shop. Meanwhile, both Mshengu (the panel beater) and the *induna* are forever grateful for their close encounter with a white man;

otherwise, they would not be at Kwa Mai Mai. Moreover, for as long as the village horse races in Matatiele and the Dundee July exist, Sithole's horse-saddle business will not run out of customers.

It remains to be seen whether the trending *ukuthwasa* phenomenon will still be in fashion in a few years' time, as rising numbers of young women and celebrities aspire to become *sangomas*. For now, both Mkhulu Mamba and Gogo MaNsimbi are not short of initiates and business is booming. In addition, the jury is still out on whether the *induna*'s council (*isigungu*) and Malibongwe Sithole's traders' committee will ever find common ground and be able to collectively devise a strategy for holding the City Council and the JPC responsible for maintenance and basic service delivery at the compound.

I salute all the reluctant village migrants who, against all odds, fought to stay afloat in a concrete jungle that was hellbent on making them anonymous. Everyone at Kwa Mai Mai is the embodiment of what can be achieved through reimagination and grit.

Welcome to Kwa Mai Mai, or should I say 'Maye Maye'!

*2021 matric learners and beneficiaries of the Kwa Mai Mai Varsity Legacy Project (Photo: Siphiwe Mhlambi)*

*Kwa Mai Mai Varsity Legacy Project committee and directors, Dr Sipho Sithole, Ms Jane Ngwabe and Mr Malibongwe Sithole (Photo: Siphiwe Mhlambi)*

*Kwa Mai Mai Varsity Legacy Project cheque presentation by Dr Judy Dlamini and Sizwe Nxasana (Photo: Melisa Peter)*

*Kwa Mai Mai Varsity Legacy Project cheque presentation by Dr Sipho Sithole (Photo: Diliza Moabi)*

# Notes


1    *Natal Mercury*, 27 July 1905.

2    *Natal Mercury*, 5 and 6 May 1905.

3    https://www.sahistory.org.za/article/zulu-kingdom-and-colony-natal

4    General Circular No. 37 of 1940 by DL Smit, Secretary of Native Affairs, Union of South Africa, dated 14 October 1940.

5    https://en.wikipedia.org/wiki/Salisbury_Claims

6    Letter to the Town Clerk from LG Heard for Central Rand Freehold Proprietary Limited, dated 6 September 1913.

7    Letter to the Town Council from Mining Commissioner, JL van der Merwe, dated 25 September 1913. File No. M.C./A. 557/12.

8    Letter to the Provincial Secretary from the Johannesburg Municipal Town Clerk, 26 September 1913.

9    Archive 3814/13/F. 724 Lease of Salisbury and Jubilee Compound, 6 November 1913.

10    Letter from Provincial Secretary authorising the lease of Salisbury and Jubilee compound, dated 4 December 1913. File Rs/R. 4.12.

11    Administrative File No. 2/7596. Executive Committee of the Johannesburg City Council, 14 December 1914.

12    Letter from the General Manager of the Municipal Council of Johannesburg, dated 20 November 1913. File No. 2322/13.

13    Letter from the Secretary of Native Affairs. No. 51/313, dated 24 December 1927.

14    City of Johannesburg, Ref. No. 29/214/2, submitted by the Town Clerk. Johannesburg, 2 August 1945.

15    Treasury Circular No. 1971, Municipality of Johannesburg –

Establishment of Natal Spruit Compound and the Indian and Coloured Sports Grounds as Native Locations, 13 December 1940.

16    Letter from the Town Clerk's Department to the Native Commissioner (Copy), 3 April 1941.

17    City Council Urgency Report of the Non-European Affairs Committee. Stands 768-9-70, City and Suburban: Expropriation. Reference No. 122/6/131, 25 March 1946.

18    https://www.sahistory.org.za/people/saul-msane

19    http://www.theheritageportal.co.za/article/mai-mai-market-place-healers

20    'Oldest town of Johannesburg, Marshalltown, is planned', *South African History Online*.

21    http://www.theheritageportal.co.za/article/80-albert-street-nerve-centre-controlling-black-peoples-lives-during-early-stages-apartheid

22    Interview with Mtutuzeli Matshoba, Protea North, Soweto, Sunday, 21 February 2021.

23    'Crime in a compound: Conditions at Salisbury and Jubilee: Strictures from the bench', *Rand Daily Mail*, 11 January 1922. National Archive 2322/13/97.

24    Dingaan's Day was, until 1994, celebrated on 16 December to commemorate the Voortrekkers' victory over the Zulu army led by the Zulu king, Dingaan, at the Battle of Blood River. Today, 16 December is celebrated as the Day of Reconciliation (between blacks and whites).

25    The Salisbury and Jubilee compound: Reply to a magistrate's criticism. Thos G. Jones, letter to the editor of the *Rand Daily Mail*, 13 January 1922.

26    'Magistrate taken to task. His location criticism resented. Defending the Salisbury and Jubilee', *The Star*, 12 January 1922.

27    'Salisbury compounded raided: Big force of police engaged: 1000 natives drunk before 10am: Black brewers' big bank balance', *Rand Daily Mail*, 25 July 1922.

28    Minutes of the Ordinary Meeting of Council, 31 August 1962, Minutes 1930 (Sp. Mtg. 30.8.62.).

29    https://www.prnewswire.com/news-releases/the-minibus-taxi-and-bus-services-industry-in-south-africa-2016-300556238.html. Accessed 19 March 2018.

30    South African Government Online. 'Shell House massacre', 8 April 1994. Available at www.gov.za

31    Greg Marinovich, 'The truth elusive: Shell House massacre, 20 years

later', *Daily Maverick*, 28 March 2014.

32    Letter from the Town Clerk, Johannesburg, to the Native Commissioner, 26 October 1955. Reference No. 122/6/385.

33    Report of the Commission of Inquiry into Witchcraft Violence and Ritual Murders in the Northern Province of the Republic of South Africa [microform] to his excellency, the honourable member of the Executive Council for Safety and Security, Northern Province, Advocate Seth Nthai.

34    '6 South African celebrities who are sangomas. Some of Mzansi's biggest stars have heeded their ancestral calling', ZAlebs, 16 August 2020.

35    Karabo Disetlhe-Mtshayelo, 'Are celebrities with a calling real sangomas?', *Soweto Live*, 30 January 2019.

36    https://www.joburg.org.za/media_/Newsroom/Pages/2014%20Articles/Tourists-flock-to-Kwa-Mai-Mai.aspx

37    Kwa Mai Mai Committee Terms of Reference 2017-18, entered into between the Department of Economic Development, the City of Johannesburg, and Kwa Mai Mai Traders' Interim Committee.

38    http://www.pikitup.co.za

39    City of Johannesburg. Final Integrated Development Plan 2020/21.

40    'South Africa: What does "service delivery" really mean?', Blog post by Guest Blogger for John Campbell, 15 May 2014. https://www.cfr.org/blog/south-africa-what-does-service-delivery-really-mean

41    International Labour Organization. 2002. 'Resolution and conclusions concerning decent work and the informal economy. Resolution adopted by the 90th session of the International Labour Conference'. Geneva: ILO.

42    International Labour Organization. 2015. 'Resolution on transition from the informal to the formal economy. Resolution No. 204'. Geneva: ILO.

43    https://www.polity.org.za/article/creating-jobs-reducing-poverty-v-is-formalising-the-informal-sector-the-answer-2018-08-21

# References


Bank, L.J., Posel, D., Wilson, F. 2020. *Migrant Labour after Apartheid: The Inside Story*. Cape Town: HSRC Press.

Barrett, C.B. 2005a. 'On the relevance of identities, communities, groups and networks to the economics of poverty alleviation.' In *The Social Economics of Poverty: On Identities, Communities, Groups and Networks*, edited by Christopher B. Barrett. London and New York: Routledge, pp. 1–11.

Barrett, C.B. 2005b. 'Smallholder identities and social networks: The challenge of improving productivity and welfare'. In *The Social Economics of Poverty: On Identities, Communities, Groups and Networks*, edited by Christopher B. Barrett. London and New York: Routledge, pp. 214–45.

Benatar, S.R. 2001. 'Health in developing countries: Cultural concerns'. *International Encyclopedia of the Social & Behavioral Sciences* 6566–70.

Blokland, T., Hentschel, C. and Holm, A. 2015. 'Urban citizenship and right to the City: The fragmentation of claims'. *International Journal of Urban and Regional Research* 39(4), July. https://doi.org/10.1111/1468-2427.12259=

Brettel, C.B. 2015. 'Migration: Anthropological perspectives'. *International Encyclopaedia of the Social & Behavioral Sciences* 2:422–26.

Britannica. 1999. 'Boomtown – History of Johannesburg: The early period, 1853–1930'. https://www.britannica.com/place/Johannesburg-South-Africa/additional-info#history

Broster, J.A. 1981. *AMAQHIRHA: Religion, Magic and Medicine in Transkei*. Cape Town: Via Afrika.

Butchart, A. 1996. 'The industrial panopticon: Mining and the medical construction of migrant African labour in South Africa, 1900–1950'. *Social Science and Medicine* 42(12):185–97.

Buthelezi, M. 1995. *Studies of The Nazareth Baptist Church Ibandla Lamanazareth: The story of Isaiah Shembe* (H. Becken, Trans). New York: Edwin Mellen Press. https://people.ucalgary.ca/~nurelweb/books/shembe/sos/sos3.html

Bye, S.N. and Dutton, M.F. 1991. 'The inappropriate use of traditional medicines in South Africa'. *Journal of Ethnopharmacology* 34:253–59.

Cabrita, J. 2012. *Patriot and Prophet: John Dube's 1936 Biography of the South African Churchman Isaiah Shembe*. London: SOAS, University of London.

Callinicos, L. 1994. 'The migrant labour system'. In *Work and Industrialisation in South Africa: An Introductory Reader*, edited by E. Webster, L. Alfred, L. Bethlehem, A. Joffe and T.-A. Selikow. Randburg: Ravan Press, pp. 94–100.

Cameron, T. (ed.) 1986. *An Illustrated History of South Africa*. Johannesburg: Jonathan Ball Publishers.

Casserley, J.V.L. 1955. 'The children of God in the city of Man'. In *The Metropolis in Modern Life*, edited by R.M. Fisher. New York: Russel & Russel, pp. 333–43.

Charman, A. and Govender, T. 2016. 'The relationship economy of informality: Spatial dimensions of street trading in Ivory Park, South Africa'. *Urban Forum* 27(3):311–28. http://doi./10.1007/s12132-016-9290-z

Charman, A., Petersen, L. and Govender, T. 2020. *Township Economy: People, Spaces and Practices*. Cape Town: HSRC Press.

Chidester, D. 1992. *Religions of South Africa*. London: Routledge.

Christensen, C.M., Raynor, M. and McDonald. R. 2015. 'What is disruptive innovation?'. *Harvard Business Review* 93(12):44–53. https://go.exlibris.link/svljZ70t

Cohen, R. 2006. *Migration and its Enemies: Global Capital, Migrant Labour and the Nation-State*. Hampshire, England: Ashgate.

Cripps, E.A. 2012. 'Provisioning Johannesburg 1886–1906'. MA diss., Unisa, 174–76. http://hdl.handle.net/10500/5966

Crush, J. 1994. 'Scripting the compound: Power and space in the South African mining industry'. *Environment and Planning D: Society and Space* 12(3):301–24. https://doi.org/10.1068/d120301

De Kiewiet, C.W. 1941. *A History of South Africa: Social and Economic*. London: Oxford University Press.

Delius, P. 2017. 'Migrant labour in South Africa (1800–2014)'. In *Oxford Research Encyclopaedia of African History: Economic and Social History, Southern Africa*. http://oxfordre.com/africanhistory/view/10.1093/acrefore/9780190277734.001.0001/acrefore-9780190277734-e-93.

Demissie, F. 1998. 'In the shadow of the gold mines: Migrancy and mine housing in South Africa'. *Housing Studies* 13(4):445–69.

Dube, J.L. 1936. *Ushembe*. Pietermaritzburg: Shuter & Shooter.

Du Bois, W.E.B. 1903. *The Souls of Black Folk: Essays and Sketches.* Chicago: A.C. McClurg & Co.

Fenyane, T. 2016. 'Project implementation of the hostel upgrade programme in City of Johannesburg'. Research report for Master's degree, University of the Witwatersrand.

Fobosi, S.C. 2020. 'South Africa's minibus taxi industry has been marginalised for too long. This must change'. *The Conversation*, 14 July.

Foucault, M. 1977. *Discipline and Punish: The Birth of the Prison.* London: Penguin.

Fourie, F. (ed.) 2018. *The South African Informal Sector: Creating Jobs, Reducing Poverty.* Cape Town: HSRC Press.

Grant, G. and Flynn, T. (eds). 1992. *Watershed Town: The History of Johannesburg.* City Engineer's Department, Johannesburg City Council.

Gunner, E. 1982. 'New wine in old bottles: Imagery in the Izibongo of the Zulu Zionist Prophet, Isaiah Shembe'. *Journal of Religion in Africa* 5:32–53.

Gunner, E. 1986. 'The word, the book and the Zulu Church of Nazareth'. In *Oral Tradition and Literacy: Changing Visions of the World,* edited by R. Whitaker and E. Sienaert. Durban: Natal Oral Documentation and Research Centre, pp. 179–88.

Gunner, L. (ed.) 2004. *The Man of Heaven and the Beautiful Ones of God: Isaiah Shembe and the Nazareth Church.* Pietermaritzburg: University of KwaZulu-Natal Press.

Guy, J. 2006. *Remembering the Rebellion: The Zulu Uprising of 1906.* Pietermaritzburg: University of KwaZulu-Natal Press.

Harris, C.B. 1954. 'How the compound system came into existence in Kimberley'. *The Diamond News and the South African Watchmaker and Jeweller*, 18–21 August.

Harrison, P. 2004. *South Africa's Top Sites Spiritual.* Kenilworth, Cape Town: Spearhead.

Harvey, D. 1985. *Consciousness and the Urban Experience.* Oxford, UK: Blackwell.

Harvey, D. 1989. *The Urban Experience.* Baltimore and London: Johns Hopkins University Press.

Hastings, A. 1976. *African Christianity.* New York: The Seabury Press.

Hexham, I. 2011. *Isaiah Shembe: Zulu Religious Leaders.* Canada: Department of Religious Studies, University of Calgary.

Hickel, J. 2015. *Democracy as Death: The Moral Order of Anti-Liberal Politics in*

*South Africa*. Berkeley, CA: University of California Press.

Igwe, L. 2014. 'The untold story of Africa's secular tradition'. *Conscience Magazine*, 19 February. https://www.catholicsforchoice.org/resource-library/the-untold-story-of-africas-secular-tradition/

Kaschula, R. 1997. *Xhosa*. New York: The Rosen Publishing Group, Inc.

Keith, M. 2005. *After the Cosmopolitan?: Multicultural Cities and the Future of Racism*. London: Routledge.

Kiaga, A. and Leung, V. 2020. 'The transition from the informal to the formal economy in Africa'. *Global Employment Policy Review*, Background Paper No. 4, International Labour Organization, 2–65.

Kiernan, J.P. 1978. 'Saltwater and ashes: Instruments of curing among some Zulu Zionists'. *Journal of Religion in Africa* 9(1):27–32.

Knox, P. and Gutsche, T. 1947. *Do You Know?* Johannesburg: Unie-Volkspers, Beperk.

Krige, E.J. 1950. *The Social System of the Zulus*. Pietermaritzburg: Shuter & Shooter.

Kubukeli, P.S. 1999. 'Traditional healing practice using medicinal herbs'. *The Lancet*, December 1999, p. 24. doi:https://doi.org/10.1016/S0140-6736(99)90367-7

Kumalo, S. and Mujinga. M. 2017. 'Now we know that the enemy is from within: Shembeites and the struggle for control of Isaiah Shembe's legacy and the Church'. *Journal for the Study of Religion* 30(2). http://dx.doi.org/10.17159/2413-3027/2017/v30n2a6

Laband, J. 1995. *Robe of Sand: The Rise and Fall of the Zulu Kingdom in the Nineteenth Century*. Johannesburg: Jonathan Ball Publishers.

Lambert, J. 1995. *Betrayed Trust: Africans and the State in Colonial Natal*. Pietermaritzburg: University of Natal Press.

Lee, S.G. 1969. 'Spirit possession among the Zulu'. In *Spirit Mediumship and Society in Africa*, edited by J. Beattie and J. Middleton. London: Routledge and Kegan Paul.

Lefebvre, H. 1974 [1984]. *The Production of Space*, (D. Nicholson-Smith, trans 1991). New York: Wiley-Blackwell.

Levitt, P. 2001. *The Transnational Villagers*. Berkeley, CA: University of California Press.

Lewis, S. 2016. 'Formalising the informal', International Institute for Environment and Development. https://www.iied.org/formalising-informal

Leyds, G.A. 1964. *A History of Johannesburg: The Early Years*. Cape Town: Nasionale Boekhandel Beperk.

Macpherson, C.B. 1961. *The Political Theory of Possessive Individualism: Hobbes to Locke*. Oxford: Oxford University Press.

Magwaza. T. 2011. 'Empowering women or gender equality: Conversations with women of the Shembe Church: Self perceptions and the role of Zulu culture in formulating status'. *Agenda* 18, 60:136–45.

Makhathini, N. 2020. *Modes of Communication: Letters from the Underworld* (Album). Universal Music (Pty) Ltd, South Africa.

Masikane, F.G. 2017. 'Indigenous religious values: Understanding work and rest'. MA diss., University of the Witwatersrand.

Masondo, S. 2004. 'Three generations of Shembe: Leadership contests within the Nazareth Baptist Church (1935–1989)'. *Journal of Theology for Southern Africa* 118:69–79.

Matshoba, M. 1980. 'To kill a man's pride'. *Staff Rider* 3(1):4–6.

McClendon, T.V. 2002. *Genders and Generations Apart: Labour Tenants and Customary Law in Segregation-Era South Africa, 1920s to 1940s*. Portsmouth, NH: Heinemann.

McClendon, T.V. 2010. *White Chief, Black Lords: Shepstone and the Colonial State in Natal, South Africa, 1845–1878*. Rochester, NY: University of Rochester Press.

Mndende, N. 2014. 'African traditional religion'. In *Sensible Religion*, edited by C. Lewis and D. Cohn-Sherbok. London and New York: Routledge.

Mokgobi, M.G. 2014. 'Understanding traditional African healing'. *African Journal for Physical Health Education, Recreation, and Dance* 20(2):24–34.

Mothibe, M.E. and Sibanda, M. 2019. 'African traditional medicine: South African perspective'. *Intechopen*, 1–27.doi: 10.5772/intechopen.83790.

Muller, C. and Mthethwa, M. (eds), 2010. *Shembe Hymns*. Pietermaritzburg: University of KwaZulu-Natal Press.

Muller, C.A. 2004. *South African Music: A Century of Traditions in Transformation*. Oxford, England: ABC-CLIO.

Ngcobo, L. 1999. *And They Didn't Die*. Pietermaritzburg: University of Natal Press.

Ngubane, H. 1977. *Body and Mind in Zulu Medicine: An Ethnography of Health and Disease in Nyuswa–Zulu Thought and Practice*. London: Academic Press Inc.

Ogana, W. and Ojong, V.B. 2015. 'A study of literature on the essence of ubungoma (divination) and conceptions of gender among izangoma (diviners)'. *Journal for the Study of Religion* 28(1):52–80.

Oosthuizen, G.C. 1968. 'Isaiah Shembe and the Zulu world view'. *History of Religion* 8, 1.

Oosthuizen, G.C. 1979. *Afro-Christian Religions. The Iconography of Afro-Christian Religions*. Leiden: E.J. Brill.

Oosthuizen. G.C., Hexham, I., Edwards, H.D. and Wessels, W.H. 1989. *Afro-Christian Religion and Healing in South Africa*. New York: Edwini Mellen Press.

Organisation for Economic Cooperation and Development (OECD). 2007. 'Removing barriers to formalisation'. In *Promoting Pro-Poor Growth: Policy Guidance for Donors*. Paris: OECD Publishing. doi: https://doi.org/10.1787/9789264024786-8-en.

Organisation for Economic Cooperation and Development (OECD)/ International Labour Organization (ILO). 2019. *Tackling Vulnerability in the Informal Economy: Development Centre Studies*. Paris: OECD Publishing. doi: https://doi.org/10.1787/939b7bcd-en.

Parsons, T. 1971. *The System of Modern Societies*. New Jersey: Prentice-Hall.

Peté, S.A. 2019. 'Keeping the natives in their place: The ideology of white supremacy and the flogging of African offenders in Colonial Natal – Part 2'. *Fundamina: A Journal of Legal History* (25)1.

Pewa, S.E. 1997. 'Song, dance and worship in the Zionist Christian Churches: An ethnomusicological study of african music and religion'. MA diss., University of Zululand.

Phiri, L. 2016. 'Construction sites: Exploring queer identities and sexuality at the intersections of religion and culture in Zambia'. PhD diss., University of KwaZulu-Natal.

Pirie, G.H. 1988. 'Housing essential service workers in Johannesburg: Locational constraint and conflict'. *Urban Geography* 9, 6:568–83 https://doi.org/10.2747/0272-3638.9.6.568

Potenza, E. 2016. 'All that glitters – The glitter of gold'. South African History Online. https://www.sahistory.org.za/archive/all-glitters-glitter-gold-emilia-potenza

Rais, B. 2016. 'Informal economy – What is it and how can we formalise the sector?' WSP, https://www.wsp.com/en-gb/insights/informal-economy-what-is-it-and-how-can-we-formalise-the-sector

Sacks, A. 1973. Justice in South Africa. Berkeley: University of California Press.

Schilliger, S. 2019. 'Undoing borders in solidarity cities'. *Global Dialogue* 3:35–6.

Shange, N. 2013. 'Shembe: Religion's integration with African traditional religion and Christianity: Case study'. Unpublished MA diss., Rhodes University.

Shorten, J.R. 1970. *Die Verhaal van Johannesburg*. Johannesburg: Voortrekkerpers.

Simelane, T.S. 1996. 'The traditional use of indigenous vertebrates'. PhD thesis, University of Port Elizabeth.

Simmel, G. 1964. *Conflict and the Web of Group Affiliations*. New York: Free Press.

Skinner, W. 1902. *The Mining Manual for 1902: A Record of Mining Companies*. London: W.R. Skinner.

Skinner, C. 2018. 'Informal-sector policy and legislation in South Africa: Repression, omission and ambiguity'. In *The South African Informal Sector: Creating Jobs, Reducing Poverty*, edited by F. Fourie. Cape Town: HSRC Press, pp. 412–38.

Statistics South Africa (StatsSA). 2021. *Mining Industry Report 2019*. http://www.statssa.gov.za/publications/Report-20-01-02/Report-20-01-022019.pdf

Stuart, J. 1913. *A History of the Zulu Rebellion of 1906 and of Dinuzulu's Arrest, Trial and Expatriation*. London: Macmillan and Co.

Strijdom, J.M. and Scharnick-Udemans, L.S. 2018. 'Materializing religion: Essays in honour of David Chidester'. *Journal for the Study of Religion* 31, 2:1–6. doi: http://dx.doi.org/10.17159/2413-3027/2018/v31n2a0

The Missionary Herald. 1853. *Proceedings of the American Board of Commissioners for Foreign Missions with a View of other Benevolent Operations for the Year 1853*. Boston: T.R. Marvin Press.

Thurman, S. 1997. 'Umzamo: Increasing hostel dwellers' accommodation in South Africa'. *Environment and Urbanization* 9(2):42–61.

Trapido, A. 2020. 'Snuff is existentially essential to many South Africans'. *City Press*, 12 April. https://www.news24.com/citypress/trending/snuff-is-existentially-essential-to-many-south-africans-20200412

Tsedu, M. 2017. Obituary of Bishop Tshamano P Makwarela. *Limpopo Mirror*, 25 August. https://limpopomirror.co.za/articles/news/43707/2017-08-25/-bishop-tshamano-p-makwarela

Turrell, R.V. 1987. *Capital and Labour on the Kimberley Diamond Fields, 1871–1890*. Cambridge: Cambridge University Press.

Urry, J. 2010. 'Mobile sociology'. *The British Journal of Sociology* 61(1):347–66.

Van Dyk, A.C. 2001. 'Traditional African beliefs and customs: Implications for AIDS education and prevention in Africa'. *South African Journal of Psychology* 31(2):60–6.

Van Onselen, C. 2001. *New Babylon, New Niniveh*. Cape Town: Jonathan Ball.

Velicu, A. 2011. 'Cultural memory between the national and the transnational'. *Journal of Aesthetics & Culture*, 3. doi: 10.3402/jac.v3i0.7246

Verovšek, P.J. 2016. 'Collective memory, politics, and the influence of the past: The politics of memory as a research paradigm'. *Groups, Politics, and Identities*. 4(3):529–43.

Vilakazi A., Mthethwa, B. and Mpanza, M. 1986. *Shembe: The Revitalisation of African Society*. Johannesburg: Skotaville.

Vosloo, C. 2020. 'Extreme apartheid: The South African system of migrant labour and its hostels'. No. 34, The School of Arts, University of Pretoria. http://dx.doi.org/10.17159/2617-3255/2020/n34a1

Wacquant, L. 2008. *Urban Outcasts: A Comparative Sociology of Advance Marginality*. Cambridge: Polity Press.

Walton, J. 1984. 'Culture and economy in the shaping of urban life: General issues and Latin American examples'. In J.A. Agnew, J. Mercer and D.E. Sopher (eds). *The City in Cultural Context*. London: Routledge.

Watson, S. 2009. 'The magic of the marketplace: Sociality in a neglected public space'. *Urban Studies* 46(8):1577–91.

Werbner, P. 2004. 'Theorising complex diasporas: Purity and hybridity in the South Asian public sphere in Britain'. *Journal of Ethnic and Migration Studies* 30(5):895–911. doi: 10.1080/1369183042000245606

Wertsch, J.V. and Roediger III, H.L. 2008. 'Collective memory: Conceptual foundations and theoretical approaches'. *Memory Journal* 16(3):318–26.

Whiting, M.J., Williams, V.L. and T.J. Hibbitts. 2011. 'Animals traded for traditional medicine at the Faraday Market in South Africa: Species diversity and conservation implications'. *Journal of Zoology* 284:84–96.

Williams, C.C. 2005. 'Formalising the informal economy: The case for local initiatives'. *Local Government Studies* 31(3):335-49.

Wilson, F. 1972. *Labour in the South African Gold Mines*. Cambridge: Cambridge University Press.

Wirth, L. 1964. *On Cities and Social Life*. Chicago: University of Chicago Press.

# Index


**A**

*acacia nilotica* 58

Acts of the Nazarites (aka Third Testament) 157

African National Congress (ANC) 54, 55, 118, 120, 121, 122, 218

African traditional medicine 178

Africanist churches 152, 154

Afrikaans 16, 18

Albert Street 63–71, 80, 82, 83, 85, 91, 174

Alexandra township 34, 200

amaBhaca 120

*amabhunguka* 3

*amabutho* 181

*amahubo* 5

*amakhathakhatha* 133, 175

*amakholwa* 166

*aMakhosi* 123, 200, 201, 202

*amaNazaretha* 159

*amandawe* 189

*amandiki* 189

*amaqaba* (aka *umhedeni*) 153, 166

*amathwasa* 187, 189, 190

*amazimuzimu* 110

American Board of Commissioners for Foreign Missions 166

ancestors (aka *amadlozi*) 5, 58, 97, 151, 155, 159, 160, 162, 163, 166, 167, 169, 172, 173, 178, 179, 182–184, 186–190

Anglo-Boer War (see 'South African War')

apartheid 65, 66, 67, 92, 121, 122, 178, 195, 196, 226, 248, 249

*assegai* 120, 160

**B**

Bambata Rebellion 156

Bantu 55, 63, 66

Bantu Affairs Department 91

Bantu Affairs Office 68

baPedi (see 'Pedi')

beer 70, 71, 72, 130 (see also 'kaffir beer' and '*skokian*')

beer hall 71, 80, 130, 212, 215

Bezuidenhout, Barend 64

Bhambatha ka Mancinza, Chief 29, 120

Big Zulu 106

black magic (see 'witchcraft')

black medicine 95

Buthelezi, iNkosi uMangosutho (see 'Buthelezi, Prince Mangosuthu')

Buthelezi, Nhlanhla 145, 250

Buthelezi, Prince Mangosuthu 113, 121

**C**

Cape Colony 20, 28, 32

Carlos I of Portugal 17

Central Rand Freehold Proprietary
     Limited 42, 43, 44
Centre Syndicate 44
Cetshwayo, King 27, 113, 156
Chauke, Mama (see 'Chauke, Nkiyase
     Rose')
Chauke, Nkiyase Rose (aka Mama
     Chauke) 123–125, 141
Chauke, Thomas 124
Chiefs' and Headmen's Act (No. 8 of
     1974) 123
Christian Apostolic Church 165
Christianity 151–155, 157, 159, 160,
     162, 163, 165–167, 169, 172, 178
Church of Zion (see 'Zionist Christian
     Church')
City and Suburban 32, 48, 49, 50, 51,
     200, 223, 226, 233
City Power 215, 226, 248
City of Gold xi, 16, 18, 83, 225 (see
     also 'Johannesburg')
City of Johannesburg's Economic
     Growth Strategy (EGS) 228
City of Johannesburg's Strategy 2040
     224
colonial(ism) 3, 5, 8, 11, 20–26, 29, 63,
     77, 80, 92, 113, 120, 121, 156, 178,
     181, 195, 201, 243, 248
Commissioner of Native Affairs 249
Committee on Native Affairs 33, 34
Community Residential Unit (CRU)
     Programme 196, 197
compound 1, 4–6, 14, 20, 35, 37–40,
     42, 47–50, 52, 56, 57, 65, 71, 72,
     74–77, 80, 82, 92, 94, 96, 119, 123,
     128, 129, 133, 155, 161, 174, 198,
     199, 209, 211, 212, 229, 233, 241,
     244, 247–249 (see also 'hostel')
Consolidated Gold Fields 16
Constitution, South African 224
Constitution Hill 223
Constitutional Court 210
Covid-19 95, 96, 97, 133, 134, 215
cultural weapons (see 'traditional
     weapons')
culture xi, xii, xiv, 1, 2, 4–11, 55, 89, 90,
     92, 94, 103, 105, 106, 109, 111, 113,
     114, 117, 118, 123, 125, 140, 143,
     153–157, 169, 172, 173, 177, 181,
     198, 218, 221–223, 227–230, 232,
     233, 235, 237, 245, 246, 248, 249
customs 4, 152–155, 221, 233

**D**
Democratic Alliance (DA) 218
Denver (Wolhuter) hostel 82, 155, 200
Department of Economic
     Development (DED) 212, 217,
     226, 229, 248
Department of Native Affairs 33, 34
Department of Social Development
     215
Department of Tourism 226
Dingane, King (aka Dingaan) 27, 74,
     113
Dinuzulu, King 27, 113, 156
diviner 90, 95, 97, 99, 116, 151–153,
     155, 167, 170–172, 174, 177, 179,
     181, 182, 184–188, 190, 237
Dlamini, Dr Judy 252
Dobson, JH 43
*dompas* 65
Doran, Magistrate TM 72, 74
dualist approach 244 (see also 'legalist
     approach', 'structuralist approach'
     and 'voluntarist approach')
Dundee July 112, 251
Dutch East India Company 77
Dutch Reformed Church 154

**E**
Eastern Native Townships 34 (see also
     'Soweto')
economic trade zone (see 'trade zone')
*edlozini* 189
Ekuphakameni 156, 157, 164
eMakhosini Valley (Valley of the
     Kings) 113
eMoyeni Temple 128, 160, 161, 162, 164
End Street Park 64
entrepreneur(ship) xi, 7, 9, 10, 55, 72, 76,

88–91, 103, 109, 140, 186, 222, 223, 229, 232, 235, 240, 241, 243, 246, 248, 249
eQhudeni 111
Esibayeni 69
*esilungwini* 2
Ethiopian Church 153
*ezintabeni zokhohlambo* (aka Drakensberg Mountains) 112

**F**
Faraday Muthi Market 95
Ferreira's Camp 49
Foucault, Michel 38, 39, 40

**G**
Gauteng Enterprise Propeller 112
Gauteng Tourism Authority 226, 229, 230
George Koch hostel 82, 155, 200
*Giya* 118
Glen Grey Act 28
*gobela* 182, 187, 189, 190
Group Areas Act No. 41 of 1950 245

**H**
Heald, CA 52
Heard, LG 42
*hele* 124
herbalist (see 'traditional healer')
heritage 4, 5, 6, 9, 10, 89, 92, 112, 114, 124, 125, 222, 233, 246, 248, 249
hostel 6, 8, 37, 48, 51, 52, 57, 71, 87, 102, 105, 121, 176, 195–197, 201–205, 210, 211, 215, 218, 219, 227, 228, 232, 243, 245, 249 (see also 'compound')
housing 31–35, 37, 42, 44, 71, 196
Human Rights Commission 210, 218, 219

**I**
*ibhande* 116
*iBandla lamaNazaretha* (aka Nazareth Baptist Church or Church of the Nazarites) (see 'Shembe Church')

*ibhayi* 125
*ibheshu* 162
*ibhimbi lokukhuluma* 175
*ibovu* 187
*idlozi* 187, 189
*idzilla* 125
*iklwa* 160
*ikolwa* 166
*ilobolo* 166
*imigcagco* 118
*imphepho* 163
*impi yamakhanda* 120
*induna* 75, 90, 111, 117, 176, 200–207, 214, 216, 219, 250, 251
*induna yezinsizwa* (or *umphathi wezinsizwa*) 118
informal economy 6, 102, 235–240, 242–245
*ingqwele* 118
Inhlangakazi 156
*inkabi* 203
Inkatha Freedom Party (IFP) 113, 118, 120, 121, 122, 123
*inkehli* 125
*inkonzo* 169
Integrated Development Plan 2020/21 224, 228, 233
International Labour Organization (ILO) 236, 239
*intombi* 125
*inyanga* 173, 187, 203
*iporiyana* 15
*iPulmende* 130
*iSabatha* 159
*isangoma* 163, 182, 184, 187
*isembatho* 174
*isibhaca* (or *ubhaca*) 94, 120
*izibhobo* 182
*isicathamiya* 82
*isicholo* 125, 127, 162
*isidwaba* 125
*isigcino* 162
*isigege* 125
*isigolwani* 125
*isigungu* 90, 200–207, 214, 219, 251

*isikhali* 168

*isinene* 162

*isinyama* 168

*isiphephetu* 125

*isiphika* 127

*isiqalo* 162

*isita sa Bantu* 54

*isiwasho* 170

iSizwe saMaNgwane (aka AmaNgwane
      Clan) 112

*isosha elifele empini* 122

*ithwasa* 182, 189

*itwetwe* 115

*izagila namawisa* 117

*izagwaca namathendele* 117

*izangoma* 95, 181, 182, 184, 189, 190

*Izibongo* 157

*izifebe* 104

*izigodi* 25, 94, 200, 201

*Izihlabelelo zama Nazaretha* (see
      'Shembe Hymns')

*izimbadada* 94

*izimbizo* 117

*izindlela zabo zikhanye* 183

*iziNduna* 24, 25, 123, 201, 202

*izingxabulela* (see *'izimbadada'*)

*izinsizwa* 116, 118

*izinyanga* 95, 181, 184

*iziphuku* 110

*izithunywa* 167


**J**

Jeppe hostel 82

Jeppe Police Station 208, 211

Jeppestown 223

João V of Portugal 17

Joburg (see 'Johannesburg')

Johannesburg xii, xiii, 3, 4, 8, 13,
      15–19, 22, 30–35, 41, 43, 48,
      51, 52, 54, 63, 66, 67, 72, 77, 80,
      82, 88–90, 94, 98, 104, 110, 112,
      116, 118–122, 130–134, 147–149,
      174, 186, 187, 199, 200, 203, 205,
      206, 210, 211, 214, 218, 222–226,
      229–232, 247, 249

Johannesburg City Council 18, 33–35,
      41–44, 48, 49, 52, 66, 67, 71, 72,
      74–76, 80, 96, 196, 198, 206, 207,
      210–212, 217–220, 222–229, 232,
      233, 235, 245, 246, 248, 251

Johannesburg Executive Council 48, 51,
      52

Johannesburg Metropolitan Police
      Department (JMPD) 208,
      211–213, 215, 226

Johannesburg Municipal Ordinance of
      1906 43

Johannesburg Non-European Affairs
      Department (JNEAD) 66, 67, 70,
      71, 74, 80

Johannesburg Property Company
      (JPC) 198, 199, 205–219, 226–228,
      248, 251

Johannesburg Roads Agency (JRA)
      226, 248

Johannesburg Technical College 130

Jones, Thos G 74

Joubert, Christiaan Johannes 17, 19
      (see also 'Johannesburg')

Joubert, General Piet 63

Jozi (see 'Johannesburg')

Jubilee Gold Mining Company 41, 217


**K**

kaffir beer (aka mai mai) 55, 71, 77, 80
      (see also 'beer' and *'skokian'*)

*khonza* 200, 202

Khumalo, Elizabeth 138, 139, 140

Kimberley archetype 39

Kliptown 32

*kraal* 25

Kruger, Paul Johannes 17, 63 (see also
      'Johannesburg')

Kwa Mai Mai xi, xiii, xiv, 1, 6–9, 13,
      18, 35, 47, 48, 50, 52, 55, 56, 58–
      61, 71, 72, 80, 84, 85, 87, 89–98,
      100–107, 109–114, 117, 119, 121,
      123–125, 128–130, 132–140, 142,
      144, 145, 151, 153, 155, 159–161,
      164, 172–174, 176, 180, 183, 186,

187, 190, 197–201, 203–219, 223,
225–229, 232–235, 237, 241–251
(see also 'Mai Mai hostel and
bazaar' and 'Maye Maye')
Kwa Mai Mai Varsity Legacy Project
250–252
Kwa Maye Maye 88
kwa Xhosa (see 'Xhosa')
KwaZulu-Natal 50, 82, 94, 105,
111–113, 119, 121, 130, 195, 200
(see also 'Natal')

**L**
Labour Party 65
Lace, Mrs J Dale 64
Lace Diamond Mines 64
Langlaagte 14, 15
*lebole* 124
legalist approach 244 (see also 'dualist
approach', 'structuralist approach'
and 'voluntarist approach')
*lobola* 2, 120
Local Government Ordinance of 1912
43

**M**
Maboneng 90, 223, 234, 235
Mahlabathini 113, 115, 116, 120
Mai Mai hostel and bazaar 6, 44, 48,
51, 54, 55, 74, 80, 87, 88 (see also
'Maye Maye' and 'Kwa Mai Mai')
*makhosi* 182, 189
Makhubo, Councillor/Mayor Geoff
210, 211, 215
Malandela 118
Mamba, Mkhulu 186, 187, 188, 189,
190, 191, 230, 251
MaNdlovu (see 'Mkhize, Landiwe')
MaNsimbi (see 'Nsimbi, uMama
Zilondile)
*maredo* 125
Market Square 32
Market Theatre 90
Marshalltown 223
maskandi 82, 105, 115
Matatiele 111, 251

Mathang, Councillor Ruby 198, 210,
211, 219
Matongo, Councillor Jolidee 215, 216
Matshoba, Mtutuzeli 69, 70, 71, 72
Mavuso, Priest 172–176, 193, 204, 250
Maye Maye 6, 54, 88, 251
(see also 'Mai Mai hostel and
bazaar' and 'Kwa Mai Mai')
MBA hostel 200
Mbhele tribe 110
Meadowlands 34
*mealiepap* 105
Melville 223
Member of the Mayoral Committee
(MMC) 198, 216
metropolis 3, 9
metropolitan 3
metropolitan man 8, 9
*metsheka* 124
Meyer, Johannes 17 (see also
'Johannesburg')
Meyer's Camp 49, 50 (see 'Natal
Camp')
*mfundisi* 173
Mhlongo 145
migrant workers (see 'migrants')
migrants xiv, 1–10, 13, 20–23, 28–31,
35, 40, 55–57, 66, 71, 88, 89, 92–
94, 106, 109, 130, 131, 133–135,
153, 195, 196, 202, 210, 220, 234,
243, 248, 249, 251
minerals xii, 30
mining industry 13, 21, 22, 133
missionary villages 154
Mkhize, Landiwe (aka MaNdlovu)
128, 142
*mkhulu* 186
Moerane, Mpho 211, 216–218
Mohlakeng 35
Moravian Brethren 154
*moruka* 124
Mpande, King 27, 113
Mpungose, Khuzani (aka Khuba or
Indlamlenze) 105
Msane, Saul 54

Mshengu xiii, 136–140, 142, 250
Municipalities Powers of
    Expropriation Ordinance of 1903
    49, 51
Murray & Roberts hostel 82, 200
*muthi* 100, 112, 116
myths xi, 7

**N**
Natal 14, 20–25, 30, 31, 41, 50, 54, 77,
    113, 122, 156, 181
Natal Camp 49, 50 (see also 'Meyer's
    Camp')
Natal Native Code 122, 181
Natal Native Congress (NNC) 54
Natalspruit compound 48, 51, 52
National Hostel Redevelopment
    Programme 196, 197
National Party 65
National Small Business Act No. 102
    of 1996 245
native locations 32
    'Coolie Location' 32
    'Kaffir Location' 32
    'Malay Location' 32
native reserves 21, 24–26
natives 1, 24, 27, 29, 37, 42, 43, 48, 49,
    51, 52, 63, 66, 71, 72, 74, 76, 91,
    131, 166
Natives Land Act No. 27 of 1913 21, 156
Natives (Urban Areas) Act No. 21 of
    1923 33, 35, 50, 71
Natives (Urban Areas) Consolidation
    Act No. 25 of 1945 49, 52
Nazareth Baptist Church (aka Church
    of the Nazarites or *iBandla
    lamaNazaretha*) 155 (see also
    'Shembe Church')
Ndebele 4, 5, 52, 123, 124, 125, 141
Ndlovu, Duma 176
Ndlovu, uMshumayeli Mphatheni
    160–162, 175, 192
Ndwandwe (aka Nkab'ewrong)
    112–117, 119, 176, 203, 204
Newclare 34
Newtown 223

Ngalonkulu, Justice 210, 211, 215
Ngejane, Simphiwe 211, 213
*ngelekejane* 136
Ngwabe, Jane 252
Nguni 52, 88, 123, 200
Nkab'ewrong (aka Ndwandwe) 191,
    203
Nkandla 119, 120
Nkosinkulu (aka Senzangakhona ka
    Jama) 113
Non-European Affairs Committee 67
*Nongoloza* 136
Nongoma 113, 120
Nsimbi, uMama Zilondile 184–186,
    191, 230, 237, 251
Ntabazwe Mountain 156
*ntepa* 124
Ntshangase 113 (see also 'Ndwandwe')
Nxasana, Sizwe 252

**O**
*oBhekeni* 25, 201, 219
Office of the Mayor 205, 207, 211, 215,
    216, 218, 219, 227
Order of the Immaculate Conception
    of Vila Viçosa 17
Organisation for Economic
    Cooperation and Development
    (OECD) 236, 237
Orlando 34

**P**
Paarl Camp 49
Paarl's Hoop 32
pass laws 65, 66, 69
Pass Office 66, 67, 70
Pedi 123, 124, 141, 248
Pentecostal 154, 167
Pikitup 199, 209, 215, 226, 248
Pikoli, Mama 144
Pimville 32
platinum 133
poll tax (see 'taxes')
prospecting 13, 14, 15, 16
Protestant 154, 159

**Q**

*qhata* 118

**R**

race 3, 5, 18, 92, 155, 195
Ralushai Commission Findings 181
Randjeslaagte 15, 17, 49, 50
red-light district 83
reference books 67
Rhodes, Cecil John 16, 28, 40
Rissik, Johann 17, 19 (see also
      'Johannesburg')
rituals xi, 7, 92, 95, 152, 157, 159, 160,
      169, 175, 190, 200, 201
Roever, Sally 241 (see also 'Women in
      Informal Employment: Globalizing
      and Organizing (WIEGO)')
*rondavel* (aka *kwaGogo*) 184
Ruda, Mbulelo 211, 212, 215
rural 3, 7, 9, 10, 20, 23, 28, 30, 31, 92,
      195, 196, 200, 201, 202, 220, 234,
      243, 248

**S**

Salisbury Claims 41
Salisbury Gold Mining Company 41
Salisbury and Jubilee compound 35,
      42, 43, 51, 54, 72, 74, 78, 79, 80,
      88, 97
sangoma 181–184, 187, 189, 204, 230,
      251 (see also 'traditional healer')
Senzangakhona ka Jama 113
Shaka, King 24, 27, 110, 113, 118, 120,
      160, 203
Shangaan 4
Shell House (massacre) 118, 120–122
Shembe, Galilee 157
Shembe, Prophet Isaiah 126–128,
      155–159, 162, 164
Shembe Church (aka Nazareth Baptist
      Church or Church of the Nazarites
      or KwaShembe or *iBandla
      lamaNazaretha*) 98, 126, 128, 142,
      155–165, 168, 173
Shembe Hymns 157
Shembe, Nkosi 163

Shepstone, Theophilus 111
*shisanyama* 93, 98, 99, 104, 105, 213
Shongwe, Themba 119, 120, 143
Sibeko, Lwando 211
Sigananda ka Zokufa Shezi, Chief 120
Sithole, Dr Sipho 252
Sithole, Jobe 110, 111
Sithole, Malibongwe 146, 207, 208,
      213, 214, 218, 219, 251, 252
Sithole, Matshana 110, 111
Sithole, Sandile 129–135, 144
Sithole, Tholukhazi 110–112, 141
Sithole Furniture 241, 251
Sjava 106
*skokian* (aka 'kill-me-quick') 72, 74, 76,
      80 (see also 'beer' and 'kaffir beer')
slaves 77
Smuts, General Jan 65
Sophiatown 34, 35 (see also 'Triomf')
Sotho 4, 5, 52, 123
South African Bureau of Standards 134
South African Native National Congress
      54
South African War (aka Anglo–Boer
      War) 124
South-Western Townships (see
      'Soweto')
Soweto 33–35, 161, 186, 200, 223
snuff 55, 94–97
*spruit* 14
stable (for horses) xiii, 6, 14, 49, 51, 60,
      61, 89, 109, 110
structuralist approach 245 (see
      also 'dualist approach', 'legalist
      approach' and 'voluntarist
      approach')
Swati 52, 123

**T**

tax(ation) 20, 22–30, 238
      dog tax 20
      hut tax 20, 27
      poll tax 20, 26, 120
      Poll Tax Act 26
      rent 27, 30
taxis 103–105, 137–139, 186, 216

*thokosa* 189

Thompson, Francis 40

*tinguvu* 124

*thwasa* 189

township 5, 6, 33, 34, 35, 37, 82, 97, 121, 196, 234, 244

trade zone xiv, 6, 48, 52, 55, 84, 89, 93, 96, 97, 102, 105, 174, 199, 204–206, 213, 226, 228, 229

traders xi, xii, xiii, 8, 9, 13, 48, 50, 52, 58, 92, 93, 98, 100, 106, 109, 119, 129, 140, 160, 161, 174, 198, 199, 204, 205, 207, 209, 210, 212, 213, 216, 217, 224, 226, 227, 229, 233–235, 237, 243, 248

traders' committee 204–208, 211, 212, 214, 218, 219, 251

tradition xi, xii, xiv, 3, 4, 7, 55, 89, 92, 97, 106, 118, 123, 125, 140, 157, 162, 166, 167, 221, 222, 228, 249

traditional beer 70 (see also 'kaffir beer' and '*skokian*')

traditional healer 56, 90, 94, 95, 97, 99, 100, 113–115, 117, 152, 153, 162, 174, 176–179, 184, 190, 198, 229, 234, 237 (see also 'sangoma')

traditional medicine 93–96, 99, 114–116, 119, 177–179, 229, 249

traditional weapons 100, 117–120, 122, 123

Transkei 95

transnationalism 1

Transvaal 14, 18, 19, 20, 21, 32, 54

Transvaal, Eastern 14

Transvaal Graphite Company 51, 52

Transvaal Native Congress (TNC) 54

Transvaal Republic 16, 17 (see also 'Zuid-Afrikaansche Republiek')

tribal system 23, 24, 25

tribal wars 21

Triomf 35 (see also 'Sophiatown')

Truth and Reconciliation Commission (TRC) 122

Tshabalala, Sizeka 211, 212, 215

Tsonga 5, 123, 124, 141, 248

Tucker, Kidger 63

Twelve Apostles 155

**U**

*ubabamkhulu* 162

*ubhekeni wezinsizwa* 201

*ubhoko* 117, 120

*ubungoma* 179, 181, 182, 183

*ucu* 125

*udelunina* 185

*udengezi* 183

*uitlander* 17

*ukubholofida* 167

*ukuboniswa* 167

*ukudla* 104

*ukugiya* 117

*ukuhlatshelwa* 172

*ukuphuma inqina* 29

*ukushela* 181

*ukuthwasa* 179, 182–184, 187, 189, 190, 251

*uLoliwe* 103, 130

Ulundi 113

*umabuya* 185

*umbilo* 131

*umemulo* 117

*umgangela* 118

*umgobo* 120

*umhlonyana* 96

*umkhokheli* 127, 128, 175, 176

*umkhosi womhlanga* 117

*umnazaretha* 126, 127, 128

*umngqayi* (aka *umantshingelani*) 173

*umnikelo* 164

*umnqawe* (tree) 58

*umnumzane* 166

*umoya* 170, 171, 172

*umphako* 133

*umquele* 126

*umsamo* 168, 183, 184

*umshumayeli* 128, 164

uMsinga 82, 110, 111, 130, 131

*Umtelebhelo* 111

*umthandazi* 187

*umuthi* 116, 170

*umuthi wenhlanhla* 184
*uMvelinqangi* (aka *uNkulunkhulu* or *uHlanga*) 152, 162, 172, 176
*umzansi* 94
uMzimkhulu 120
*uNdunankulu* 201
Union of South Africa 77
United Party 65
*uNkulunkulu* 152
uNyazi lwe Zulu 161, 162
uPikoli, Mama 250
urban 1, 3, 7–10, 20, 23, 28, 30–32, 35, 65, 66, 90, 92, 106, 156, 196, 201, 202, 219, 221, 234
*ushiyamen* 94

**V**
Van der Merwe, JL 42
Venda 4, 5, 123–125, 141, 248
Verwoerd, Hendrik 65
Vha Venda (see 'Venda')
villagers, transnational 2
village xi, xii, xiii, 3, 4, 6–9, 13, 20–24, 27–30, 37, 52, 54, 66, 80, 84, 88, 89, 92, 94, 96, 103, 104, 107, 109–111, 128, 131–134, 195, 197, 201–203, 220, 243, 248, 251
voluntarist approach 245 (see also 'dualist approach', 'legalist approach' and 'structural approach')
*vukuzenzele* 90

**W**
wasbank 131
*waslap* 133
wedding kist (aka mai mai) 56, 57, 93, 103, 129, 130–132, 144, 161, 242
Wemmer hostel 155, 200
Wemmer and Jubilee compound 41, 48, 71, 130, 134
*wenda* 125
Western Cape 105
Western Native Townships 33 (see also 'Soweto')
white medicine 95

white monopoly capital 243
(1996) White Paper on the Development and Promotion of Small Business 245
witchcraft 115, 179, 181, 185
Witchcraft Suppression Act No. 3 of 1957 181
Witchcraft Suppression Amendment Act No. 50 of 1970 181
Witwatersrand 13, 14, 30, 31, 35, 37, 40, 41, 54, 58, 121, 122, 223
Witwatersrand Native Labour Association (WNLA) 31
Women in Informal Employment: Globalizing and Organizing (WIEGO) 241 (see also 'Roever, Sally')
World Health Organization (WHO) 179

**X**
Xhosa 4, 5, 52, 124, 248
*xibelani* 124

**Y**
Yeoville 32

**Z**
Zakwe, Mr 205, 208, 213
Zakwe, uMama uMaNhlangwini (aka Mama Zakwe) xiii, 143, 250
Zamxaka, Saki 112
Zionist Christian Church (aka *Isonto lamaZayoni*) 153, 155, 159, 165–169, 172–175, 204
Zondo, Councillor 211–215
Zuid-Afrikaansche Republiek (ZAR) (see also 'Transvaal Republic') 16, 17
Zulu xii, 4, 5, 22, 26–28, 52, 57, 58, 88, 94, 114–126, 145, 155–157, 166, 195, 196, 200, 201, 218, 234
Zulu High Church 156
Zulu Kingdom 22, 58, 95, 113, 121, 122, 155, 156, 166, 202
Zululand 21–25, 30, 31, 113, 119, 120, 202, 248